Images of Incar
Representations of Prison in Film and

David Wilson is professor of criminology at the Centre for Criminal Justice Policy and Research at the University of Central England in Birmingham. A former prison governor, he is the editor of the *Howard Journal* and a well-known author and broadcaster, having presented various TV and radio series for the BBC, ITV and Channel 4.

Sean O'Sullivan is a lecturer in sociology based within the Centre for Criminal Justice Policy and Research, at the University of Central England. He is the coordinator of the Prison Film Project—an initiative that aims to utilise interest in prison films and TV drama as a means to stimulating debate on real world experiences of incarceration. His published work includes articles on prison and on the death penalty as portrayed in Hollywood cinema.

Images of Incarceration
Representations of Prison in Film and Television Drama
David Wilson and Sean O'Sullivan

Published 2004 by
WATERSIDE PRESS
Domum Road
Winchester SO23 9NN
United Kingdom

Telephone or fax: 01962 855567
Orderline e-mail: enquiries@watersidepress.co.uk
Online catalogue and bookstore: www.watersidepress.co.uk

Copyright: David Wilson and Sean O'Sullivan. All rights reserved. No part of this book may be reproduced, stored in any retrieval system or transmitted in any form, including in electronic form or over the Internet, or by any means without prior permission. The rights of the authors in this regard are hereby asserted.

ISBN 1 904 380 08 5

Catalogue-In-Publication Data: A catalogue record for this book can be obtained from the British Library

Printing and binding: Antony Rowe Ltd, Chippenham

Cover design: Developed by John Good Holbrook, Coventry/Waterside Press from a poster created by Artichoke Design Studios, Birmingham

The Prison Film Project: *Images of Incarceration* was created as part of the Prison Film Project sponsored by the Esmée Fairbairn Foundation as part of its Rethinking Crime and Punishment initiative. For further information visit www.theprisonfilmproject.com

Images of Incarceration
Representations of Prison in Film and Television Drama

David Wilson and Sean O'Sullivan

Acknowledgements

This book has been produced as part of a wider set of activities, collectively known as the Prison Film Project. Briefly, this project is an initiative which seeks to explore the ways in which dramatic representations of prison in film and on television might be used as a springboard to debating real world experiences of prison and to help give a higher profile to the need to reduce the UK prison population.

The Prison Film Project has been funded under the Esmée Fairbairn Foundation's Rethinking Crime and Punishment initiative. We are immensely grateful to Rethinking Crime and Punishment, and to Rob Allen in particular, for supporting and funding the activities that have allowed us to develop the materials for this book. We hope that what we have written will in some way contribute to the aims of that initiative.

In the course of developing the Prison Film Project we have met and talked with many people about prison film. Everyone who we have spoken to has contributed ideas that have shaped our thinking on these issues. We wish to thank them all for their contributions but particularly the members of the Steering Group who supported us.

Finally, we wish to thank Dr Mike Nellis who, in the earlier stages of the project, acted as our external consultant. Mike's vast knowledge of prison films and his generous supply of printed and visual materials have helped make this book possible. More than anyone Mike has a longstanding interest in wishing to see representations of prison and prisoners in popular film and on television given the attention and interest that they deserve. Again we hope that what we have written here might contribute in some way towards this goal.

David Wilson and **Sean O'Sullivan**

January 2004

Images of Incarceration

Contents

Acknowledgements	iv
A Guide to Using this Book	vi

CHAPTER

1   Introduction: Prisons and Prison Drama   7

Prison Film in Britain and America

2   The British Prison Film Revisited   24
3   Tracking the US Penal State: Issues and Eras   58
4   Tracking the US Penal State: In Defence of
    Hollywood   88

The Smaller Screen

5   Origins and Intentions: In Praise of *Bad Girls*   116
6   Hidden From View: *Buried* and *Ghosts... of
    the Civil Dead*   136
7   Inside the Predatory Prison: *Oz*   148

Reform and Change

8   On Being 'the Man': the Prison Governor   156
9   In and Around the Penal State: Escaped
    and Released Prisoners   169
10 Film, Television and Popular Culture: A Note   183

Bibliography   186

Index   189

A Guide to Using this Book

We have written this book in an attempt to provide a reasonably comprehensive introduction to the topic of dramatisations of prison in film and on TV. But readers will most likely approach it for different reasons and with different aims in mind. In view of this we have tried to present each chapter largely as a self-contained entity. Although the book develops arguments progressively and can be read from 'cover-to-cover', we also hope that it will also be possible for readers to 'dip into' it to sample those chapters that most interest them at the outset.

When reviewers or critics write about a film, they most often write in a style that gives the reader enough information to assess whether they might wish to watch the film in question, but without divulging enough of the plot or ending to ruin the reader's subsequent enjoyment of the film. In the kind of analysis developed in this book this concealing of plot development and endings is not always possible. To suggest 'a reading' of what a film is doing or how its moral or message might be interpreted, it is often necessary to disclose details of significant plot developments and endings. All chapters therefore come with a 'spoiler alert'. If a chapter discusses a film that is still on your list of films to see, then you might wish to see it first before reading the chapter in question too closely.

Chapters 2 and 4 supply select *Filmographies* of the main prison films cited in the relevant chapters. Prison films or significant prison-related films are identified by title and date. We believe that this is sufficient to identify the film in question, the details of which can easily be found, for example, at websites such as Internet Movie Database (www.imdb.com). Non-prison films which are only mentioned in passing are generally not dated and do not appear in the filmographies.

Following the *Introduction* in *Chapter 1*, *Chapters 2, 3* and *4* provide broad brush surveys of the prison film in the UK and USA. These chapters seek to chart the general trends in the development of the prison film and, particularly in *Chapters 3* and *4*, to review existing academic literature on the prison film. The next three chapters deal mainly with prison in TV drama and consider the cult series *Bad Girls*, *Oz* and *Buried*. *Chapters 8* and *9* return to the subject of film looking at certain prison film issues—the significance for the reform-minded warden and the experience of escaped and released prisoners. We conclude in *Chapter 10* with a note about popular culture and the way in which screen representations can influence the progress and development (or otherwise) of penal reform.

David Wilson and **Sean O'Sullivan**

CHAPTER 1

Introduction: Prisons and Prison Drama

Without wishing to seem unduly provocative or controversial, we start our discussion of the depiction of prison in film and TV with the suggestion that probably the major influence on the British public's understanding of prison today is a situation comedy made some 30 odd years ago. The most famous and most 'visited' nick in Britain is likely to be one Slade prison, home to Norman Stanley Fletcher and his chums, the cast of the fictitious BBC situation comedy *Porridge*. Here Fletcher, the seasoned old con, struggles stoically to deal with life's little emergencies and attempts to weather the trials of incarceration.

As a situation comedy the storylines in *Porridge* disclaim any pretence to seriousness. On one occasion, for example, Fletch is moved to suspect 'dishonour amongst thieves' following the disappearance or theft of a tin of pineapple chunks from his cell! On another, following a rash of petty pilfering within the prison, including the theft of hapless prison officer Mr Baraclough's 'bi-cy-cle', it is announced, much to Fletcher's consternation, that Christmas in Slade prison will be cancelled that year! There are no doubt many similar examples that could be added to the list of trials and tribulations endured by the inmates of HMP Slade.

Of course *Porridge* did not entirely revolve around such mock tragedies. In one episode early in the first series, 'A Night In', Fletcher encourages his new cellmate, young Lenny Godbar, to adjust to the loss of liberty entailed in imprisonment by thinking of each night of his sentence as one where, rather than getting dressed up and going out up-town, he has instead opted for 'a quite night in'. More generally the point of the show, to the extent that there was one, revolved around the issue of whether Godbar, the likeable young man with an O-level in geography, would leave Slade prison relatively unscathed by his experience or go on to become, like Fletcher, a repeat offender and an habitual criminal. But *Porridge* is most likely to be remembered for thefts of 'bi-cy-cles' and pineapple chunks and mock tragedies like the cancellation of Christmas, rather than for the discussion of any weighty penal reform issues. Arguably, the series constructed a sanitised view of prison in which:

> the day is filled with humour and attempts by various prisoners to 'get one over' on their fellow prisoners or the staff. In short, prison isn't too bad; a bit of a laff and no one comes to too much harm. (Wilson, 2003: 28)

This view is, of course, radically out of step with what we know about British prisons in the 1970s, the time when *Porridge* was conceived and first aired. If today we were to read the accounts of prisoners who were in custody at this time we might be surprised at how far their view of 'the reality' at that time diverges from *Porridge's* version of events. The 1970s was a time of widespread unrest in Britain's prisons with a wave of roof-top protests, riots and sit-ins (see, for example, Fitzgerald and Sim, 1979). Organizations were formed to defend prisoners' rights, and, if the contemporary accounts of these organizations are anything to go by, relations between 'screws' and inmates were a long way away from the sanitised antagonism portrayed in *Porridge*. But here we can begin to hear the sound of objections being raised as incredulous voices begin to chime that, 'of course *Porridge* didn't represent the reality of prison: it was and is a situation comedy'! As such, it might be suggested, the series neither sought to provide a realistic account of what prison is like, nor was it believed by anybody to do so.

This book stems, in part, from a belief that it is inadequate to regard *Porridge* as 'just a situation comedy'. After all, it is worth pointing out that the vast majority of people in this country will never serve time in a prison and most will never even have a family member or friend subject to a custodial sentence. It therefore follows that the vast majority of the general public will never see the inside of a prison, even just to visit one. Indeed it could be argued that such establishments are deliberately constructed not just to keep prisoners in, but also to keep the public out. This being the case we need to ask: from where do people get their ideas and impressions about prison? Obviously official government reports and the accounts of these in the press, the writings and autobiographies of currently serving and ex-prisoners, and media appearances by advocates of penal reform are all potential sources of information, ideas and impressions. But, if we were to be honest, outside of an already committed few, how many people engage with such sources of information? On the other hand, the current prime-time TV prison drama *Bad Girls* regularly attracts an audience of more than six million viewers and is now into its fifth series. For better or for worse, *Bad Girls* is, for very many people, far more likely to be an important source of their ideas about prison and prisoners than any number of unread, dry and dusty government reports, or campaigning documents of penal reform organizations, which are usually met with a fair degree of scepticism and disinterest by the general public.

We therefore suggest that there is a need to take seriously the possibility that representations of prison in film and TV drama are an important source of people's implicit and commonsense understandings of prison. This being so, this book seeks to develop an analysis of some of the main ways in which prison has been represented in film and TV drama and to suggest how and why these depictions might come to influence people's perceptions of actual prisons. Our main focus is on the situation in the UK although, for what we hope are fairly obvious reasons, we also consider the influence of the US prison film and the TV programme *Oz* which, although of American origin, is broadcast in the UK on Channel 4 (C4). The remainder of this chapter sets out our approach to our subject and seeks to justify why we think this approach is both necessary and beneficial. But before we turn to considering prison drama itself, we need first to say a little more about its real world referent—prison. We need to say why prison should be a cause for concern, before going on to consider the influence of film and TV on popular commonsense understandings of the subject. The chapter then concludes with a brief outline of the rest of the book.

PRISON AND PENAL REALITIES

Prison drama as a form of popular entertainment could be studied in a number of ways and from a range of perspectives. Film critics, film fans, criminologists and cultural studies academics might all study or analyse prison drama in different ways. But our own interest stems from a more general concern with the use of prison in society and recent debates about the need to rethink its role within the criminal justice system. Thus, before we can discuss why prison drama matters, we need to briefly outline recent concerns about the continued use of prison as a response to crime and the need to develop alternatives.

Rethinking prison?
There are indications that the issues of prison and prison reform are moving up the policy agenda. The UK is currently experiencing a growth in its prison population and there is, at least within some sections of the media, a perceived 'crisis' within the penal system. In July 2003, for example, it was reported that the prison population of England and Wales had exceeded 74,000 for the first time. A new record high of 74,012 represented a total incarcerated population some 45,000 higher than ten years previously. Arguably, this increase did not reflect any real increase in crime, nor in the seriousness of offending, but rather the reality that minor offenders today are more likely to receive a prison sentence than they would have been for the same offence ten years ago. The news of the record level followed on the heels of England and Wales rising to the top of Europe's incarceration league table, with the highest prison numbers per 100,000 population in the EU (Travis, 2003). In September 2003 it was reported that Scotland's prison population had reached an all time high despite it being Scottish Executive policy to reduce the figure and notwithstanding a 35 per cent increase in the number of offenders serving community sentences (Scottish Executive, 2003). Only Northern Ireland would seem to be enjoying any success in holding its prison population stable at a relatively low level (Walmsley, 2003).

For a number of good and understandable reasons, news of the new record numbers triggered a rash of negative media reports about Britain's penal system. 'UK Europe's prison capital', 'Prisons crisis grows as population reaches record 74,000', screamed the newspaper headlines. These particular headlines, which appeared in the broadsheet press in July 2003, followed on from a stream of previous news features reporting that rising prison numbers were making it difficult for prison staff to provide opportunities for the 'purposeful activities' that might encourage rehabilitation. Overcrowding was said to be contributing to rising tensions within Britain's jails, with assaults by prisoners, both on staff and on each other, rising to new highs. Suicides and incidents of self-harm were also reported to be on the increase. Finally, a series of earlier negative reports by the government's prisons inspectorate in England and Wales on particularly bad prisons, combined with reported incidents of riot and protest, contributed to a sense that Britain's penal system was in 'crisis'. However, before we rush headlong to join this clamour about a 'prisons crisis' it is worth noting the opposing view. Namely that conditions in our prisons have improved dramatically over the last five, ten, 20 and 30 years.

Are Britain's prisons getting worse? Recent disturbances in UK jails have not been on anywhere near the scale of those which occurred during the 1970s, when discontent was more prolonged and more widespread (Fitzgerald, 1977). It is quite possible that prison regimes which were then accepted and taken for granted would now be deemed unacceptable. The point of the above discussion is not to deny that there are real problems within Britain's penal system—which do need addressing—but to suggest that there is a need to question accounts that focus entirely on the negative aspects and deny improvement has taken place, or that campaigns for penal reform can have an impact. It is beyond the scope of this book to provide a fully worked out solution to all the problems of penal policy, or of campaigns for penal reform. We cannot, for example, determine what the ultimate aims of penal reform should be; whether to campaign for the outright abolition of prison, or merely to insist that prisons should be well run, adequately resourced, and provide opportunities for activities which encourage rehabilitation. Nor can we resolve all the outstanding issues of penal policy. What role should prison play within the criminal justice system? For whom and for how many is incarceration an appropriate response to their offending behaviour? There will always be outstanding unresolved issues of principle and practice concerning the appropriate use of prison in society. Having said this, we do not think that it is possible, or desirable to approach the issue of the influence of prison drama in a neutral way. Any discussion concerning what prison drama is, what it does and how it works, must entail the analyst adopting some kind of view about the actuality of prison, and so we feel it desirable that we should indicate our own stance here.

This book originates from a belief that the current prison population of the UK is too high. Like many other people we would question, for example, whether there really is a need for some 45,000 more individuals to be incarcerated in England and Wales than there were ten years ago. It has been suggested by the *Rethinking Crime and Punishment* initiative that:

> It is widely agreed that the British penal system is not working as it should for victims, offenders or the wider community. The prison population is increasing but society does not feel increasingly protected from violence and crime. High proportions of prisoners re-offend and are not equipped for constructive employment in society. Yet prison, in spite of its costs, enjoys growing popularity as a policy response and receives often uninformed support from the public.
>
> (*Rethinking Crime and Punishment,* Bid Guidance Document, p.1)

We agree with these sentiments and point out that alternatives to custody do already exist in a variety of forms. The question that arises then is: if prison is an expensive and counter-productive mistake and as alternatives do exist, why is there not more support for a reduction in the prison population? We believe that part of the answer to this must lie in the way in which prison is represented in popular culture—and in film and TV drama in particular. For example, one of the effects of prison drama could be to encourage complacency about prison. We develop this argument below, but first need to say a little more about the nature of prison.

The unique culture of prison
We suggest that it is not possible to understand what prison drama is, what it does and how it works without having some view as to the nature of real prisons. This is not to say that it is possible to determine 'the reality' of prison. But there is a need to have an appreciation of the issues raised and the possible ways in which prison can

be conceived of and thought about, in order to examine the extent to which these issues and perspectives are represented in, or omitted from, the products of prison drama.

From the outset it should be emphasised that establishing 'the reality of prison' is no easy matter. Problems arise even at the most obvious level of developing basic empirical statements about the size and character of the inmate population. Once we move from these problems to consider if it is possible to make any evaluative judgments on the quality of the experience of the prisoner population, it is easy to see how the problems involved multiply. For example, any estimate of the current prison population will refer to a large number of people housed in a diverse range of penal settings, each with its own differences in regime. In the UK there are differences between the criminal justice systems of England and Wales, Scotland and Northern Ireland. Prisons themselves can vary from maximum security establishments to open prisons and even within these categories there may be significant variations in the ethos, culture and regime as between particular institutions. In the US, prison can vary from a county jail, which might be no more than a row of tents in a field, to a super-maximum security facility with an architecture and regime orientated almost entirely to 'inmate control'. Prisons also vary over time. So, as already suggested, we cannot assume that autobiographical accounts produced by prisoners in say the 1970s would necessarily be useful sources of information on the reality of prison today. In short, it seems safe to say that 'what prison is really like' is a complex and contested reality.

Having raised these problems, should we then accept the view that there is nothing that can reliably be said about prison? Or do prisons share some identifiable characteristics, albeit that not all of them will be shared equally? Can we theorise the characteristics of prisons as organizations and prison as a social institution? Again, there are no clear answers. Different sociological and criminological perspectives would provide different answers to these questions. But it is perhaps worth recapping some of the things that have been said and could be said about prison. By doing so we may at least be able to identify some relevant issues, even if we are unable to provide uncontestable definitive answers to the questions that we are raising.

Firstly, as we have already noted, the general public do not have extensive contact with what goes on inside a prison. The internal reality is known to prisoners, the staff and a few other specialist professions and occupations within the criminal justice system. In terms of theory it could be argued that a prison approximates to the notion of a 'total institution'—a concept introduced by the sociologist, Erving Goffman. Briefly, Goffman (1975) specified that a total institution was an organization where, for residents of the institution, all aspects of their lives took place under one roof and under one authority. Goffman developed an analysis of the implications of this kind of setting, highlighting the ways in which inmates of such institutions (asylums, prisons) can become trapped within a system of rules and authority which they find difficult to resist. Goffman's notion of a total institution was instrumental in helping to popularise the idea of community care. Advocates of de-institutionalisation for elderly people, people with mental health problems, people with a mental handicap (now learning disability) and so forth, developed a critique of long-stay institutions as leading to the de-personalisation and institutionalisation of their client groups, promoting dependency and 'taught helplessness', and creating conditions conducive to abuse.

In Scandinavia, advocates of 'normalisation' argued that when people in danger of social devaluation are brought together in one institution, this tends to reinforce negative perceptions of that group. So, for example, where people with a mental handicap are cared for together in one establishment this leads to them being identified only in terms of their common negative characteristic—they are all seen as mentally handicapped. Negative expectations of what this client group can achieve can then become self-reinforcing. If you have low expectations of a client group, then you won't invest much effort in providing them with the services and opportunities that will enable them to achieve more; they will then not achieve much, thereby justifying the initial expectations of their limited ability. This is the vicious cycle of low expectations reinforcing poor performance (Wolfensberger, 1980).

In the field of social care the critique of large, impersonal, long-stay institutions is now widely accepted and although the policy of community care is not without its shortcomings and deficiencies, there is relatively little support for reopening such institutions, particularly not from the client groups who experienced the 'benefits' of living in them! There are of course parallels and differences between the issue of social care—with its debate about 'institution versus community'—and the debate about 'prison versus community justice'. One major difference is of course that the elderly, the mentally ill, the physically disabled and so forth were located in institutions whose overt purpose was to provide care. When such institutions were revealed to be as much about control as about care and to be conducive to the abuse of their charges, this was received as being something of a scandal. In the instance of prison the situation is immediately different. Prisoners are, almost by definition, there for the purpose of punishment and control and any care responsibility prisons might have to their charges is in a sense secondary to their main purpose. However this may be changing. Current anxieties about the numbers of young people and children in prison, also the numbers of prisoners with mental health problems, or who are drug addicted, might suggest that a shift towards a welfare model of incarceration (and then decarceration) may be possible. Dramatic representations of prisoners and prisons might be significant here and could help effect a shift in the way in which the general public think about the appropriateness of prison.

One of the main problems today is, that at a time when society seems to be willing to 'decarcerate' and 'normalise' most other groups, it is increasingly willing to incarcerate criminals. Criminological arguments against prison have been extensively rehearsed and developed over a number of years. Contrary to the view that 'prison works', it could be argued that prison fails on two of its supposed main aims—deterrence and rehabilitation. Does custody act as an effective deterrent to people committing crime? Arguably criminals do not enter into a rational calculation which weighs the extent of the possible punishment against the benefits of committing crime. If they did then the threat of stiffer sentences might be an effective deterrent. The reality is likely to be different. For example, recent concerns over gun crime in Britain's cities have led to a proposed recommendation of a five-year minimum jail term for people found carrying a firearm. This proposal is one that has come 'from above'—from a Home Secretary quite divorced from the immediate problem. People working closer to the problem suggest that by the time a (young) person has developed the mentality such that they are prepared to carry a gun and use it, the threat of a jail sentence will not act as much of a deterrent. The call for stiffer sentences for this offence is a 'knee-jerk' reaction which deflects thinking away from considering why some (young) people are prepared to carry firearms and use them in the first place. The fallacy that gun crime can be controlled through 'supply-side' measures has already been extensively examined (Shelly and Wright, 1995).

If stiffer sentences do not, in fact, deter crime then the effect of their introduction would, assuming that offenders can be apprehended and convicted, lead to fuller prisons with more people in them serving longer sentences. Many criminologists and penologists would suggest that this is likely to be counter-productive. The longer an offender stays in prison, the more likely he or she is to have lost touch with the contacts that might have helped to re-integrate them into society on their release. Longer sentences might lead only to more hardened and embittered criminals finally coming out on to the street to commit more crime. Whilst longer sentences might be seen to be necessary for prison to act as a deterrent or punishment, they are likely to run contrary to any aim of rehabilitation.

Arguably prisons have a 'unique culture' that is not found in any other institution in society. A group of socially marginalised and stigmatised citizens are coercively detained in a rigidly structured 'closed institution'. The institution's goal of punishment leads to regimes which deprive inmates of access to those things regarded as normal by the rest of society such as family relations, access to normal paid employment, and so forth. Attempts to allow prisoners access to those activities which maintain their connection with society and which might encourage their eventual rehabilitation tend to be seen as working against the notion of prison as a form of punishment. Despite modern day attempts at greater standardisation, how the prison authorities and staff balance the conflicting demands between punishment and rehabilitation, care and control, segregation and integration may well vary from one establishment to another. But whether they do a good or bad job at reconciling those demands depends on the extent to which society sees prison as a merely place of punishment, or as a structure to encourage rehabilitation. If, as it is reported, more than 50 per cent of prisoners serving a custodial sentence will re-offend within two years of their release, then the more we wish rehabilitation to be the goal of prison the more we would judge prisons to be a failure.

BELIEVING IN PRISON

Given the weight of criminological and sociological evidence together with the testimony of offenders and ex-offenders against the effectiveness of prison, how should we account for society's continuing faith in it as a response to crime? Scandinavian sociologist Thomas Mathiesen is one of several commentators who lay a large part of the blame at the door of the media. Mathiesen (2000) believes that there is overwhelming evidence to suggest that prison is an expensive and counter-productive mistake. It is, he believes, a policy that could not be justified in a fully informed, rational debate. The continuing resort to the use of custody depends on a series of processes which conceal and mystify the reality of prison. People who work within the penal system may realise the futility of sending people to prison, as they see the ways in which it often does as much to confirm people in patterns of offending behaviour as to deflect them from them. But this futility is rarely recognised in the wider society.

Arguably, part of the responsibility for this problem lies with the news media and the way in which they report on and cover crime issues. Walmsley (2000) maintains that the public have a poor understanding of the characteristics of offenders and their offending behaviour—the public, for example, tend to overestimate the seriousness of the crimes offenders need to have committed in order to receive a custodial sentence. The idea that many prisoners are relatively minor offenders, who could be dealt with differently, has not been part of our popular common sense. So are the media giving us the right messages about crime? Drama may again play a role here. Prison films, for example, have a bias towards being set in maximum security prisons and, particularly the US action-adventure variety, tend to depict their inmates as hardened convicts. This is a misrepresentation of the characteristics of the inmate population, both in the UK and in the US, where most prisoners would not fit this description. But do screen representations influence peoples' perceptions of real prisons and can we not trust people to distinguish fact from fiction?

Believing in prison: the role of prison drama?

We have already intimated that prison constitutes something of a 'secret world', beyond the direct experience of the majority of the population. Nonetheless people do have ideas about what prison is like. These come from a variety of sources, but we cannot assume that the general public have more access to and interest in factual information about the nature of prison rather than its fictional representation. If anything, the reverse is likely to be true. Given this assumption, we need to consider the possibility that fictional representations of prison are an important source of these ideas and understandings. The problem is to identify ways in which dramatic representations come to influence peoples' perceptions of 'the real'. The approach taken below is to suggest that drama provides people with imaginative resources which help them to visualise, or imagine the nature of the world. It can be suggested that people are much more receptive to arguments about things outside of their own experience if they possess a cultural model or metaphor which helps them to visualise it. The idea that prison drama can act as an 'imaginative resource' can be developed in the form of five specific propositions.

Thus, we argue that (prison) drama:

- helps to set the limits of what we take to be the plausible range of interpretations of the world;
- translates or transcodes ideas and arguments from specialist sources (official reports, social scientific research, experiential writings) into accessible popular forms;

- can commit sins of omission as well as commission: dramatic products may help create a view of the world as much by what they leave out as through what they include;
- gives people access to models of, or metaphors for, other people's experiences which they don't experience themselves directly; and
- may evoke feelings of empathy and attach sentiment to subjects which cannot be entirely reduced to matters of rational debate.

These ideas are elaborated on below (and in the rest of this book), in an attempt to move beyond the view that fictional screen representations of prison are recognised as fiction and as such have no bearing on peoples' ideas and understandings of reality. But, what do we mean when we say that drama helps set the limits of plausibility? And how might this argument help us to move beyond the view that *Porridge* is 'just a sit-com'.

Porridge: a sanitised prison?

It could be suggested that any fictional product implicitly stakes some claim to plausibility. Although *Porridge* is 'only' a sitcom, as one set in a prison it needs to include or retain some recognisable aspects of real world prisons in order to establish its setting. *Porridge* is not set in some future world, or fantasy world but is clearly presented as being set in the present day (i.e. the then 1970s). *Porridge* retains, or includes, some aspects of real world prisons including: a set featuring prison landings, cells and an association area, plus other aspects and features (the governor's office, the prison farm, the hospital wing, etc.); prison officers and prisoners wear uniforms; and the latter are subject to regimes including 'bang-up' and 'slopping out'. The prison is shown as a hierarchy of authority, from the Governor, through chief officer, rank and file prison officers and inmates. There is a clear division between staff and inmates, with further divisions within those two groups arising within an overall structure of 'them' and 'us'. Through its inclusion of these and other features, *Porridge* constructs a view of prison and its regimes which is intended to approximate, in some way, to an idea of what prison is actually like. But in constructing this approximation, some aspects of real world prison have been left out and various things modified in the process.

No drama can fully capture the reality it purports to describe. Any dramatic product, whether a play, film or TV programme, is limited by the technology of its medium and the conventions of drama which usually require that the narrative products be comprehensible and entertaining. These constraints do limit what it is possible for drama to show and it is also true that any dramatic re-enactment of prison will still only be a representation of 'the reality', not reality itself.

But the criticism of *Porridge* is not that it failed to show 'the reality of prison', but that the approximation that it constructed was selective and sanitised. Even recognising that 'what prison is really like' is problematic—which prisons are we considering and whose account of them are we taking to constitute the reality—we can still identify the ways in which *Porridge* either excluded or reworked elements which clearly would be agreed aspects of prison. We might note, for example, that throughout three series and two Christmas specials the show never featured a suicide. The use of solitary confinement is alluded to but never actually shown and the idea that British prisons would use excessive, prolonged solitary confinement is nowhere present. Some aspects of prison life are shown but softened in the process. So, for example, the relationship between 'screws' and inmates is portrayed as a structured, mild antagonism. This is in marked contrast to the reality of the 1970s when UK prisons were affected by a wave of roof-top demonstrations and riots in protest against poor prison conditions, inflexible regimes and allegations of officer brutality. In *Porridge* McLaren goes on a roof-top protest and has to be talked down by Fletcher. But, as it turns out, the escapade is just a scam cooked up by the pair to wangle Fletcher a job in the library and McLaren one in the hospital. Similarly, one episode features a riot in which the prisoners trash the kitchen and dining area. Fletcher advises the Governor that there is only one person who can end the disturbance and so the hapless prison officer Mr Baraclough is sent in to quell the riot. 'Now, you men, just stop all this and get this mess cleaned up', he implores. Much to his surprise, the riot subsides and his instructions are followed. The disturbance has been staged to make 'soft screw' Mr Baraclough look good and prevent his transfer from the wing. Prison riots and *Porridge* riots are two different things. Is *Porridge* rewriting history before our eyes?

But are we also taking things a little too seriously here? Does the selective and sanitised representation in *Porridge* matter? Surely the fictional portrayal of prison, prisoners and prison staff in the series is *so far away from* reality that viewers recognise it as such and do not confuse it with the actuality?

Imagination and 'discounting towards the middle'
In considering how dramatic fictional products might effect our understandings and impressions of prison, our concern first is with the 'uninformed viewer' with no direct experience of prison nor particular expertise, nor interest in penal affairs. Querry (1975) suggests that because many people are ignorant about prisons:

> we are forced to call upon the powers of our imaginations—or the imaginations of someone else—to help us with the details of an institution about which we really know very little. (Querry, 1975:147 cited in Mason, 2003b)

Querry also gives examples (now somewhat anachronistic):

> Perhaps we didn't really believe that convicts danced to Elvis's guitar, but who doubted that grizzled cons on Death Row played mournful tunes on harmonicas. And while we may be skeptical of the mole-like tunneling abilities of the average prison inmate, we do tend to assume that escape is uppermost in his mind at all times. (Querry, 1975:7 cited in Mason, 2003b)

Querry's examples don't seem all that persuasive, but his observation contains a suggestion that we view fictitious dramatic products through a process of discounting and *unconscious* acceptance. We do not take fictional representations to be literally true, but once we discount the element in them that we regard to be dramatic licence what remains unconsciously influences our implicit beliefs. People clearly do not accept fictional representations as true. But it seems equally unrealistic to suggest that such representations have *no impact at all* on our thought processes and imaginations.

To develop this idea of discounting and acceptance it might be suggested that in arriving at our implicit commonsense understandings of prison we (the uninformed general public) have a tendency to 'discount towards the middle'. We do not take *Porridge* to be a literal and accurate description. Recognising the show to be both a comedy and fictional most viewers assume, or recognise, that some elements of prison life have been softened. If *Porridge* does influence their implicit commonsense view of what prison is like, they are likely to 'factor up' from that representation. Prison isn't as easy as it is depicted, the reality is likely to be worse.

But by how much does our hypothetical viewer 'factor up' from the sanitised prison of *Porridge*, and how does the implicit commonsense conception arrived at compare with the actuality of prison? This will depend on a number of things, including available alternative sources of information. If we continue with our hypothetical uninformed viewer we could suggest that alternative sources of information would include media reports of prison and other fictional dramatic representations. Media reports might provide a stream of generally negative assessments—'Inspector's Report Slams "A Bad Prison which Just got Worse"', 'Suicides and Assaults Rising as Prison Numbers Hit All Time High'. These negative reports no doubt provide ideas and information to counterbalance the sanitised view portrayed by *Porridge*. But neither are such reports necessarily accepted at face value. The public may expect inspection reports to have a bias towards identifying failings in the system and the media to be more likely to report problems and crises, rather than instances of improvement. The public may therefore 'ratchet down' from these negative assessments, assuming them to represent a potential 'worst case scenario'.

A similar process might be at work with regard to dramatic representations which portray prisons as violent, dangerous places. A number of US films released from the late 1980s to the mid-1990s depicted American prisons as battlegrounds between warring prison gangs. The death-count and degree of violence depicted in such films almost certainly exceeds the actuality of prisoner assaults which occur in US prisons. But again viewers most certainly recognise that the films' producers are taking dramatic licence and 'ratchet down' from this depiction. Prisons are not as violent and dangerous as shown in the US action-adventure prison movies, although these representations may still leave a taint of residual plausibility with prison being viewed as in some way a 'dangerous' environment. Even if UK viewers unconsciously subtract for dramatic licence, they may still be left with the idea that these screen prisons must in some ways approximate to the American penal system and the audience may inherit, for example, the notion that US prisons are racially divided.

In these ways drama may help set the limits of plausibility. Is prison the sanitised 'holiday camp' portrayed in *Porridge*, or a kill-or-be-killed playground for hard-core gang members? We, the uninformed viewer, do the subconscious mental arithmetic. The reality lies somewhere between these poles. But having done the arithmetic and arrived at our implicit commonsense view, where does the mid-point that we arrive at lie, and how does it compare with the actuality? This is a difficult question to give a precise answer to. Different people will make their own unconscious calculations differently, depending on their background, interests, information and the imagery available to them. So implicit common sense is likely to encompass a range of perceptions. Similarly the actuality of prison is itself a variable, with different institutions and regimes which vary in place and time. Saying precisely how common sense and 'reality' converge or diverge is no straightforward matter, but one way into this would be to consider the accounts of people who have experienced prison. How did their experience relate to their expectations?

Commonsense expectations, actual experience and dramatic preparation
There is not sufficient space here to develop a comprehensive survey of all the relevant contributions, but one example might provide us with some insight. In 1993 Sandra Gregory, a British citizen working in Thailand as a teacher, fell ill and lost her job. Having no money to afford the plane fare home to Britain for treatment, she unwisely agreed to act as a drug mule to obtain her passage. Subsequently she was arrested at the airport, charged with drug smuggling, convicted and sentenced to 25 years in the Lard Yao prison, also known as 'the Bangkok Hilton'. Later, writing of her experience, she said:

> What I sensed immediately is that prison is not like the movies, or television dramas. It's far more insane, terrible, emotional and disgusting than any of those.
>
> (Gregory, 2002)

Sandra Gregory's comments do not appear to be aimed at the Thai system of criminal justice or that penal system. She says simply that her impressions of prison, gained from film and TV drama, did not prepare her for the reality. And if one reads her account of her case, being repatriated to Britain to serve out her sentence in a UK prison was a long way from being the end of her problems. But to return to Gregory's words: prison is far more 'insane, terrible, emotional and disgusting'. This is in a sense surprising, as any number of prison movies, including the women-in-prison sub-genre and particularly those featuring prisons abroad, surely have the recurring theme of just how awful prison is! But, if Gregory's experience is anything to go by, why does the screen depiction not prepare us for reality?

Can drama educate us to 'the reality of prison'? Could film and TV provide us with an understanding of what prison might be like, such that if we were to 'do time', whether in the Bangkok Hilton or an average British medium secure prison, our entry into the 'secret world' of prison would not be as much of a culture shock as it might otherwise be? One view suggested already is that screen drama can never fully represent the awfulness of prison. There is an element of truth in this. A film will always be just a film. The medium possesses a necessary degree of artificiality. The most commonly cited example here is the difference between the run-time of a film and the run-time of a prison sentence. Can film show the extended stretches of boredom that prison entails? Films have a degree of artificiality in other ways too. For example, they tend to use photogenic stars who are likely to be untypical of the people you would meet in a prison. This artificiality might be one reason why people, consciously at least, tend to discount 'film-prisons' as unlike 'real-prisons'.

It could be argued that there is something about film (or television) as a medium that makes it unsuitable to convey 'the awful reality' of prison. But should we accept this idea? The autobiographies and other writings of people who have experienced prison are a source of insight into what the reality is like. Anyone reading Jimmy Boyle's (1977) autobiographical account of Scottish prisons in the 1970s could not help but be struck by the extent to which his version of events portrays a view of prison markedly different to that conveyed by *Porridge*. Not everyone might agree with Boyle's account of his life and career within the penal system as recounted in his book *A Sense of Freedom* and this makes his version a contested one. It does not, however, establish that his experience is *unrepresentable*. Boyle's book was adapted for TV and screened as a one-off drama special, which arguably did succeed in capturing some of the insights provided by his book. Again the point here is not so much that drama can fully capture reality or 'tell the whole story'. Rather, it is that drama can help set the limits of plausibility and through its inclusion or exclusion of particular issues help shape perceptions of reality. To the extent that *Porridge* never showed prison officer brutality or suicides, these issues were absent from our screens and to that extent much less visible in popular debate. *A Sense of Freedom* provided a very different account, despite the fact that both it and *Porridge* were reflecting on prison in the 1970s.

Expanding the range of dramatic representations
Alternatives to the sanitised view of prison portrayed in *Porridge* were produced both at the time and then later, but for a variety of reasons these more hard-edged, critical alternatives are much less often seen. As it is usually quite difficult for anyone to come up with ideas and insights about subjects which are beyond their own experience, then one of the things that film and TV drama can do is to give people ideas that they might not have otherwise had. If more people had the opportunity to see the TV version of *A Sense of Freedom*, for example, or other similar products, rather than endless reruns of *Porridge* then their understanding of a life in custody might well be different. It is not so much that there is anything wrong with the fact that *Porridge* was made and shown, or that it is endlessly repeated, but that other representations of prison found it harder to get into production and those that did are seen less often. Whilst this is partly explicable in terms of the 'entertainment value' of the products concerned, it is not the whole story.

One example that might help to convey the point here is the film *Silent Scream* (1990). It tells the story of Larry Winters and his experience of the Scottish penal system in the 1960s and 1970s. In 1964 Winters was convicted of the murder of a barman in a London pub but was given a life sentence as opposed to hanging, apparently on the basis that he had some kind of psychological or mental instability. Winters found it difficult to cope with the inflexible regimes of Scottish prisons. His mental health worsened and he became addicted to drugs. Like other lifers in the Scottish penal system at the time, Winters came into conflict with the authorities about the conditions of his incarceration and was involved in peaceful protests, demonstrating against the extended periods of solitary confinement and prison officer brutality. He was also involved in several violent assaults on prison officers.

Silent Scream presents a fairly sympathetic portrayal of Winters. He is shown to be a disturbed but sensitive young man who could have led a productive life in prison, if accommodated within an appropriate regime. One significant scene in the film comes early on, just as Winters is about to be admitted to the Special Unit at

Barlinnie prison. A small group of prison officers are discussing his impending arrival, with one of them expressing strong reservations about accepting him into the unit. The officer knows of Winters by his reputation and quite frankly admits that he is scared of him. When Winters actually arrives we see a tall, thin, slightly dishevelled man wearing blue and white striped pyjamas open at the top. Winters appears slightly edgy and somewhat traumatised, but is able to accept a cigarette when it is offered to him. Overall it is clear that he is reasonably non-threatening and has far more to fear from the prison officers than they from him.

Silent Scream is not easy to watch. It has only a loosely chronological narrative, interspersed with flashbacks which have no clear order. The overall style of the film is fragmentary, disconnected and impressionistic. Nonetheless it succeeds in conveying the impression of a man whose mental and physical health has been totally wrecked by the prison system. Ironically the film succeeds in getting this across, despite the fact that much of its narrative centres on the efforts of the staff in the Barlinnie Special Unit to reconnect Winters with his family and reality. The film succeeds not only in showing the harm prison did to Larry Winters but is also able to suggest that things could have been different. The drama is possibly too sympathetic towards Winters. It shows his original crime more as an act of confusion than malice. It also tends to show the violence inflicted on him, but not that inflicted in the opposite direction. But the point is not really whether the film succeeds in telling everybody's version of the story of Larry Winters, for it obviously cannot. Its significance is that it gives a radically different version of prison to that presented by the comedic prison of *Porridge* or the stylised Hollywood action-adventure prison movie. It is an example of the ability of drama to convey an idea powerfully and in so doing to give some insight into reality. It is not being suggested that *Silent Scream* is a 'better', or more realistic view of prison than *Porridge*, although arguably it is. Rather its significance is in its difference and that it adds to the range of representations available which people can draw on in order to make sense of prison.

THE WAY FORWARD

Prison is a complex and contested reality and thus there is no agreement as to whether prisons in the UK are getting better or worse. Whilst many believe that prison is an expensive and counter-productive response to crime, the government plans to expand the number of prison places and the prison population is predicted to continue to rise. Whilst all this is happening, the general public seem relatively indifferent to the cause of penal reform. Reformers tend to talk in terms which mean little to the general public, most of whom have no experience of working with offenders. It could be suggested then, that penal reform and issues of prison policy and management can and should be left to those politicians, policy-makers, professions and activist groups with a particular knowledge of and interest in penal affairs. There is surely some evidence that improvements in prison regimes have taken place without any level of mass interest, or involvement from the public. However, if we are to have an informed debate, which accommodates more than the professionals and activists who already have an interest in this subject, the public need to be equipped with models and metaphors that enable them to connect with the issues being discussed. Until the public can be encouraged to see offenders as people, who have a life before and after the crimes that they have committed, then it may be hard to convince people of the value of alternatives to custody. Drama can be one way of providing the imaginative apparatus necessary to enter the debate.

In the past one of the main tasks of penal reform has been to improve prison regimes. Arguably prisons *have* improved and practices that were accepted in previous eras would now be frowned upon. But the paradox of penal reform may be that as prison improves, then so too does society become increasingly willing to resort to prison as a response to crime. Objections to this counter-productive strategy have already been extensively rehearsed and there is little point going over them here (Mathiesen, 2000; Wilson and Ashton, 1998). But if the prison population is to be reduced, then alternatives need to be popularised and legitimated and rethinking the prison may require the rethinking of our conception of justice .

It could be suggested that at present our criminal justice system operates on a notion of 'punitive justice'—those who have done a wrong shall have a wrong done back to them. As Mathiesen (1990; 2000) pointed out some time ago, this model of justice gives nothing positive back to the victims of crime. They receive no reparation or compensation. It is also a model of punishment that sees no possibility that any good can come out of tragic events, and amounts in effect to arguing that 'two wrongs do make a right'. More recently, a lot of effort has gone into developing an idea of Restorative Justice (Braithwaite, 1989), whereby criminal justice systems look for ways to put victims and offenders in contact with each other so that victims can receive back some material or symbolic compensation or reparation for any hurt they have suffered. But at present the term Restorative Justice, and the practical schemes it gives rise to, have a relatively low profile within the public's imagination. If the public are to be included in the process of rethinking crime, punishment and prison, then they will need a non-technical/non-expert appreciation of what Restorative Justice means. Popular film and TV drama is one of the main ways in which people might acquire such an understanding.

The rest of this book: scope and methods
What we hope we have established so far, if only in outline, is the proposition that film and TV drama matter. They are not just entertainment products: they also help shape our understanding of the world. Drama can give us impressions which fill in those places, or aspects of society, of which we have little direct knowledge. Drama can rehearse arguments drawn from specialist sources of knowledge and diffuse these in a popular form. Drama can give us, or fail to give us, the models and metaphors we need to understand and debate issues outside (or even within) our own immediate experience. All of these functions are particularly relevant to the case of prison, for reasons which we hope we have already given. Drama can help raise the level of awareness of and interest in particular issues, or equally can convince us that we already know all we need to know about a particular topic. It is for these reasons that we need to investigate the repertoire of prison drama. What representations of prison have been presented to us in film and on TV and what impact have they had on popular understandings of prison, prisoners and punishment? Does prison drama allow us to think critically about prison, or does it encourage us to believe that prison is something that we need not worry about?

Immediately we begin to think about these questions we start to see some of the problems involved in answering them. A number of difficulties arise concerning the scope and method of our enquiry. Our discussion so far has tended to use the term 'prison drama'. By this we mean fictional, dramatic representations of prison in film and on TV. We start by examining 'the prison film', partly in the belief that every generation has one classic prison movie that operates as some kind of benchmark for unconscious understanding of prison. What role do these classic prison films play in shaping our understanding and in influencing real world penal realities? We explore this issue firstly in relation to the British prison film and then with respect to the US prison movie. Hollywood has long been an integral part of British culture and it makes little sense not to engage with the US prison movie, which in turn requires us to engage with US penal realities.

It should be said that no authoritative list exists of every prison film ever made and even if there were such a list, it is unlikely that any one analyst, or even group of analysts, could locate and view all such films. When attempting to develop an analysis of prison films there is no ready made guide as to which films should be chosen for consideration. Should the analyst attempt to view and analyse as comprehensive a range of films as possible, or concentrate on the few big prison movies, those which are the most well known and most often seen? How much effort should go into locating and analysing films on the margin of the category? In the analysis that follows we attempt to provide both some broad-brush surveys, which map out the historical development of the prison film, both in the UK and USA, and to analyse some less well-known films, some of which might not usually be included within the category of prison film. We cannot claim to have identified, still less have seen, every possible film that could qualify. Nevertheless we believe our analysis to be reasonably comprehensive, both charting what are the generally agreed key texts within the prison film tradition and identifying some interesting lesser known films that may have some qualitative bearing on our analysis. We also look at some selected examples of representation of prison in TV series. Although our approach here is not comprehensive, we hope to demonstrate the significance of the examples we have chosen.

In the material that follows we identify a number of prison film traditions. We chart the development of the prison film in Britain, identifying both a comedic and a social realist tradition and a more recent group of films which would seem to constitute a newly emerging tradition. We similarly chart the development of the prison movie in the USA, from its pre-war origins up until the present day. We identify the similarities of films within these traditions, in terms of both style and structure and the issues they raise or fail to raise about prison. The categories identified are not intended to imply that films within any given identified tradition constitute a unified whole. There is always a need to examine individual films and assess each in its own right. Our discussion contains elements of broad-brush survey and in-depth examination of individual films, or groups of films. In addition to considering the main traditions of prison film we also devote some attention to analysing certain sub-categories, including, for example films featuring escaped and released prisoners. For Britain, where the distinction between prison film and TV drama is more permeable than in the US, we discuss significant TV prison dramas alongside films where this seems appropriate.

Any discussion of prison, or prison drama should recognise the structuring influences of race and gender. One definitional and methodological issue which arises is how to treat films that deal with women's experience of prison. Do women-in-prison films constitute a distinct sub-genre? Here, in our survey chapters, we have kept films dealing with women's experiences within our main surveys. In addition to this, we also provide a chapter dedicated to dealing with women's prison drama. When considering issues of race and racism we need to recognise that, in Britain and the USA, visible minorities and people of colour are over represented within the prison population, although they are perhaps under represented on screen. Although we do not devote a specific chapter to race and prison drama, discussion of the relevant issues is included within our general surveys. In Britain there has been no black equivalent to the women's prison drama. We do however provide a chapter analysing the recent C4 TV series *Buried* (*Chapter 6*) and another analysing the racially-divided prison depicted in America's HBO cult TV drama *Oz* (*Chapter 7*).

The concluding chapter pulls together the whole discussion and makes some suggestions about the ways in which prison film might be used as a springboard to debate the nature of prison and its role within the criminal justice system. Our discussion of the prison film and its TV relations is not intended to be merely an academic exercise, or a 'fan-appreciation'. Rather, we hope to stimulate interest in the idea that prison film and TV drama can be a valuable penal reform resource. At the most obvious level films can be rich in visual information. One scene—or even just one shot—in a film can convey a very nuanced understanding of a social situation that might be nearly impossible to convey by verbal or written description. If 'a picture paints a thousand words' then it should be remembered that a film runs at 24 frames per second.

CHAPTER 2

The British Prison Film Revisited

If asked to name the stars and titles of three British prison films the average member of the public would probably struggle to formulate an answer. A particularly game respondent might venture the films *Scum* or *McVicar*, or perhaps one of the more recent offerings, say, Vinny Jones's *Mean Machine*. But, it seems safe to say that the British prison film does not enjoy that high a profile. Indeed some of the key films within this tradition have the status of being little more than cult movies. At a time when the prison population of England and Wales has reached an all-time high, when Scotland and Northern Ireland are similarly wrestling with the problem of restraining prison growth, and whilst the UK has the highest incarceration rates in Europe, can an interest in the British prison film be justified? Is the cataloguing and recovery of this 'lost cultural heritage' little more than a frivolous exercise for anorak film buffs? We hope that it is not—and in this chapter argue that the British prison film tradition is a subject worth studying. 'What films have been made?', 'When were they released?' and 'How did they portray prison?' are among the questions that we ask.

There is of course a common sense tendency to deny the significance of film and TV in shaping perceptions of social life. The idea that such drama influences the way in which we see prison is not broadly accepted. For example, the suggestion that the widely seen BBC situation comedy *Porridge* has been a significant source of people's understanding of prison was met with derision by some sections of the press (see, for example, 'Sitcoms Miss the Boiling Issues', *London Evening Standard*, 16 July 2003). To those who would reject the suggestion that *Porridge* may have contributed to public complacency about prison, we would pose the question as to why there has been so little outcry at Britain's current record high prison population. Why are the public prepared to accept, without any apparent qualms, the current record incarceration rates? Are the public generally well informed on penal affairs or are they, to a degree, systematically *misinformed* as to the nature of prison? If the latter is true, where does this misinformation come from and what roles do film and TV drama play in shaping the public's perceptions of prison?

The following discussion is informed by a view that the general public, or at least those amongst the public who do not have any direct experience of prison, are for the most part both uninformed and misinformed on penal affairs. It will be suggested that popular common sense notions of prison systematically underestimate 'the pain of incarceration' (Mathiesen, 2000). A very brief history of prison in Britain will be introduced to support the argument that there is always a *discrepancy* between 'the reality of prison' at any given time and the public's perception of it. This will then allow us to discuss the role of prison drama in highlighting or concealing this discrepancy. A periodisation of the historical development of the prison film in Britain is introduced. Both general tendencies within this tradition and the significance of individual films are discussed. In particular the discussion focuses on the ways in which prison has been represented and the penal issues that the films under consideration raised, or excluded. In conclusion it is argued that the British prison film has had an ambivalent and contradictory quality. It tends to operate in two opposing directions at the same time. Firstly, it contributes towards the creation of a misperception of prison and deludes the public into thinking that they have some basis for estimating the nature of prison—it encourages us to think that we 'know prison', when in fact we don't. But, at the same time prison drama alerts the public to the failings of prison as an institution and to the need for change. This underlying dynamic can be shown to manifest itself in different eras from the 1930s through to the 1980s, although this relationship has perhaps changed slightly in the present day.

Prison films do many things. They comment on the way in which society sees prison. They also reflect ideas about crime, concerns about delinquency and debates about the nature of masculinity and femininity. How are men and women encouraged to see themselves and what are they encouraged to aspire to? Our discussion is mainly concerned with the ways in which prison films comment on prison, although in examining these some of the other issues that are raised will need also to be considered. The analysis presented here does not claim to be fully comprehensive, and seeks to do no more than map out the general territory of the British prison film and to indicate where possible significant areas where there is room for further discussion and analysis.

PRISON AND THE PUBLIC

Whilst many academic criminologists would argue that prison is a counter-productive and ineffective response to crime, and that alternatives to prison do exist, some politicians and some sections of the media subscribe to an alternative point of view: that society needs to be tougher on crime and that this in turn may mean harsher sentencing, leading to longer prison sentences and hence a need for more prisons. The current New Labour government appears to subscribe to both views simultaneously, its 'Janus-faced' policy stance advocating both the use of alternatives to custody wherever possible, whilst at the same time planning for more prisons, recognising that this will inevitably be accompanied by further growth in prison numbers.

Should prison capacity be expanded to facilitate 'tough on crime' sentencing? Or should prisons be closed and the money that would have been spent on them be redirected into alternative ways with which to prevent crime and to work with offenders? It could be argued that with the prison population of England and Wales currently standing at some 45,000 higher than it was ten years ago it would be possible to cut the prison population drastically in a short space of time. The point here is not really whether the arguments for a drastic reduction in prison numbers are correct or not, but whether they get a fair hearing. Many people would argue that in a democracy we can and should let elected politicians decide on what is the appropriate course of action. The government can make its choices on prison policy and the public can chose either to re-elect or vote out a government on the basis of its record in office. But there are many reasons why electoral politics works as a blunt instrument of democracy and this is particularly so in relation to prison and penal affairs, where democratic debate would work best if the public were appropriately informed as to the true costs of prison and its alternatives (Walmsley, 2000). But, if the public are systematically misinformed then they have little basis for judging whether the politicians' record of managing the penal system should be reckoned a success or a failure.

One common sense view of prison might be to deny that there is any problem of misinformation and to insist that the current prison population is not a cause for concern. Simple populist reasoning might run something like this: *criminals* commit *crimes* and get sent to *prison* for *punishment*. In this light complaints by prisoners (or their families, academics or penal reformers) about prison conditions might be met with the adage, 'If you can't do the time, don't commit the crime'. Such a view accepts that prison is a distasteful and unpleasant experience, but insists that so is it intended to be! But, we would argue, this simplistic argument does implicitly assume that some kind of proportionality exists between the offence and the punishment. Even those who believe that criminals should not whinge about 'taking their punishment' must surely recognise that there is some degree of hardship and punishment which would not be acceptable for a given offence, and which could not be dismissed in terms of 'don't do the crime'. Yet arguably the problem is that public perception tends to assume that this proportionality—between the harshness of prison and the offence committed—actually exists, when in fact the public has little real basis for knowing whether this is the case or not.

One way to demonstrate that the public tends to systematically underestimate the awfulness of prison is to consider the accounts of people who have been incarcerated, such as Sandra Gregory (see *Chapter 1*). Gregory's observation is instructive: prison was worse than she had expected. This is significant because, at heart, the case against prison is a moral one. The question we need to ask is: 'Is it just for one group of people (the unimprisoned), to impose on another group of people (the imprisoned) an experience that they would not accept for themselves in similar circumstances?' If Gregory's experience is anything to go by the general public tend to underestimate 'the pain of imprisonment' because this is, at the end of the day, an experiential quality. Prisoners know this pain of imprisonment and can convey something of its experience through their writings and autobiography. Prisoners are also more aware than most of the 'irrationality of imprisonment' and the ways in which prison as a place of punishment confounds any goals of rehabilitation. But the processes by which these experiences 'get out', and are relayed to the general public are mediated ones. Inevitably something is lost in the process, although this is not to say that experience cannot be shared or communicated. There is, for example, a long tradition of middle-class people who serve a custodial sentence going on to write about their experiences and to become campaigners for penal reform (for a discussion see Morgan, 1999). The experience of 'the middle-class ex-prisoner turned penal reformer' does suggest that we allow prison because we have a degree of ignorance of it. The experiences of working-class (ex)prisoners and their writings are of course also relevant (see Nellis, 2002).

But what role does film (and TV) drama play in all this? Can the prison film be accused of encouraging the public to underestimate the awfulness of prison, when surely one of the main themes of the movies is just that—its awfulness! As was suggested in *Chapter 1*, film and TV drama have an influence on common sense perceptions of prison through the ways in which they help to define the limits of plausibility. In relation to prison, drama delineates the bounds of plausibility as stretching from the sanitised comedic prison, most notably depicted in the BBC TV series *Porridge*, through to the infernal hell-holes of Devil's Island in *Papillon*, Alcatraz in *Murder in the First* and *Escape From Alcatraz* or the Turkish prison depicted in *Midnight Express*.

Although we cannot say precisely how people arrive at their common sense understandings of prison, it is surely not unreasonable to suggest that they in some way find a (weighted) 'midpoint' between the available representations. Clearly people do not believe that prison is as 'easy' as it is portrayed in *Porridge*. The reality is assumed to be worse. However, conversely, viewers may not believe that cinematic representations of Devil's Island or Alcatraz are reliable guides to reality either. These prisons are often represented in film as being exceptional regimes, the abuses of which have now been revealed and discovered. Various processes of distancing may lead us to believe that these cinematic prisons are worse than our currently existing actual prisons (Nellis, 1988). We argue in the discussion of British prison film developed below, that in the British context, this last belief is generally not true and that even critical depictions of the worst excesses of the British experience of prison may actually understate the reality. The public may be midpointing between two already sanitised (or at least softened) versions of penal realities. We argue that a series of formal and informal processes can be identified as operating to mute the critique of prison and limit the revelation of some of its more distasteful aspects. This is so even in portrayals of prison which are believed to be 'gritty', 'realistic' and 'truthful'.

As noted in *Chapter 1*, we recognise that establishing the above proposition does rely on us being able to give some kind of account of the actuality of prison with which to compare the cinematic representation. This is problematic as 'the reality' of prison is complex, contested and changing. Nevertheless we need some account of penal realities in order to arrive at an understanding of prison film. The strategy adopted here is to take some aspects of prison which are, if you like, agreed historical fact and to supplement these where possible with prisoners' accounts of their experience of penal realities, to provide some kind of benchmark with which to compare cinematic representations. The aim of our discussion thus developed is to show that film (and TV) soften the representation of prison regimes and may thereby contribute to the misperceptions. But we need to also record that penal realities change over time and we will go on to suggest that film representation may be one of the ways in which the need for penal reform is recognised and disseminated.

CHANGING PENAL REALITIES

It is beyond the scope of this work to provide anything more than a brief outline of the historical development of prison in Britain. What follows is a very schematic outline of some of the milestones. An attempt is made to identify certain basic propositions about penal realities in the following periods: the 1600s and the emergence of houses of correction; the 1850s and the emergence of the state prison system; the inter-war period; the post-war welfare state period; the 1960s; the 1970s; the late 1980s/early 1990s and the present day. The aim is to make some suggestions about prison regimes and how they were experienced, prior to moving on to examine how prison has been represented in British film.

The forerunners of modern prisons began back in the 1600s when in Britain and across Europe a system of houses of correction emerged to deal with the perceived problem of vagrants, beggars and the poor. Strictly speaking the houses of correction were not prisons as we understand them today since people could be confined within them for reasons other than having committed a criminal offence. Nevertheless the offence of vagrancy was one route into these institutions. Houses of correction were intended by their advocates to encourage the poor and the homeless to improve themselves to become sober, industrious, responsible members of society. The inmates were to be subject to a regime of work, schooling, education and discipline to improve their moral character. Matheisen (2000) argues that in reality the 'improving' aspects of purposeful work, schooling and religion all quickly withered as elements of the institutional regimes, leaving only basic repetitive work, done as punishment and/or a means of contributing to the financial support of the institution itself. Discipline was perhaps the one aspect of these institutions that was particularly emphasised and detailed systems of rules decreeing the punishments for a variety of infractions were developed. Prisoners could be restricted to bread and water rations, confined in the dungeon or whipped for a variety of offences ranging from cussing, through disobeying a member of staff, to refusal to work or escape. Although the regimes in these institution might not always have matched the harshness of some of the rules proposed by the more zealous advocates of 'Correction', there is evidence that refusal to work, for example, was taken very seriously and that people were whipped for this. One of the harsher methods of discipline for the particularly troublesome inmate was the 'water cellar', in which the prisoner had continually to pump out water to avoid drowning (Mathiesen, 2000: 39).

The houses of correction had, by the 1700s, developed into a system of local jails specialising in the confinement of offenders, although at this time the main response to offending was transportation. In 1776 the American Declaration of Independence ended the transportation of offenders to the American colonies and we begin to see the emergence of penitentiaries that were run, owned, managed and controlled by the state, accompanied by a fierce and detailed debate as to the design of these institutions and the regimes that would characterise them. The Penitentiary Act 1779 allowed for state-run prisons and envisaged that prisoners would be subject to solitary confinement, have religious instruction, be required to work and be subject to a coarse diet (Wilson, 2002: 368). The same Act also recommended use of the treadmill in the belief that prisoners required:

> labour of the hardest and most servile kind in which drudgery is chiefly required and where the work is little liable to be spoiled by ignorance, neglect, or obstinacy.
> Cited at: http://www.uh.edu/engines/epi374.htm

Wilson (2002) outlines the origins and development of the first state (central government) run prison at Millbank in London, built between 1812 and 1822. The establishment, which was planned to house 1,200 prisoners, began accepting inmates in 1816. As a new purpose-built prison its architecture was designed to suit its proposed regime. Prisoners were to be held one to a cell in silent solitary confinement, being allowed out to work and able to graduate to periods of association with other inmates only after a period of good behaviour. The regime was held to be 'progressive' in as much as it did not feature the use of a treadmill! But despite this apparent boon, the prison experienced difficulties from the outset. In 1817 prisoners rioted over their food allowance and between 1822 and 1824 30 prisoners died from diarrhoea. A Parliamentary Commission recommended changes to the regime of the prison to 'improve its cheerfulness', but there were riots again in 1826 and 1827, with prisoners trying to bring to the authorities their complaints about prolonged use of solitary confinement and brutality by some of the staff. The response of the authorities was to allow the prisoners to be flogged and for the 'ringleaders' to be transferred to the 'prison hulks' (converted ships in the Thames estuary where conditions were even worse). The belief that the trouble had been caused by 'indiscriminate association' amongst the inmates (i.e. too lax a regime) led to increased use of solitary confinement and restrictions on association, following which the prison is reported to have been affected by an epidemic of suicides. The establishment was superseded in 1842 when the newer, but not necessarily more progressive, HMP Pentonville opened. Millbank was converted to a women's prison in 1877 and closed in 1893 (see Wilson, 2002).

At the most obvious level, unrest within the prison would suggest that its inmates were somewhat unhappy with their lot. However there is little by the way of inmate writing or autobiography to provide us with a first hand account of how the regime was experienced. At this time it was left to novelists such as Charles Dickens to attempt to bring a sympathetic account of penal realities to a working-class audience, although Dickens himself never actually served a custodial sentence. A little later we have the experience of the playwright, author and poet Oscar Wilde (1854–1900) to draw upon. Wilde was a notable celebrity in Victorian London but in 1895 he was found guilty of having committed an act of gross indecency and received a two year prison sentence. Wilde served his sentence in Pentonville and Reading prisons, where his celebrity afforded him little protection and he was subject to the same regime as other prisoners: minimal diet, attendance at chapel daily and twice on Sundays, and six hours' a day working on the treadmill. Wilde's relatively short sentence ruined his health and he died just over two years after his release. He lived to see published his classic poem *The Ballad of Reading Goal*, an account of the horrors of prison based on his own experiences. Wilde's awareness of the discrepancy between the reality of prison and its social acceptance, based on ignorance of this reality, is expressed in one particular verse which appears at the start of *Chapter 7* of this work. The treadmill continued to be used in British prisons well into the twentieth century and it seems not unreasonable to suggest that improvements in prison regimes lag behind developments in wider society. Not only are prisons usually worse at any given time than the public would think, and hence the impact of Wilde's *Ballad of Reading Gaol*, but also as social standards change regimes that might once have been acceptable come to be viewed as archaic.

So, to continue our history, it could be argued that the end of the 1914-18 war prompted a period of reform. Returning soldiers were to be greeted with 'homes for heroes' and the immediate post-war period saw a boom in state housing construction and an improvement in housing standards, in both the public and private sectors. Whilst the inter-war years were once seen by historians as a period of prolonged, widespread depression and mass unemployment, later accounts stress the growth of new Fordist industries, the spread of the ownership of consumer durables, the rise of mass cinema attendance, and other technological advances such as the introduction of radio (Smith, 1989). Despite the experience of the Depression, the 1930s could be seen as an era of social progress and optimism. But to what extent did this climate extend to Britain's prisons?

In 1932 there was a prison mutiny at Dartmoor Prison in which the inmates briefly took control of the prison. On the face of it the mutiny arose out of complaints about the inedible nature of the food, but a better appreciation of why the revolt occurred might be gained by outlining the regime in the prison at that time. Despite recent improvements conditions were still harsh. Inmates would work a seven hour day and for the remainder of each 24 hours would be locked up alone in their cells. An inmate would have to serve two-and-a-half years before being allowed the privilege of reading newspapers and four years before he was allowed to smoke and enjoy limited periods of association (Fitzgerald, 1977: 122). The average cell was small, damp and draughty, with bare granite walls and rudimentary furniture. Punishment cells, another focus of complaint by the mutineers, were half the size of a standard cell, taking the form of a sound proofed cell within a cell. In the punishment cells inmates could spend 23 hours a day alone with little light (Fitzgerald, 1977: 122). The mutineers briefly took control of the prison for some two hours before it was taken back by armed prison officers. The leaders of the mutiny were subject to court proceedings and received additional sentences increasing their time to be served.

But we should not assume that the conditions that existed within Dartmoor were acceptable at that time. The 1930s were characterised by an extensive debate on penal reform and the period saw a number of plays and novels based on the experiences of prisoners beginning to document the reality of the prison regime (Nellis, 1988). At around the same time as Dartmoor maintained its regime of discipline and control the first open prison was built at New Hall Camp near Wakefield. We shall see later how the Dartmoor mutiny was indirectly reflected in film.

Just as the First World War had prompted social reform in the form of 'homes for heroes', so similarly did the Second World War promise not just that but also a 'cradle to grave' welfare state. The penal system could not remain unaffected by welfare state thinking and the Criminal Justice Act 1948 ended hard labour and flogging in British prisons, although the post-war welfare state optimism fell well short of envisaging an end to crime. The immediate post-war period was characterised by fears of a crime wave driven by spivs, black-market racketeers, and disgruntled, de-mobbed ex-servicemen. But as the perceived post-war crime wave of the 1940s petered out, it was replaced by concerns about a rise in delinquency by both juveniles and females. At the same time notions about the prevention and treatment of delinquency started to gain credibility, suggesting a need for a broader response to the problem of crime, rather than reliance on prison alone.

It seems quite reasonable to suggest that following the 1948 Act regimes in the post-war prisons of the 1950s were an improvement on those of their pre-war counterparts. However, such improvements seemed merely to encourage the use of custody and prison numbers rose during the 1950s and 1960s. At the same time the proportion of long-term and life-sentenced prisoners was increasing, a trend symbolically confirmed with the abolition of hanging in 1965.

It has been suggested that these changes were perceived, particularly by prison officers, as presenting a problem in terms of maintaining discipline and control (Fitzgerald, 1977; Boyle, 1977). Allegations of prison officer brutality directed against inmates, particularly those who questioned the adequacy of conditions, and of inappropriate and excessive use of punishment cells surfaced in the late 1960s. In 1969 Parkhurst prison on the Isle of White experienced the worst prison riot in the UK since the 1932 Dartmoor mutiny. Thirty-five prison officers and 28 prisoners were injured, some of them seriously. The complaints of the prisoners centred particularly around the use of punishment cells and allegations that the prison officers staffing these cells would regularly dispense 'vicious beatings' to the inmates detained there (Fitzgerald, 1977: 131). The 'ringleaders' of the riot were subject to court proceedings and received additional sentences, whilst allegations against prison staff of brutality led to no official prosecutions, leaving the prisoners to pursue their own private ones. Outside of prison the 1960s were characterised by mini-skirts, Mini cars, the Beatles (singing *All You Need is Love* and *Give Peace a Chance*) and 1969 was dubbed the 'Summer of Love'. But this changing social climate seems to have been slow to penetrate the UK prison system.

Under the influence of nostalgia TV (programmes such as *I Love 19...*, etc.), the 1970s are in danger of becoming remembered mainly for 'clackers', the pop group Mungo Jerry and the heatwave of 1976. Although the 1970s were all these things, this was also the time of: the 1972 miners' strike; the three day working week; unemployment rising to the one million mark; civil disturbances after the Notting Hill Carnival; Punk Rock and Rock Against Racism; and the 1979 Winter of Discontent (marked by widespread public-sector strikes) amongst other things. The world of prison was similarly eventful. In 1971 an uprising took place in the Attica penitentiary in upstate New York. The prisoners took control and held it for four days, before being overcome in a display of force that led to the deaths of 29 of them and ten of their hostages (Fitzgerald, 1977). At this time prison riots also occurred in Italy and elsewhere in Europe, and British prisoners were aware of this. In Britain, prison in the 1970s was characterised by riots, sit-down and roof-top protests, with prisoners' complaints centring around prison officer brutality, prolonged and excessive use of solitary confinement and the use of drugs and medication to control the inmate population (Fitzgerald, 1977). One difference between the 1960s/1970s and earlier periods is that accounts by working-class prisoners of their experiences were gaining in popularity. So, for example, both *McVicar, by Himself* (1974) and Jimmy Boyle's *A Sense of Freedom* (1977) provide insider accounts: a richer description of the experience of prison than is possible in official reports or historical summaries.

In 1979 the Conservative Party, led by Margaret Thatcher, came to power, promising to cut public expenditure, taxes and crime. Accordingly the Thatcher era saw unemployment rise to three million and a long running contest between the National Union of Mineworkers and the government. The 1984/5 miners' strike ended in defeat for the miners and was duly followed by the planned programme of pit closures that had been at the heart of the dispute. Of course the 1980s was also the era of the newly affluent young professionals dubbed 'Yuppies'; the introduction of mobile phones; the expenditure of billions of pounds on the redevelopment of London's rundown docklands and other deprived areas; and the emergence of 'Basildon man'—affluent, new working-class and Conservative voting. With the Conservatives promising to be tough on law and order, the prison population at first rose but then later fell during the 1980s. The fall was too little and too late to avert the crisis developing in some of Britain's local jails.

In April 1990 Strangeways prison in Manchester was taken over by its inmates in the worst prison riot in British history and later a series of copycat disturbances occurred in 20 other prisons across the country. The Strangeways disturbances lasted 25 days, saw 147 injuries to staff and 47 to prisoners, caused an estimated £60m worth of damage, and one prisoner—segregated for his own protection under 'Rule 43' (now rule 45 whereby vulnerable prisoners are separated from the others for their own protection)—died (Woolf, 1991). What caused this major riot? There seems to be agreement that at the time the prison was suffering from chronic overcrowding and related problems. Some 1,700 prisoners were crammed into an establishment originally designed to hold 970; most were 'doubled-up' two (or three) to a cell. It seems to be agreed that for many prisoners there was no association, nor purposeful activities. Most of the prisoners were on 23-hour-a-day 'bang-up' (confinement to cells), in overcrowded cells which had no sanitation, and therefore were still—as late as 1990—relying on 'slopping out'. The significance of this practice was not so much the routine of emptying the chamber pots at morning 'unlock', but the fact that the contents of the pots remained in the cell throughout the time prisoners were locked up (Woolf, 1991). The above details form the 'official' agreed features of the situation at Strangeways. However, prisoner accounts add that the protest was not just about living conditions but also violence and brutality perpetrated by prison officers on inmates.

The Strangeways disturbances prompted an enquiry by Lord Justice Woolf. The Woolf Report (1991) argued that prison regimes had to be perceived by prisoners as being fair and a period of liberalisation was initiated in the early 1990s. As the 1990s wore on prisoner numbers rose significantly, overcrowding increased and it is possible to paint a very negative view of prisons at the end of the 1990s/beginning of the new millennium, with suicides rising again from the late 1990s and further disturbances and roof-top protests in 2002/3.

British prisons are regulated in a number of ways. In the 1990s the Incentives and Earned Privileges Scheme was introduced as one means of maintaining control through the granting or withholding of a series of petty privileges defined through three levels of prisoner regime identified as 'basic', 'standard' and 'enhanced'. The withholding of advancement through these levels can be used as a way of punishing prisoners who are perceived to be 'trouble makers'.

Some prisoners would argue that prison still relies on abusive power (rather than management by consent as recommended by Woolf) and that punishment blocks continue to be used in inappropriate and excessive ways. Other sources suggest that regimes are improving, citing as evidence the amount of time devoted to purposeful activity, the number of education qualifications gained, access to telephones, and visitor contact (Leech and Cheney, 2002).

The accounts we have given above are provided in an attempt to support a more general point, that the public systematically underestimate the harshness of penal conditions. So, for example, conditions in Strangeways would have become known to the general public only after the 1990 riot and even then through sources which could only give a mediated and limited account of the factors underlying the disturbances. More generally, the public misperceive prison simply because they lack the hard information about what regimes/conditions are like and also because they lack the ability to translate the information they do have into an assessment of the reality.

Prison regimes do improve over time. UK prisons today do not have water cellars or treadmills, although some would argue that they have equally cruel forms of mental torture. But in general standards have improved. 'Slopping out', which was once accepted practice, has now all but disappeared and where it does occur, by the back door, is seen as a failing. Despite the improvements that have taken place, problems still remain relating to overcrowding and the record prisoner numbers. And prison will always manifest conflicts and tensions which are to an extent inherent in its nature. But we need to remind ourselves again that a *discrepancy* always exists between: the public's perceptions of prison; what they would accept for themselves if they were imprisoned; and the penal realities, which will always be harsher. How can the public be alerted to this discrepancy and what role might film (and TV) drama play in the processes?

THE BRITISH PRISON FILM

As already indicated, no complete or authoritative list exists of every prison film ever made in Britain. Some of the early examples may be lost in the mists of time and even a list of post-war films will necessarily reflect only those known to the compiler. But although it has been said that the prison film is notoriously difficult to define, this doesn't seem to be a major problem in the case of the British prison movie. The *Filmography* provided at the end of this chapter identifies some 30 instances. Most of the films included in the list would generally be accepted as instances of the British prison film tradition—broadly defined, and including portrayals of male and female, adult and adolescent experiences of prison, and of young offender institutions, but excluding prisoner of war movies. Boundary problems still occur. Should capital punishment films featuring death cell inmates count as prison films or constitute a category on their own? What about courtroom dramas which feature scenes of the accused in prison? However the majority of the films noted are clearly prison films or relevant to prison. Inevitably it may be possible to pull other films into the analysis or exclude some of those considered, but in the main there is a degree of agreement as to the films which merit discussion.

How should we approach the analysis? The approach adopted here is to introduce a periodisation of the British prison film—division into chronological periods—both to facilitate discussion of the films themselves and to suggest their relationship to changing penal realities. This periodisation is inspired by, but reworks earlier work by Nellis (1987) who in particular has done much to map out the earlier periods of the British prison film.

Firstly, we can identify a period pre-1939 when relatively few prison films were produced—this can be characterised as a period of 'restriction'. Then 1945-59 when the number of prison films increased and those that were produced could be said to reflect a degree of 'post-war optimism'. By the 1960s prison films continued to be made but began to question the concept of prison and to 'retreat' from the post-war optimism about reform. Next came a burst of films in the late 1970s/early 1980s, which tended to be critical of penal institutions and to varying degrees identified problems within them. Prison film here reflected a 'crisis and concern' about penal institutions. Then, between the mid-1980s and the end of the 1990s there appears to have been a relative hiatus in British prison film—a period of 'disappearance'. Finally, from the late 1990s into the new millennium, we see the emergence of a new style of British prison film which does not immediately appear to be related to changing penal realities. The rather whimsical, 'English' view of prison portrayed in the films produced here suggests that the period be identified as one of 'knowing nostalgia'

This periodisation, illustrated in *Table 2.1*, is expanded on and explained below. It is not being suggested that in any given period all prison films reproduced the characteristics of the dominant tendency, nor that films within a tendency should be seen as being the same in intent or effect. The films are discussed mainly in terms of the penal issues they raised, or excluded, and the film style in which this was done. It is suggested that the films, particularly for the earlier periods, in some way reflected a series of formal and informal social pressures which shaped the manner in which prison could be represented. One further issue that will arise from the discussion is that of the origins of the film product. Is there any significant difference between films which were conceived of firstly as dramatic/entertainment products, which then researched prison as their topic and those films which originated in real world experiences of prison which were then dramatised?

Pre-war restriction (the 1930s)
As Nellis (1987; 1988) has rightly pointed out the pre-war period in Britain is marked by a relative absence of prison films. In Britain there was no equivalent of the US prison movie as made under the Hollywood studio system. Whereas the 1930s saw some 60 or more US prison movies, in Britain there were few if any 'pure prison movies'. *Escape* (1930 and remade in 1948) was a film adaption of a John Galsworthy play, but its story of a middle-class convict on the run from Dartmoor dealt relatively little with the prison itself. The 1935 film *King of the Damned* told the story of revolt by prisoners on a Caribbean island penal colony.

Table 2.1: *A periodisation of the British prison film*

Era	Prison film trend	Events and background	Indicative films	Type/Comment
1930s	Pre-war restriction: few British prison films produced and distributed.	Dartmoor mutiny (1932). Debates about flogging in prison.	*Convict 99* (1938)	Comedy
1945–59	Post-war, welfare state optimism: more prison films produced reflecting optimism about improved regimes.	Concerns about 'post-war crime wave' and rise in delinquency.	*Good Time Girl* (1949) *The Weak and the Wicked* (1953) *Now Barrabas* (1948)	Drama
1960s	Retreat from optimism: doubts about prison as achieving reform and rehabilitation.	Growth of prison population, abolition of hanging (1965).	*The Criminal* (1960) *The Pot Carriers* (1962) *The Loneliness of the Long Distance Runner* (1962)	A variety of different film styles reflecting a shift away from the respectable, serious drama of the previous decade.
Late 1970s/ early 1980s	Crisis and concern. Prison as problem: burst of film (and TV) activity reflecting conflict within the prison system.	Growth of control units, riots and roof-top protests, organizations for prisoners' rights.	*Scum* (1979) *A Sense of Freedom* (1979) *McVicar* (1980)	TV/film crossover. Influence of the bio-pic.
Mid-1980s/ late 1990s	Disappearance: few prison films made.	Thatcherism etc., Majorism, Strangeways riot (1990).	No indicative films.	Emergence of the 'prison-dentistry movie'.
New millennium	Knowing nostalgia: reappearance of the Brit-pic prison film.	Continued prison growth/ perceived prisons crisis	*Greenfingers* (2000) *Lucky Break* (2001) *Mean Machine* (2001) *Tommorrow La Scala* (2002)	Nostalgia, whimsy and Englishness.

It's Never too Late to Mend (1937) was a historical drama which was a critique of the Victorian prison, but not necessarily translatable into a view on current penal realities. *Prison Without Bars* (1938) was an English remake of a French film set in a women's reformatory, which retained the French setting of the original. Nellis (1988) suggests that the only real candidate for a contemporary set 'pure prison movie' at this time is a Will Hay comedy, *Convict 99* (1938) (see Nellis, 1988: 5). Some movie databases record the existence of a 1931 British prison film, *The Shadow Between* but this film does not seem to be available and so the discussion below will follow Nellis in discussing *Convict 99* as indicative of the period.

How should we account for the relative absence of British prison movies in this period? Nellis (1987; 1988) suggests three reasons. Firstly, the British prison authorities actively discouraged any interest in penal affairs. Access to prisons was restricted and staff were dissuaded from co-operating with film makers. Former prisoners and ex-staff were frowned upon for producing accounts of their prison experience. The authorities believed that prison should be a secret world, of which the public enjoyed a fearful ignorance.

Secondly, film makers were discouraged from taking on prison topics because of the formal processes of the British Board of Film Censors (BBFC). This was an industry-established body but located within the Home Office. Its task was to provide self-regulation of the film industry, as a means of avoiding more formal regulation. The BBFC followed the official line on prison, seeing it as a subject that was sordid rather than uplifting, and actively discouraged its representation. In the 1930s a system of scenario censorship operated whereby screenplays would be vetted by the board prior to production. A restriction on the inclusion of objectionable prison scenes was stated in the board's criteria for scene refusal (Nellis, 1988: 6).

A third, more general, reason for the restricted development of the British prison film would relate to the culture of the industry at the time. By as early as the 1920s Hollywood film products had come to dominate British cinema screens. The weakness of the British film industry required it to continually petition the government for protection from US imports and/or support for the domestic industry on the grounds that this was in the national interest. In the light of this, British film makers tended to avoid challenging dominant interests and subscribed to prevailing notions of respectability and national consensus. This is clearly reflected in the films of the time and so precluded prison becoming the topic of a 'social problem film'. Indeed, arguably no tradition of a 'social problem film' existed in Britain prior to World War II (Nellis, 1988: 7).

Convict 99

In the context of the 'climate of restriction' described above, it is significant that the closest thing to a contemporary British prison movie surviving from this period is a Will Hay comedy *Convict 99*. The film features Hay as a roguish headmaster who has been unceremoniously booted out of his previous job for an impropriety. By a farcical error he attends an interview and is unwittingly appointed Governor of Blackdown Prison. As Hay arrives drunk to take up his new post he is caught up in a riotous melée and admitted to the prison as an inmate—Convict 99. Later, when it is 'realised' that Convict 99 is their new Governor, Hay is put in charge of the prison and immediately begins to devolve the running of the institution to its occupants. Before long the prison has deckchairs in the exercise yard, with the cons and Hay vying for control of the illicit scams run from inside the prison. But when one of the prisoners—'The Rat'—fraudulently makes off with the scam money that has been accumulated in the prison bank account, Hay has to travel to London to recover it and avoid official discovery. Fortunately a group of prisoners 'break out' of the prison and travel to London to assist. They succeed in recovering the money, break into the bank to replenish the prison bank account and return to prison by morning. The arrival of the prisoners back at the prison in the nick of time leads to Hay's efforts in running the prison being proclaimed as 'a great day for penal reform'.

There are several things that could be added to this brief plot summary (again the discussion here draws on Nellis (1988)). Firstly Blackdown, the prison in the film, is clearly intended to be a stand-in for HMP Dartmoor—scene of the Dartmoor mutiny only six years previously. Hay is shown travelling cross-country to reach the West Country location of his new establishment. However, the representation of the prison is a problem for the film's makers as they have no means of depicting visually the interior of a prison to which they had been denied access. As Nellis suggests, some of the scenes, particularly early on in the film, clearly draw on American movie tradition. Indeed, at the start the prisoners are represented as being unmistakeably hostile and belligerent, with scenes of riot and confrontation that could have come straight out of a 1930s American prison movie. But as the film progresses the comedy takes over and 'the crims' become less threatening and more accepting of their incarceration.

Nellis (1988) reports that *Convict 99* was criticised at the time for its depiction of prison life, which was at some remove from the known penal realities of the day. The film has clearly softened prison and, arguably, started a tradition of prison comedy that was continued later in *Two-way Stretch* (1960) and then the TV series *Porridge* and its film (1979). If we believe that these film images do influence people's common sense understanding of prison, then *Convict 99* is clearly operating to cause people to underestimate the awfulness of it. On the other hand it might be argued that prison comedy, from *Convict 99* to *Porridge*, does humanise the prisoners and so unwittingly contributes to penal reform. After all *Convict 99* does carry the message that attempts to contain the prisoners within a harsh regime will be met with belligerence and resistance, whilst a more relaxed regime might bring out their more cooperative qualities. Regardless of what weight one would wish to give to this argument, the film clearly did succeed in arriving at a formula for producing a representation of prison that was acceptable within prevailing social norms. It at least made prison visible—and stood there to be disagreed with.

Post-war welfare state optimism (1945–59)
Following the restriction of the pre-war era, the post-war period saw a significant increase in the number of British prison and prison-related films. The 1940s and the 1950s saw the production of: *Now Barabbas* (1948), *Boys in Brown* (1948), *Good Time Girl* (1949), *Turn the Key Softly* (1953), *The Weak and the Wicked* (1953) and *Yield to the Night* (1956). The significance of these films is firstly the fact that they were made, in some cases, with a degree of official cooperation, usually in the form of advice on prison routines and regulations from former staff. In the post-

war welfare state era it became less acceptable to see prison as an entirely closed institution. The war itself had seen an emergence of documentary film making and the idea of film as a form of education had taken hold. The post-war period was characterised by concerns about crime and delinquency and its treatment and prevention. The films of this era clearly reflect these concerns, with film itself being seen as part of prevention and treatment.

The increased licence of British film makers to portray prison has been investigated by Nellis (1998) with regard to one film that he feels is particularly significant—*Now Barabbas* (1948). This was a film about capital punishment which followed a motley group of prisoners during the countdown to an execution. Each of the men is given a character and the film shows in flashback the circumstances of the crimes they have committed. Nellis suggests that the significance of *Now Barabbas* was that it was set entirely within a prison and was the first attempt at a realistic portrayal of a British prison. The origins of the film are interesting in as much as it was an adaptation of a play by William Douglas-Home, based on his experience of serving an eight month sentence in Wakefield Prison during World War II. Although Douglas-Home was critical of the conditions that he experienced there, both in the film and the earlier play, his criticisms are to an extent muted, as he attempted to phrase his critique within an account that was acceptable to the authorities. The film shows British prison officers to be generally decent and well meaning and there are no indications of brutality, intimidation or sarcasm. The play also featured an exploration of homosexuality within prison, which processes of censorship (formal and informal) ensured was dropped from the film (Nellis, 1988).

In the same year, *The Boys in Brown* (1948) was a similar depiction of life in a borstal. The film again provides a sympathetic portrayal of well meaning staff within the institution doing their best to redirect their charges away from a life of delinquency. A year later, *Goodtime Girl* (1949) dealt with the topic of female delinquency and the road to offending behaviour, and featured an early portrayal of an approved school for girls. The 1953 film *The Weak and the Wicked* depicted the regime inside an adult women's prison and a women's open prison. Finally, *Turn the Key Softly* (1953) followed three women, all of whom were released from prison on the same day and the temptations and pitfalls they had to overcome in order to avoid a return to custody. These films clearly reflected concerns of the time about adult and youth offending. They are generally aware of the failings of the institutions that they portray, but are, nevertheless, optimistic that reform and improvement is possible. These themes can be seen in particular in two films, *Goodtime Girl* and *The Weak and the Wicked*, which are worthy of further examination.

Goodtime Girl
Released in 1949, *Goodtime Girl* is part 'spiv movie', part social message film. The film follows Gwen Rawlings, a sixteen-year-old young woman who wishes to escape the family home and gain independence. She wishes both to earn and control her own income, to spend money on clothes, make-up and dancing. Unfortunately the escape from her (abusive) home background leads her into bad company as she mixes with the petty spivs of the underworld. Rejecting the advances of Jimmy Rosso, the spiv who obtained her a job as a hat-check girl in a

nightclub, she comes to be framed for the theft of a piece of jewellery and, unable to establish her innocence, is sentenced in the then juvenile court to three years in approved school. This (unjust) sentence is shown to accelerate Gwen down the path to delinquency. Unable to accept the regimented and petty regime, she escapes and returns to the world of nightclubs, spivs and racketeers. Here her problems worsen, as a life of partying with bad company leads her to become involved in the death of a police officer in a hit and run accident. Gwen then goes on the run, hooking up as partner to a pair of deserting American soldiers, before becoming an accessory to murder.

Goodtime Girl is a reasonably hard-edged film. Men are almost always portrayed in quite unflattering terms and criminals and crime are presented in a thoroughly de-glamorised manner. But being set in a world of seedy nightclubs, spivs and razor gangs, the film could easily have been accused of pandering to salacious bad taste and so this is offset by its 'social message' aspect. The fact that Gwen's story is intended as both a warning and an educational message is brought home by the film's frame story. It starts with a police officer bringing a young Lyla Lawrence (Diana Dors) to the female youth magistrate for an informal talk. Gwen's story is told by the magistrate to Lyla who at the end of it agrees to return to her family home (see Chadder, 1999). It is in this successful outcome that the film displays its post-war optimism rather than in Gwen's story which indicates the failure of the residential institution to divert her from the path to delinquency and crime.

It is not entirely clear from watching *Goodtime Girl* what its origins and intentions were. Did its makers intend producing a 'spiv-cycle' movie which they sought to get by the censors through including a social message? Or did they intend to portray female offending and criminal justice institutions, and include the underworld element to help hook in the audience?

The Weak and the Wicked
The origins of the later film *The Weak and the Wicked* are clearer. Released in 1953, it was seen by many at the time as an eminently saleable, if lightweight, 'convicts in skirts', women's prison melodrama (see Nellis, 1993). The film tells the story of Jean Raymond (played by Glynis Johns), a middle-class girl who is convicted of a minor fraud offence and sentenced to a year in prison. Whilst there she meets a variety of female offenders, each with a story to tell, including Betty Brown a young, slightly naïve first-time offender played by Diana Dors. The film follows Jean and Betty though a stint in HMP Blackdown (a stand-in for HMP Holloway and coincidentally the same title as given to the prison in *Convict 99*) and then in The Grange (at the time Askham Grange was the only women's open prison in Britain).

The film was based a book, *Who Lie in Gaol* (1952), a first hand account of the experiences of Joan Henry who had, like the character Jean in the film, been sentenced to a year's imprisonment for fraud. The book, a best-seller, caused something of a sensation on its release and was widely regarded as an authoritative account of women's prison conditions. The film toned down the book's representation of the conditions within Holloway (Blackdown), excluding, for example, examination of Henry's claim that that younger prisoners were sexually exploited by older female staff (Nellis, 1993: 45).

Nonetheless it was still significant in indicating a harsh regime and the regime of Askham open prison is compared favourably to that of Blackdown. The film indicated that different women come to offend for different reasons, and, for some, rehabilitation and reform are possible.

Although dealing with the female experience of incarceration both *The Weak and the Wicked* and *Goodtime Girl* illustrate some of the more general characteristics of prison films of this period. The films had a social message and an educational purpose. They were allowed to visualise and represent contemporary prisons in an apparently realistic way. Their portrayal of penal institutions was softened, with prison regimes being represented as strict rather than cruel. The critique of the institutions was that they were ineffective and that more progressive interventions were to be recommended. In this sense the films did reflect an ethos of welfare state optimism.

Despite their similarities the two films differ in various ways. *Goodtime Girl* appears to have its origins as a dramatic product which its makers thought would make an entertaining commercial film. It is basically a dramatic recreation of what criminologists or sociologists might call the 'labelling theory' of deviance. (Originating in American sociology, this theory examined how labelling a person, e.g. as a 'troublemaker', a 'delinquent', or 'mentally ill', might exacerbate their deviant behaviour and become a 'self-fulfilling prophecy'. Interestingly, *Goodtime Girl* proposes informal cautioning and diversion from custody as the counter to this.) *The Weak and the Wicked* on the other hand is a dramatisation of a first-hand account of the experience of prison. Although both films could be argued to fit a simplistic definition of 'the prison film genre' neither of them is a straightforward 'genre pic'. Although both contain recognisable elements of prison films (a 'prison innocent', initiation rituals, fights among prisoners, etc.) in these films these elements have not yet become clichéd and formulaic.

Space does not allow full development of a discussion of the gender politics of these films here (see Chadder, 1999 for a discussion of *Goodtime Girl* and Morey, 1995 for a discussion of American women's prison films of the same era). For present purposes suffice it to say that both films illustrate a welfare state ideology of (middle-class) women managing (mainly) working-class women, although this relationship is not necessarily one group of women contributing to the oppression of another. *The Weak and the Wicked* suggests a possibility for cross-class sisterhood—the middle-class Governor of The Grange and Jean combine in their efforts to save Betty going down a similar path to Gwen Rawlings. The film could be criticised for its portrayal of middle-class Jean as being the saviour of working-class Betty, although this in part reflects its origins in Joan Henry's original experience. The theme of middle-class women learning from their experience of prison is returned to, and arguably improved upon, in the more recent TV series *Bad Girls* (see *Chapter 5*).

Retreat from optimism (the 1960s)

From 1960 the representation of prison in British film changes. British prison films of the 1950s displayed a degree of respect for the institutions that they were criticising. In the 1930s film makers had hardly dared portray prison at all. But by the 1960s representations of prison begin to diversify and in so doing lose some of the respect and optimism displayed in previous periods. These changes can be seen in: *The Criminal* (1960); *In the Nick* (1960); *Two-way Stretch* (1960); *So Evil So Young* (1961); *The Loneliness of the Long Distance Runner* (1962); *The Pot Carriers* (1962); *The Quare Fellow* (1962); *The Hill* (1965) and *The Smashing Bird I Used to Know* (1969). A brief discussion of some of the key films listed above should be sufficient to establish the point. Again some of this discussion is informed by Nellis (1987), although as this source is not generally available some repetition of it is permitted here.

The Criminal
Regarded by many as a landmark film, *The Criminal* (1960), directed by Joseph Losey and starring Stanley Baker, has been described as 'a haunting and unique portrayal of prison and criminal life in Britain in the early 1960s' (Internet Movie Database: user comment). Having appeared in previous films such as *Hell Drivers* (1957), the film's star, Stanley Baker, was being groomed as Britain's tough-guy actor. *The Criminal* took the tough-guy and put him in a prison. The resulting representation of prison is distinctly different from the films of only a few years before. Baker's prison adversary, the chief warder, is portrayed as sadistic and corrupt, and the prison's reform minded Governor as weak and ineffective. Prisoners are presented as incorrigible offenders for whom aspirations of reform are a waste of time (Nellis, 1987).

The Loneliness of the Long Distance Runner
A film which reached an equivalent conclusion albeit from a different perspective is *The Loneliness of the Long Distance Runner* (1962). The film follows the borstal career of Colin Smith, played by Tom Courtney, and is usually cited as an instance of British Social Realism, a film movement which attempted to portray working-class life and its discontents from a working-class perspective. In the film, Colin's offending behaviour is represented as being a natural aspect of (male) working-class life, with nothing to look forward to but the conveyor belt of a low paid job followed by marriage. Borstal is represented as being a system of oppression, punishing those working-class kids who do not or will not toe the line. Borstal punishes, with some minor concessions for those who show due deference and conformity, but Courtney, the anti-hero, ends up rejecting deference and pays the price for his actions. The film leaves us not only with the idea that borstal will fail to reform its charges, but that the institution itself cannot be reformed or improved upon (Nellis, 1987). In this period female representations of approved school/borstal make an appearance in *So Evil So Young* (1961) and *The Smashing Bird I Used to Know* (1969). Neither of these films is currently easily available but descriptions of them suggest that they both represent a move towards clichéd girls' reform school genre pics. Both feature 'prison innocents' battling against instances of cruelty and sadism within institutions, although it would be unfair to reach a final judgement on these films without further analysis.

The Hill
The final film worth discussing here is *The Hill* (1965). Starring Sean Connery, Michael Redgrave and Ian Hendry amongst others, *The Hill* might be considered out of place in our list, as it concerns the experience of incarceration within a

British military stockade located in North Africa. Although not dealing with civil incarceration, the film does address the punishment of soldiers who have offended against military discipline and it is clearly not a prisoner of war movie. The significance of *The Hill* is that it raises an issue perhaps neglected in previous films, although relevant to understanding *Loneliness* and later films such as *Scum*. This is the issue of the necessity and inevitability of authority. The film proposes that armies need rules and discipline. Soldiers should obey, rather than question, even bad orders and so should they accept even excessive punishment and discipline. *The Hill* outlines a challenge of the prisoners of a military stockade to harsh and excessive punishment but poses the question that—if the prisoners are allowed to triumph—will authority itself unravel? One possible message of the film is that abuses of authority are part of the price we pay for having authority in the first place!

The films of the 1960s were more critical of penal institutions than the films of the 1950s. It does seem fair to tag the period as representing a 'retreat from optimism' about the possibility of reforming institutions and developing a welfare-based approach to offending. As Nellis (1987) has suggested, films of this period do display a generally unflattering representation of prison officers and the rise in the tensions between staff and prisoners. But it is equally clear that film in this period almost certainly understated the hostility between staff and prisoners and the degree of institutional violence within penal institutions at the time. Jimmy Boyle's account of his career through approved school, borstal and then prison, the experience of Larry Winters as documented in the later film *Silent Scream* (1990), and accounts of the events leading up to the Parkhurst riot of 1969 (Fitzgerald, 1977) arguably all give a more accurate picture of the tensions within prison at the time. Contemporary film only allowed these tensions to appear in a refracted and muted form.

Crisis, concern and critique (the late 1970s/early 1980s)
Both inside and outside prison, the 1970s kicked off with a bang and continued to be a rollercoaster ride of social tension and crisis, even if it might not always have seemed so at the time. As already mentioned, from the outset of the decade British prisons were hit by a wave of unrest and protest. Surprisingly these events do not really begin to register in film until the end of the decade with a clutch of films (some originating in TV) appearing at the end of the 1970s and the beginning of the 1980s. The representation of British prison in the early 1970s was dominated by the BBC TV sit-com *Porridge*, originally broadcast between 1974 and 1977, with the film version appearing in 1979. There is some irony that the film *Porridge* appeared in the same year as *Scum* and *A Sense of Freedom*. Both of the last two are 'anti-Porridge'—they attempt to provide the view of prison that *Porridge* never did.

The other films from around this time that require discussion or mention are: *McVicar* (1980), *Burning An Illusion* (1981), *Made in Britain* (1982) and *Scrubbers* (1983). When discussing dramatic products from around this period we do need to be aware of a possible definitional issue as to what constitutes a film. The story of *Scum* (1977) is relatively well known. *Scum* was originally written to be made into a one-off TV play for the BBC. The programme was made from a script provided by writer Roy Minton and directed by Alan Clark. However, on seeing the finished product the BBC refused to screen the programme, believing that its violence and the disparaging representation of the system for young offenders could not be justified as legitimate social comment. Two years later the BBC's rights to the script lapsed and writer Roy Minton and director Alan Clark remade the programme, shooting it as a film for Channel 4. *Scum* (1979) clearly counts as a film, although its style does owe something to its TV origins. *A Sense of Freedom* (1979) is more problematic. This was a TV dramatisation of Jimmy Boyle's autobiography of the same name. This was originally made for Scottish Television (STV) and screened as a one-off drama. The programme later went to video and was for a while available and could have been watched as if it were a film. The same is true of *Made in Britain* (1982), which was a one-off TV drama that later went to video and then DVD. These products will be discussed here 'as if' they are films, although it should be recognised that if they were excluded from the analysis our assessment of this period might be quite different.

Scum

Released in 1979, *Scum* tells the story of Carlin, played by Ray Winstone, and Archer, played by Mick Ford, in their own different ways two rebellious young men trapped inside the borstal system. The film begins with Carlin and two other relatively minor young offenders being inducted into the borstal regime, after having been transferred from a less demanding regime. Carlin has been involved in an assault on a member of staff in his previous establishment and is identified by the receiving staff as a 'tough-nut' who needs slapping down. Whereas *Porridge* never showed any instances of staff brutality against prisoners, or even petty injustices, *Scum* from the outset reveals both to be accepted aspects of institutional life. On his induction into the institution Carlin is punched and threatened by staff. Soon after his arrival he is beaten up by fellow prisoners, at the implicit behest of the staff and as a result is put on report and given solitary confinement for fighting. At first Carlin attempts to keep a low profile, but it becomes apparent that his reputation as a 'hard-case' marks him out for intimidation and assault by staff and prisoners. He becomes obliged to live up to his reputation and prove himself. Meeting violence with violence, he succeeds in becoming top dog—'the daddy', a role that is represented as being some kind of perverse 'head boy'. Carlin is expected to keep order and maintain the status quo in return for a few perks and privileges.

But Carlin's willingness to cooperate with the authorities is never more than grudging. At the same time Mick Ford plays Archer, the upper working-class/lower middle-class youth who is too intelligent for his captors and engaged in an on-going war of resistance against the system. Archer declares himself a vegetarian to cause problems for the institution, and at one point tells the Church of England Governor that although his religion is declared as atheist, exempting him from chapel, he is thinking of becoming a Sikh. Archer disrespects and mocks authority wherever possible. In *Scum* 'the system'/authority is the staff who run the institution and they are generally portrayed as being incompetent, uncaring and unimaginative. Their concern is to maintain order, by intimidation if necessary, with few tears shed for the casualties. Staff indifference leads to one attempted suicide (later successfully carried out elsewhere) and a male rape overlooked by a staff member, leading to the preventable suicide of the victim.

The deaths of two of their peers underlines the prisoners' shared hostility to authority and leads to a riot as a protest over conditions.

Scum was intended as a revelatory critique of the system for young offenders as it existed in the 1970s and was indeed received as such. On its release the film was seen as shocking and violent, but also acclaimed as a 'must see' indictment of the borstal system. It is possible that at the time of its release *Scum* benchmarked borstal as a failing institution (see *Chapter 8*). But the extent to which the film succeeds in providing a more lasting critique of these institutions is open to debate. Although the film has received occasional screenings on UK TV, it has to a large extent acquired its cult status through the video market and has now been re-released on DVD.

What accounts for *Scum*'s cult status and how successful is it as critique and social comment? There are quite a number of things going on in *Scum*. Firstly, to state the obvious, it should be said that the film does not follow the formula of a standard Hollywood 'prison genre pic'. In one version of the Hollywood tradition a prison innocent endures a series of indignities at the hands of an oppressive regime before triumphing over them. In *Scum* Carlin does not really fit the character type of the prison innocent, nor does he enjoy a Hollywood style happy ending. The film operates more within a tradition of 'social realism', an attempt to portray and take seriously working-class dissatisfaction with social institutions. Carlin is an offender, although he believes that his subsequent institutional career is an excessive response to his initial crime—'nicking 30 bob's worth of scrap'. *Scum* seeks to portray the borstal system as illegitimate (excessive, arbitrary and ultimately counter-productive) and to align the viewer with the point of view of Carlin and Archer, the film's anti-heroes.

There are two problems with the film's attempt to achieve its aims. Firstly although it attempts to critique the legitimacy of the institution this might backfire. After the riot nothing changes and authority re-asserts itself. In avoiding a pat happy ending the film may unwittingly subscribe to the view that 'resistance is futile'—the authorities will always prevail. As with *The Hill* (1965) above, *Scum* may unknowingly contribute to the view that excesses of authority are an unavoidable aspect of having authority.

A further problem with *Scum* is that it cannot entirely control the ways in which its viewers interpret the violence in the film. Generally, although not always, the violence portrayed serves a purpose in relation to the film's intentions. So, for example, the male rape scene leads to a suicide; bullying amongst prisoners is shown to be tolerated if not encouraged by staff. In other words the violence is generally intended as a critique of the institution—both the dramatic representation and the real world institution that it represents. The film is suggesting to its viewers, 'This is what may well be going on in borstals (now young offenders' institutions) in this country today'. However viewers may not interpret the violence in this way and might, for example, see staff assaults on Carlin as a generic convention, simply one of the things that one might expect to see in a prison film rather than a statement about actual institutions. And again we can illustrate the problem with the portrayal of violence in *Scum* by noting that the scene, (rightly) regarded by many as the key scene in the film, is the one where Carlin despatches his adversaries in quick succession in a skilfully executed series of attacks. This and the fight scene alluded to on the cover of the

DVD/video underline that for many viewers the attraction of *Scum* is its portrayal of Carlin as 'a hero with superpowers'. *Scum* trades on, rather than critiques a 'fascination with the hard man' and it is no surprise that the film is more popular with 'boys' than it is with 'girls' (see Internet Movie Database: user comments and the gender breakdown of votes posted for the film).

Scum neatly illustrates one of the paradoxes of prison film. It attempts to portray things which are aspects of penal institutions (bullying, intimidation, petty injustices, rape, suicide, etc.). If anything, it tones down some of these issues (for example the sexual exploitation of weaker prisoners was in the original BBC play but did not make it to the film). Yet *Scum* (the film they tried to ban!) is in danger of being perceived as being an exercise in dramatic excess where distasteful elements are inserted into the narrative in order to create the environment within which the (anti-)hero must struggle. On the internet *Scum* is marketed along with the video of *McVicar* as part of a 'Brit Violence Triple Pack', which suggests that its cult status most likely derives from something other than its intended aim of social comment.

McVicar

Released one year after *Scum*, *McVicar* (1980) is an overlooked film. Although easily available on budget video it is rarely seen on TV and little commented on elsewhere. The film is based on the autobiography of armed robber John McVicar, published as *McVicar, by himself* (1974). The film version starred Roger Daltrey and was made by The Who Films, with McVicar acting as co-screenwriter. The film is closer to a feature film in style and presentation than the other products considered in this section. The action is set roughly 50 per cent in Durham prison and 50 per cent whilst McVicar is on the run in London. It features plenty of 'motors', 'birds', 'blags' (armed robberies) and London villains. On inspection, it turns out to have been directed by Tom Clegg, who was responsible for the production of a number of episodes of the 1970s TV cop show *The Sweeney*. *McVicar* is in some ways closer to being an entertainment product than an attempt at social comment, although at the same time it is based on an experiential account: a real life experience.

Despite the fact that the film stars Roger Daltrey (lead singer with The Who pop group) and 1960s pop star and actor Adam Faith, it seems to succeed in recreating a fairly 'realistic' account of Durham prison in the 1960s and early 1970s. Relations between 'screws' and 'cons' are portrayed as being unrelentingly antagonistic. Officer brutality makes a couple of brief appearances, and there is a fairly even-handed portrayal of the Durham prison 'riot' when the prisoners took over E wing and presented the authorities with their demands for improvements in the regime for life-sentenced prisoners. This incident is rather mischievously portrayed as being a 'fight for the right to wear sneakers', but the film does succeed in conveying the significance prisoners attached to having to wear regulation prison issue, particularly shoes.

The second half of the film is set in London after McVicar has escaped from Durham. Here he re-establishes relationships with his wife and child and eventually decides to try and get out of a life of crime. The point of the film which is portrayed consistently and unsubtly throughout is that McVicar had to break out of prison to stand any chance of being rehabilitated. Whilst in the lifer's wing at Durham he was locked into an unprofitable conflict between staff and cons. Re-establishing family relations provided the spur to reform and the closing titles tell us that after being recaptured and sent back to prison, McVicar went on to gain a degree in sociology and was subsequently released early on parole. The in-prison scenes of the film are pervaded by an intentional 'camp mateyness' amongst the prisoners, which seems to be invoked as a contrast to the more 'natural' relations of a functional family. Essentially the film suggests that McVicar gave up crime for family.

Comparing *McVicar* with *Scum* we might suggest that, perhaps surprisingly, the former succeeds better than the latter as a piece of social comment. Despite McVicar's celebrity status as 'armed robber turned sociologist' the film manages to portray him as a fairly ordinary villain, in a fairly ordinary nick. It avoids revelling in the awfulness of prison, although it possibly does this at the expense of implying that prison is something that can be survived and overcome.

The film treatment of *McVicar* can be usefully contrasted with the TV dramatisation of *A Sense of Freedom*. This dramatisation of the prison career of Jimmy Boyle provided a much harder edged look at prison than either *Scum* or *McVicar*. Both the book and the televised versions detail how Boyle became locked into an escalating confrontation with the Scottish prison authorities, in which he spent extensive periods of time in solitary confinement, with his body and the walls of his cell smeared with his own excrement and slops of prison food in order to discourage the warders from coming in and beating him up. Interestingly, because the depictions of prison in the drama/film version are anchored in autobiography then, extreme as they are, they still come across as referring to a real world experience. Having said this *A Sense of Freedom* does not entirely escape being built around a fascination with 'the hard-man'. Briefly available on video it is listed on Internet Movie Database (IMDb) as a film where many people comment on it as such. Young male contributors to IMDb seem to agonise extensively over which of *Scum*, *A Sense of Freedom* or *Made in Britain* is the greatest/grittiest/most 'in yer face' British prison movie ever. Technically only the first one is a movie, the other two were TV dramas.

Made in Britain
First shown in 1982, *Made in Britain* was originally a one-off TV drama which since its release on DVD/video is now regarded 'as if' it is a film. Directed by Alan Clark, also the director of *Scum*, *Made in Britain* stars Tim Roth as Trevor, the rebellious skinhead in a youth detention centre. Although Trevor adopts skinhead dress, speaks in extreme racist diatribe and pursues delinquent behaviour, he is highly intelligent and articulate and his anti-authority/non-conformist approach to life is consciously chosen. Whilst social workers and probation officers may try to persuade Trevor that the path he is pursuing will lead to prison and self-destruction, Trevor maintains his attitude of 'Fuck you!' defiance.

But although *Made in Britain* is very highly rated, at least by the contributors to IMDb, it is a bit difficult to see what the point of it is. The film consists only of a stand-up bravura performance by Tim Roth railing against everyone and anyone in authority. However by the end, when his social worker and probation officer have given up on him, as Trevor sits alone in a police cell, the realisation dawns on him that this time he may well be on his way to prison and his supreme confidence seems to desert him or at least ring a little hollow. Like *Scum* and *Loneliness* the film caries a possibly unintended message about the inevitability of authority. Despite all Trevor's energies, 'resistance is futile'.

Trevor briefly adopts a younger black sidekick whom he meets in the detention centre, although the character tends to exist only to be the butt of Trevor's racist diatribes. But the film does not really develop any argument about the black experience of youth justice. During the 1970s and 1980s it was becoming obvious that black children were over-represented within the care system and black youths and adults within the criminal justice process. This over-representation is only indirectly referred to in the films of this period. In *Scum* borstal is depicted as racially mixed/divided but the film does not really comment on this and has a white main protagonist.

The nearest thing to a black British 'prison film' in this period is *Burning an Illusion* (1981). The story centres on a young black British woman, who at the start of the film aspires to success in conventional terms of job and marriage. But her view of the world changes when her boyfriend is falsely accused of a crime, arrested and sent to prison. Whilst visiting him in prison she becomes more aware of the racism in British society and politicised as a result. Including this film in our list is appropriate, as it reflects concerns that were current at the time and are still relevant today. Having said this, the film is not easily available and has not recently been shown on UK terrestrial TV.

How then should we appraise the prison film product of this period? Firstly it should be said that the appearance of a burst of prison film activity is, in part, created by our inclusion of TV dramas that later went to video. Even *Scum* would have been a TV drama and not a film if the BBC had been prepared to screen it! Nevertheless, if we include these products then this time period represents a burst of prison drama activity. In comparison with earlier periods, prison dramas do begin to present a concern about the malfunctioning of penal institutions, although this is expressed in different ways and to different extents. Taken together they reflect an unease about penal institutions. All of the films arguably understate the harm that prison can do to some people. Even *A Sense of Freedom* tones down some of the content of the book, and arguably does not match the later *Silent Scream* (1990) as an examination of the harm that can be caused by prison. Formal and informal processes of censorship are still operating (for example the BBC's decision not to screen their version of *Scum*), although they have less impact in restricting what can be shown, and prison film is restricted more by problems of the strategy of representation (such as how to portray institutional violence so as to maintain a critique of the institution, rather than to pander to a fascination with violence). As in the 1960s, prison is being represented in a range of film styles although perhaps a divide is emerging between those accounts that were conceived of as social comment drama and those which were dramatisations of experiential accounts. *Scum*, its sister film *Scrubbers* (1983) and *Made in Britain* all attempted to avoid sanitised representations of prison but struggled to avoid becoming merely cult movies for adolescent males revelling in the horror of penal institutions. Significantly the key films of this period appear to be most popular with adolescent males (based on IMDb user comments and voting patterns for the films involved). The products seem to be more masculine than in the period of post-war optimism, as above although this might have changed if we had included in our analysis TV drama series.

Disappearance (mid-1980s /late 1990s)
The period from the mid-1980s to the end of the 1990s appears to represent something of a lull in the production of British prison films. Are we justified in characterising this as an era of 'disappearance' and if so why did this occur? The apparent contenders for British prison film product would seem to be few in number for this period but it is always the case that at any time the number of British prison films being made is relatively small and a definitional decision either way may shift the numbers appreciably.

Knockback (1985) was a one-off BBC2 TV drama which featured Derrick O'Connor and Pauline Collins in a story about a life-sentenced prisoner who begins a 15 year relationship with a female prison worker. There is no evidence of this ever having been released on video and it does not feature on Internet Movie Database. To all intents and purposes it can be discounted as a film although it would be included if we widened our analysis to include TV. The difference between this and the TV dramas discussed already is that they are seen and discussed as if they were films. Apart from *Knockback* we would seem to have three items for discussion: *Silent Scream* (1990), *In the Name of the Father* (1993), and *Captives* (1994). Although each has its individual significance they do not together represent a significant burst of prison film activity comparable with earlier periods.

In the Name of the Father (1993) was a very popular film, an Eire/UK bio-pic of the experience of Gerry Conlan, who was falsely accused of having been involved in the IRA Guildford pub bombings (the 1974 IRA bombings of two public houses in which 21 people died) Although the film is partly a courtroom drama about a miscarriage of justice, enough of it is set within prison to merit inclusion in our list. It contains some significant representations of prisons and prison officers—the face of authority and therefore not to be trusted!

Captives (1994) is more curious. The film tells the story of a prison dentist (played by Julia Ormond) who becomes erotically attracted to a prisoner (played by Tim Roth) during her two-days-a-week part-time job in the prison. The film was made by the BBC films unit and briefly available on video. It is now variously described by people who have seen it as either 'a ludicrous curiosity' or 'a must see movie'.

Finally, *Silent Scream* (1990) is a highly significant film. In subject matter, although perhaps not style, it belongs with the Boyle and McVicar films of the late 1970s/early 1980s. The film, which tells the true story of Larry Winters and his experience of the Scottish prison system in the 1960s and 1970s, is arguably one of the most successful portrayals ever of the traumatising effect prison can have on some individuals. Unfortunately this is achieved by way of a fragmented, discontinuous narrative with no clear chronological pattern. Although the result is highly appreciated by some critics and analysts, this film is not widely seen. Internet Movie Database records one user comment ('bleak and Arty') and 12 people as having voted to record a rating for it. *Scum* and *Made in Britain* receive hundreds of votes (they are cult movies), whilst *In the Name of the Father* has received nearly 8,000 votes.

In terms of our periodisation, the 'disappearance' of the British prison film would appear to be an appropriate judgement. As the next spurt of prison films starts in 2000 with *Greenfingers*, we have a period from 1983 to 1999 in which it appears that only three British prison films were made. It is possible that there are other candidates for inclusion which have been neglected. These might include historical death penalty films, such as *Let Him Have It* (1991) about the 1950s Derek Bentley case, or 1985's *Dance With a Stranger* about the Ruth Ellis case—both films feature some prison scenes. *The Dunera Boys* (1985) is an historical internment/POW movie. *Some Mother's Son* (1996) is the story of Bobby Sands' 1981 hunger strike in support of political prisoner status being given to IRA prisoners in Northern Ireland. Again, does this count as a prison film? Perhaps we might refer to the period in question as being one of 'fragmentation', but if we accept the use of the term 'disappearance' then why did this occur? Firstly, such a disappearance surely cannot be explained by the profile of prison in society. The 1990 Strangeways riot was the worst prison riot in British history and might have been expected to place prison in the public imagination, although it seems to have generated no dramatic by-products. It is possible that interest in prison in this period was reflected more on television, both in documentaries and TV drama series. The representation of prison in TV drama and documentary at this time is obviously worth examining (see Mason, 1995), although even establishing a high level of TV interest would not necessarily of itself explain the relative neglect of prison in film. Finally it may be that by the mid-1980s the options for making prison films were thought to have become exhausted. Indeed the prison films of the new millennium do appear to be significantly different from those produced in previous periods.

Knowing nostalgia (the new millennium)
Prison films are like buses. You can wait an age for one and then suddenly three, or in this instance four, come along together. *Greenfingers* (2000), *Lucky Break* (2001), *Mean Machine* (2001) and *Tommorrow La Scala* (2002) are all quite clearly and unambiguously British prison films, albeit that *Mean Machine* is a remake of an earlier American movie (in the US *The Longest Yard*). In the earlier periods considered—'Restriction', 'Optimism', 'Retreat' and 'Concern', it has been suggested that prison film in some way reflected social thinking about prison and indirectly tracked penal realities. For the last period considered, 'Disappearance', it was suggested that those films that were made did not as a group exhibit any obvious relationship to contemporary penal thinking. The films in the current phase might be regarded as different again. Stylistically they do illustrate some broad similarities. All might be said to be characterised by a certain 'English' whimsy. All lie somewhere between outright comedy and drama. For reasons that will be explained below, this era is dubbed 'knowing nostalgia'. But what is going on in these films? What do they do and how do they relate, if at all, to contemporary penal realities?

Let us first take *Lucky Break* and *Mean Machine*. Both of these films most likely owe their existence to the mini-revival of the British film industry from the mid-1990s. The international success of films like *Four Weddings and a Funeral* and

Shakespeare in Love suggested that British films could sell in the American market and provided something of a leg up for UK film making. The surprise success of *The Full Monty* (1997) continued this trend. But this international success was to an extent misleading. (*Four Weddings* and *Shakespeare* were in fact Anglo-US collaborations and other films such as *Brassed-off* and *Billy Elliott* never achieved the crossover blockbuster status of *The Full Monty*, or the Anglo-US romantic comedies (*Four Weddings, Notting Hill*)). In *The Full Monty*, *Brassed-off* and *Billy Elliot* the nature of Britishness is being redefined and packaged, but for sale to the home market as much as to the international market. Such films, despite their occasional international success, are essentially parochial and could be accused of 'nostalgic rediscovery' of the British working class. In *The Full Monty* they are to be found in the former steel city of Sheffield and in *Brassed-off* in a now defunct colliery village. Arguably *Lucky Break* (the follow up film by the director of *The Full Monty*) simply takes the formula into prison. *Lucky Break* is 'The Full Monty meets Brassed-off in prison'—although this time the unemployed workers are armed bank robbers. The Vinnie Jones' film *Mean Machine* owes its existence to a revival in popularity of the British crime/gangster film, particularly the hit *Lock Stock and Two Smoking Barrels*, which turned former professional footballer Jones into a marketable commodity. As the existing film *Mean Machine* was the story of an ex-professional (American) footballer, coerced into organizing a team of cons to play a grudge match against the guards, an opportunity existed to remake an English version so as to utilise Jones's unique combination of football/acting talents. Regardless of their origins both films are set for virtually their entirety inside UK prisons and so clearly do count for inclusion in our analysis. How did these films choose to represent prison and what relation, if any, do these representations have to current penal realities?

Lucky Break
Lucky Break tells the story of Jimmy Hans, an Irish Londoner whose unsuccessful career as an armed robber lands him a lengthy sentence in a remote northern English prison. There he meets up with his partner in his last unsuccessful robbery and the two hatch a plan for escape. The plan involves using an amateur dramatics performance by the prisoners, of a musical stage play written by the prison Governor, as cover for the escape.

Lucky Break is not serious drama but equally not quite full-on comedy, although it draws on elements of previous comedic prison films. Its criminals are basically decent blokes, with the exception of one requisite heavyweight and his henchmen. The middle-class Governor is ineffectual and limited to the vague idea that participation in amateur dramatics might be good for the men. The staff feature one requisite 'nasty screw', who gets his comeuppance before the end of the film. As Jimmy and Rudy develop their escape plan, others are drawn into it (Roger and Darren assist) and the prison heavies try to crash in on it too. But the film never really explains why the prisoners wish to escape, other than through rhetorical references to 'not being able to do the time'. There is little attempt made to establish what's wrong with the regime, although one prisoner commits suicide as a result of depression brought on by niggling harassment by a 'nasty screw'. But this kind of tragedy is not out of place in films in the tradition of *Brassed-Off* or *The Full Monty* which, despite their generally sentimental depiction of working-class people, also usually seek to suggest rhetorically that life is no bowl of cherries. Probably the most irritating aspect of *Lucky Break* is its thoroughly clichéd use of a young, attractive female prison welfare officer, to operate as the 'love interest' for Jimmy Hans. Predictably the film ends with Jimmy (the well intentioned con with a heart of gold) getting 'the girl' and his collaborators Rudy, Roger and Darren effecting a successful escape. The escape in *Lucky Break* could have been a radical end to a prison film, except that it is conducted in a manner overtly suggestive of a World War II prisoner of war (PoW) movie. The cons escape by mingling in disguise with the audience as they leave the performance and have a tense moment as they go through the gate, before a quick moonlight flit through the woods takes them to a light aircraft ride to freedom.

Despite being set for almost its entirety in a prison, *Lucky Break* has very little to say about prison. The film redefines Englishness to an extent, featuring Irish Londoner Jimmy as the lead protagonist and his black British partner. The prison is depicted as weakly multi-racial. Its 'knowing nostalgia' tends to redefine and recreate a notion of Britishness, particularly through its use of the PoW motif, but in terms of prison the film does little to reference real world events—and in a sense distances itself from them. Arguably all film and TV representations of prison are significant because they help to shape perceptions of what is possible. Ironically Lenny James who played Rudy in *Lucky Break* went on to play the lead role in C4 television's *Buried*, a representation of prison in some ways as far removed from *Lucky Break* as it is possible to get. The great god of casting moves, it would seem, in mysterious ways.

Mean Machine
As already indicated, *Mean Machine* (2001) is a re-make of an existing film, the basic story of which made it an ideal vehicle for utilising the talents of its star, ex-professional footballer turned actor, Vinnie Jones. It keeps quite a lot from the original, including the basic story line and a few memorable scenes which are reproduced fairly faithfully. Despite these origins the re-make does recast the film into a recognisable Brit-pic mould and *Mean Machine* does display some stylistic similarities to *Lucky Break* (above) and *Greenfingers* and *Tomorrow La Scala* (below). All could be said to be heart-warming, sentimental tales which inject a bitter-sweet element into their narrative, before reaching a happy but understated ending.

In *Mean Machine* Jones/Danny Mehan is befriended by prison old-timer, Doc, played by David Kelly. The same actor plays a similar part and meets the same fate in that other prison Brit-pic *Greenfingers* (below). In both films the old-timer dies just over halfway through the movie. In earlier British crime comedies criminals were portrayed as loveable rogues, who commit crimes which do not cause much harm and do not seriously hurt anybody—see for example *Two-way Stretch* (1960). In the new prison Brit-pics, crime becomes a trauma from which the prisoner must recover. In *Mean Machine* this is established in the scenes in which Doc tells Danny about how he came to lob a grenade into the flat of an adversary, in the process killing the man in question, his partner and child and when Danny tells of his fall from grace as England team captain explaining to his team of footballer cons how he came to be involved in match-fixing.

Apart from the introductory credits sequence, which sets up the back-story to the film, *Mean Machine* is set in its entirety within a UK prison. But how did its makers dramatise and portray prison? Here the film operates on the principles of economy, re-cycling and cliché. In the re-make more than the original, prison is just a setting for a heart-warming-tale-cum-soccer-movie. The basic story of a grudge match between cons and guards is retained and so some scenes need to be included to establish the brutishness of the guards. Unlike in *Porridge* recognisably British prison officers are displayed as being capable of dispensing violence, sarcasm and intimidation. The Governor is represented as a pompous and slightly shady posh twit. But this character, whom we meet early on in the film, is given the most outlandishly exaggerated pair of eyebrows ever seen on film or TV, with the effect that every time he appears on screen we are being reminded that we should not be taking this portrayal of prison too seriously. The prisoners feature a recognisable crew including the prison's 'Mr Big', and 'the Rat/Snitch' who in this instance also doubles as the prison psycho. The prisoner population is a little more multi-racial perhaps than in previous British prison films, although this is generally through the inclusion of black British supporting players and extras. British Asians do not appear to feature in the film. Women do not feature at all, other than the Governor's secretary who takes a bit of a shine to 'our Mr Footballer'. The relevant scenes here are taken straight from the original. Although the clichéd and stereotypical use of the film's one female character could be criticised, the relative absence of women is not necessarily an indicator of sexism. Arguably *Mean Machine* is, like *The Shawshank Redemption*, a male recovery movie.

Although both *Lucky Break* and *Mean Machine* are set in prison, arguably neither of them is about prison. By way of contrast, although *Greenfingers* and *Tomorrow La Scala* have clear stylistic similarities to the previously mentioned films, both are intended to address prison in some way. Both are best understood as being post-*Shawshank Redemption* prison movies. Briefly, prior to *The Shawshank Redemption* (1994) the trend in US prison movies at the end of the 1980s and the beginning of the 1990s was towards violent action-adventure films, set in maximum security prisons populated by hard-core convicts (Wilson, 1993). Cinema was developing a representation of a 'kill or be killed' prison, which resonated with contemporary notions propagated by some US penal authorities that the prison system was facing a problem of how to mange a section of hard core inmates, dubbed 'the worst of the worst' (see King, 1999, for a discussion and critique). *The Shawshank Redemption* made an unwitting intervention against this trend, postulating an alternative direction for the prison movie. Basically *Shawshank* gave film makers permission to make slower-paced prison films which had no need for masculinist action-adventure elements, but which also avoided the ideological pitfalls of the American prison film genre. Prisoners were to be represented as human, mutually supportive and capable of reform and rehabilitation despite, not because of, the efforts of society or the penal authorities. Both *Greenfingers* and *Tomorrow La Scala* take up the challenge thrown down by *Shawshank*. Both deploy a degree of 'knowing nostalgia' although in a way different to that seen in *Lucky Break*.

Greenfingers

Greenfingers tells the story of Colin Briggs (Clive Owen), a man serving a lengthy prison sentence for a serious crime which we later learn turns out to be the murder of his brother. Colin is angry and at odds with the world, so much so that when informed—having already served a substantial part of his sentence—that he is to be transferred to an open prison to serve out his remaining time, he attempts to reject the offer. He is transferred anyway to a prison with a more relaxed regime and put in a room with old-timer Fergus, under whose placid influence he begins to mellow. Colin is introduced by Fergus to the joys of gardening and soon becomes a keen enthusiast with some kind of natural talent for it. Soon a whole group of cons have adopted the activity and a celebrity gardener (played by Helen Mirren) is introduced to advise them on their progress. This also allows the introduction of the celebrity gardener's daughter, as the romantic interest for Colin. He eventually completes his sentence, is released and takes up with the gardener's daughter, although this leaves his pals in the open prison without his assistance just as they are reaching the stage when they wish to enter a garden exhibit in the prestigious Hampton Court Palace Flower Show. Colin commits a minor offence (breaking a shop window) in order to get sent back to prison to lead his pals in that competition.

Although not everybody's cup of tea, *Greenfingers* is nowhere near as bad a film as its potted plot summary would make it sound. Someone watching it from the point of view of how it portrays prisons and prisoners might discern some subtle merits. For example, one of the criticisms of traditional prison films is that they often use a character type of 'the prison innocent' to create the viewer's empathy with the prisoners. The prison innocent was usually someone who was either factually innocent of the crime of which he or she was accused, or was guilty of a minor transgression for which they were being apparently harshly treated. In a sense the problem with this was that when the prison innocent then survived or overcame the prison environment it left unanswered the question of whether criminals who had committed more serious crimes should be seen as deserving and capable of similar redemption. In *Greenfingers* the main protagonist is not a prison innocent, but someone who has committed a serious crime from which they need to recover.

The film reworks some of the conventions of the prison film genre in other significant ways. It is set in an open prison not a maximum security prison. It is slower paced than most prison films, a pacing assisted by the use of incidental music, reminiscent of parts of *The Shawshank Redemption* ('Brook's theme'). And although the theme of redemption though gardening might be seen as somewhat twee, the choice of Clive Owen to play this part succeeds in bringing a slight ambiguity to the role. Despite his 'mellowing through gardening' Colin never becomes a completely sanitised criminal. Even though *Greenfingers* is apparently based on a true story, the idea of rehabilitation through gardening should probably be taken as metaphorical rather than literal. The film is not literally suggesting that if all prisoners were to take up gardening they would undergo some kind of stunning personal transformation, although it does seem to suggest that open prisons are a good thing and that it is important to keep them open.

But despite this apparent nod in the direction of penal realities, *Greenfingers* seems different to previous prison films. It has been suggested that many prison movies from the 1950s to the 1980s attempted to pitch a realistic depiction of prison, but only ever succeeded in producing something that fell short of approximating to penal realities. *Greenfingers* does not even attempt to make this approximation. It is the story of one person/group of people, in one particular institution and not necessarily a representative one at that. Its story is metaphorical rather than literal. Like *The Shawshank Redemption* before it, *Greenfingers* is a male recovery movie, with a happy ending, although this is not the same as saying that it provides a fantasy solution to the problems of imprisonment (Rafter, 2000).

Like the other films considered here, *Greenfingers* displays a degree of 'knowing nostalgia' and the film is pervaded with a sense of Englishness. The main cast are all recognisably English. The open prison is set in rural England. The celebrity gardener, her daughter and the village that they live in are all English. Gardening and the Hampton Court Palace Flower Show are recognisably English. Yet the film feels different from the other Brit-pics such as *Brassed-off* and *The Full Monty*. Both of these profess to address working-class problems and issues. Yet *The Full Monty* has actually very little to say about the problems of working-class people in Sheffield in 1997, which would be as likely to involve a young female working in a low paid retail job in the Medowhall Shopping Centre as a redundant ex-steel worker. *Brassed-off* produces a similarly backward looking view of the problems of the former mining village and only very indirectly addresses the problems of its contemporary working-class (see Turner, 2000). *Greenfingers*, by contrast, professes itself not to have any lofty purpose. It is about a flower show, not the closure of an industry, whether steel or coal. Unlike previous Brit-pics, *Greenfingers* is not nostalgic for a rediscovery of the British working-class, although prisoners are generally portrayed as being working-class.

Tomorrow La Scala

Made by the BBC films unit, *Tomorrow La Scala* (2002) tells the story of a professional opera group who put on a performance of *Sweeny Todd* inside a maximum security prison, using a group of prisoners as players in the production. The film is again a light comedy drama done with a degree of nostalgia and whimsy (amateur dramatics again!). But, despite its apparent superficial similarities, this is quite a different film from *Lucky Break* and owes little or nothing to previous prison comedies. The slightly whimsical portrayal of the opera group led by Vicky (Jessica Stevenson) is combined with a fairly deadpan one of the maximum security prison—with the character of Kevin, the prison officer assigned to look after the opera group, being depicted as a basically normal bloke trying to do a difficult job within the constraints he faces. The prison is initially portrayed in relatively harsh terms, with the pressures of coping with long-term sentences being shown to create a jittery atmosphere, where outbursts of violence can and do happen. As the opera group form their company of players and rehearsal for the production begins to progress the atmosphere starts to improve. Again hard-core cons mellow, this time through the power of opera—although here this is done as an ensemble, rather than a main character. At the same time Vicky (Jessica Stevenson), the very English leader of the opera group and the (female) main protagonist of the film, in struggling to keep the production going, finds that she needs to mellow a little herself and so becomes a better person in the process. The film ends without us seeing the performance of the production the group have been rehearsing.

Both *Greenfingers* and *Tomorrow La Scala* are different from some of the previously discussed prison films. British prison drama, from *The Weak and the Wicked* to, say, *Scum* had attempted to portray prison in a manner which in some way approximated to contemporary penal realities. In the case of *Greenfingers* and *Tomorrow La Scala*, despite their apparently realistic settings (shots of the prison set against wind turbines in *Tomorrow La Scala*), the films tell 'moral stories' (that criminals can recover from the trauma of their crimes), but do not claim to have necessarily captured or portrayed penal realities. Whether we see this as a retreat from the idea of drama commenting on the real world, or an improvement in the way in which prison drama comments on prison, depends in part on how we see *The Shawshank Redemption*. Do we need to show prisons as they actually are, or do we need to propagate the idea that prisoners as a group can be mutually supportive and capable of reform and redemption? Both *Greenfingers* and *Tomorrow La Scala* set themselves against a demonisation of criminals and a simplistic view that *criminals* commit *crimes* and are therefore sent to prison as *punishment*—full stop, end of story. It is also possible to see *Lucky Break* and *Mean Machine* as doing something similar as in all these films crime is portrayed as a trauma that criminals need to recover from.

None of the new prison Brit-pics discussed here really achieved blockbuster, 'smash hit' status. It is fairly subjective as to whether we see any or all of them as tiresome exercises in a film style that had already become a recognisable formula by the time they were made, or whether we grant them some subtlety of intent and effect. But these films will show up on video and receive occasional TV showings in the years to come and in this way will become part of our culture. Although both *Greenfingers* and *Tomorrow La Scala* in some ways disavow their ability to represent prison, they do still provide a look inside the institution; they are part of our apparatus for imagining it—a closed, secret world where anything can happen. The new prison Brit-pics do seem to comment on crime and criminals, albeit in a more mythical and indirect manner than their predecessors.

CONCLUSION AND FUTHER ISSUES

If the analysis developed above is accepted then one reasonably firm conclusion is that it is not enough to suggest that 'a film is just a film', or that prison films are 'only entertainment'. British prison films do tend to reflect the period that they were produced in. They do seem to act as a kind of social barometer, registering the concerns of their era and may have played a role in disseminating ideas and understandings about the state of penal institutions and where they might be heading. This is perhaps most clearly seen by contrasting the films of the 1950s (welfare-state optimism) and those of the 1970s (crisis and concern). Of course from the analysis developed here we can only speculate about the *effects* of the films in question. But there is in principle no reason why the analysis should not be subject to further development as an empirical investigation of the issues involved, although there would be methodological problems involved in designing and conducting appropriate studies.

One of the problems involved in investigating the *effects* of prison films is determining the ways in which they are consumed and understood. It has been suggested here that prison films have a dual and contradictory nature. On the one hand they may alert us to the state of penal institutions and the need for change. At the same time they may also contribute towards a misperception of prison. These dual properties might manifest themselves differently at different points. So if we consider the dramatic products *Scum*, *McVicar* and *A Sense of Freedom*, at the time they were first seen these may have contributed to publicising penal issues and generating debate. When *A Sense of Freedom* was first screened on TV the producers held on to their studio audience for a debate of the issues raised which was broadcast immediately afterwards. The film was clearly perceived as a social document and a stimulus for discussion. When watched today the same films might be consumed more with a view to a 'fascination with the hard man' or just enjoyment of the fact that they are more anti-authority than much mainstream film and TV product. They may simply allow their cult viewers to enjoy the pleasure of armchair identification with the rebel, without stimulating much thought at all about penal realities. Again all of this is in principle amenable to further empirical investigation, although most likely through qualitative rather than quantitative methods.

Of more interest to penal reformers might be the notion that 'meanings' of dramatic products are not necessarily fixed or given. Rather, the different meanings latent in them may be activated or suppressed depending on the manner and circumstances in which they are viewed. To take two of the films mentioned, *McVicar* and *A Sense of Freedom* can be texts which seek to bring first hand accounts of experiences of prison to a wider audience. But they can also be consumed in a manner of shallow fascination and when considered in combination with other prison dramas can allow viewers to revel in the excess of prison.

The question for penal reformers is whether there are any interventions that can be made to influence the way these cultural products are perceived and consumed. It was suggested in *Chapter 1* that, with respect to prison, film viewers may 'discount toward the middle'. As well as 'factoring up' from representations of prison which are obviously sanitised, this includes 'ratcheting down' from representations which seem to depict prison regimes as being unduly harsh or oppressive. We have suggested that we can identify a series of formal and informal processes which shape and restrict what can be shown in prison drama. So, for a variety of reasons, even apparently hard-edged and critical representations of prison may actually understate the harshness of the penal realities that they attempt to depict. But is it possible to popularise an awareness of this? One suggestion would be that it may be possible to undertake educative work where viewers are asked to watch a prison film and then discuss it. They might, for example, be asked to consider which aspects of the film they thought were realistic and which constituted fictional licence or 'dramatic excess'. If the discussion could then include a speaker who experienced prison in the time/place covered by the film it might be interesting to see where the perceptions diverged. Our suggestion is that a group of people with no direct experience of prison would systematically mistake things that can and do happen in prison for dramatic licence.

Thomas Mathiesen has, over a number of years, been developing a set of ideas and arguments about the irrationality of prison and how it survives in society. Mathiesen (2000) suggests that for society to continue building more prisons and incarcerating greater numbers of people even in the light of the overwhelming evidence that it fails to achieve any of its goals should be dubbed a 'prisons fiasco'. Prison would not be justifiable in the light of unrestricted and informed debate. But as the public underestimate 'the pain of prison' and as a series of processes operate to conceal or deny 'the prisons fiasco', prison survives as a social institution. These arguments that Mathiesen has developed at length are condensed in the discussion above into a 'discrepancy theory' of the public's relationship to prison. But the point to make here is that, although his arguments are well-known and understood in penal reform circles, there has been little success in popularising amongst the general public the idea that they systematically misunderstand prison. Perhaps more surprisingly, there has been relatively little work done to investigate how film and TV drama might contribute to the public's perception of prison, and few attempts to use the public's interest in prison film/TV as a means to pursuing penal reform, information, education and politics. How film and TV drama might be used as a springboard to debating prison is a topic for another chapter.

FILMOGRAPHY for *Chapter 2*

1931	The Shadow Between
1935	King of the Damned
1936	It's Never Too Late to Mend
1936	Prison Breaker
1938	Convict 99
1938	Prison Without Bars
1948/9	Now Barabbas (Was a Robber)
1949	Good Time Girl
1953	The Weak and the Wicked
1956	Yield to the Night
1960	The Criminal
1960	Two-way Stretch
1961	So Evil So Young
1962	The Loneliness of the Long Distance Runner
1962	The Pot Carriers
1962	The Quare Fellow [Ireland /UK]
1965	The Hill
1969	The Smashing Bird I Used To Know
1979	Scum
1979	Porridge
1979	A Sense of Freedom
1980	McVicar
1981	Burning an Illusion
1982	Made in Britain
1990	Silent Scream
1993	In the Name of the Father
1994	Captives
2000	Greenfingers
2001	Lucky Break
2001	Mean Machine
2002	Tomorrow La Scala

CHAPTER 3

Tracking the US Penal State: Issues and Eras

The 'prison film' has long been a Hollywood staple. In such a picture one can reliably predict that the warden will be evil, the inmates rough but colorful, and that a reluctant leader—usually a newcomer who does not quite fit in at first—will emerge to lead his ragtag fellow inmates to eventual triumph.

(Review of *The Last Castle*, 2001)

The United States is now 30 years into the biggest prison-building spree in all history, a binge that has led to one of the highest incarceration rates in the world and to huge, impersonal institutions disproportionately filled with people of colour. In this context, it is increasingly difficult to escape into the world of Hollywood prisons, where the good guys look like movie stars and injustices are ultimately repaired. In the face of the new realities of incarceration feel-goodism may be growing obsolete.

(Rafter, 2000:137)

The prison film and its relationship to US prison growth is now attracting a degree of academic attention, with recent contributions coming from Cheatwood (1998), Rafter (2000), Clowers (2001), O'Sullivan (2001) and Mason (2003b), following earlier work on prison film by Querry (1973), Nellis (1982) and Wilson (1993). Why this interest exists is not too hard to discern. All of the contributors believe that film has the ability to shape the way in which we see society. Given this, it seems intuitively likely that prison movies must, in some way, shape the way in which we see prison. However, once we attempt to develop our understanding of this intuitive belief a little further, things become quite complicated rather quickly.

The first of the quotations to head this chapter is taken from a review of a Robert Redford movie, *The Last Castle*, and advances a commonsense notion about prison films invoking an almost taken for granted belief that (i) there is such a thing as a prison film; and (ii) collectively such films constitute a genre, with characteristics so recognisable that they can be reduced to a neat summary. Elements of this popular belief can be seen to inform, sometimes implicitly sometimes explicitly, academic analysis of perceptions of prison. The second quote seems to be similarly incontrovertible. It contains two elements. Firstly, a belief that the US is involved in some kind 'experiment with mass incarceration' and, secondly, an implied suggestion that in the light of this, Hollywood feel-good prison movies—or, if you like, prison films with happy endings—are 'bad' from the standpoint of those who would wish to slow or possibly reverse prison growth.

The aim of this chapter is to review, clarify and if possible move-on the debate about how representations of prison in film might influence common sense understandings of prison and, in turn, contribute to US prison growth. The discussion will take issue with the quotes that head the chapter and we will argue that, despite their apparently self-evident nature and initial appeal, both are open to serious challenge.

Let us consider first the idea of 'prison film' advanced by our reviewer of *The Last Castle*. It could be suggested that virtually every element of this statement is wrong or seriously open to challenge. Is the prison film a Hollywood staple? It may be that at particular times significant numbers of prison films have been made—say for example in the 1930s—but, if we look at the evidence we might equally suggest that there have been other periods since then when relatively few prison films have been made at all. In terms of volume and commercial importance the prison film is not necessarily a staple and its popularity can sometimes be overstated. Of the prison films that have been made we most definitely could not have 'reliably predicted' that the Warden (the US equivalent of the British prison Governor) would be evil. Wardens in prison films vary from being 'evil', usually in a fairly clichéd and hyperbolic way, to being good, principled, well-intentioned people and taking in along the way a variety of shades of outlooks and personalities in between. If we knew the time period that the prison film in question came from, then we might be able to hazard a guess at the representation of the Warden but reliably predict—no. Similarly, the idea that such a film must inevitably include a reluctant leader who will steer the inmates to victory is equally suspect. As the discussion below shows, there are any number of prison films which end not in triumph but in eventual defeat for the prisoners. The reviewer here is guilty of looking at the film in front of him or her and extrapolating back from it to an imagined set of characteristics for an allegedly well-defined and well-behaved genre. The only slight redeeming feature of the statement is the placing of the term 'prison film' in inverted commas, signalling that everything is, perhaps, not quite as simple as it might seem.

The second quote would seem at first to be on firmer ground. Yes, the US would appear to be experiencing the prison-building spree complained of. Yes, inmate numbers are rising—and yes the US does have incarceration rates amongst the highest in the world. Whether the inmate population is housed in huge, impersonal institutions might perhaps require some empirical support and verification. But, if we were to quibble with the first part of the statement it might be to point out that incarceration rates vary widely between states and that some states have relatively low incarceration rates, including some with rates lower than Britain which is not a mass incarceration society (Beckett and Western, 2001: 40). So, is *the US* in the middle of a prison-building spree, or is it that some states within the US are binging on prison, accounting for all or most of the race to mass incarceration? Despite these quibbles, this book and this chapter are written in the conviction that rising inmate numbers are a real concern. But should we then grant the second part of Rafter's argument, the implication that Hollywood prison films, with heroes and happy endings, are 'bad' for those who wish to oppose the growth of the prison population? In a society, or even a world, where Hollywood is the dominant style of cinema and one to which we as analysts would seem to be according a power to shape perceptions and beliefs, can the opponents of prison growth give up on Hollywood?

PRISON FILM ISSUES

We have begun to identify some of the areas that require investigation and can suggest some of the issues that are key to our study. Firstly, there is the question of whether the significance of 'the prison film' can be understood through a notion of genre. Do prison films have recurring similarities which make them identifiable as a group of films and which allow us to understand how these films work and what they do? Some accounts of 'the prison film' suggest that there is a generic formula which Hollywood prison films work within. This is said to be good for producing entertaining, 'feel-good' movies but not good for producing films which reflect thoughtfully on US penal realities. But should we agree with this? Should we criticise or defend Hollywood? And if Hollywood cinema is not appropriate for reflecting on penal realities, what style of film is?

The discussion of these issues we offer is written in the conviction that representations of prison in film and TV drama do influence people's perceptions of it and so in some way contribute to the balance of forces that shape the reality of prison. We begin with a preliminary examination of our field of study by considering the meaning and usefulness of the terms 'prison film' and 'prison-film genre' and later widen the analysis to pull in 'prison-related film' and 'prison-in-film'. A survey and review of the US prison film is then introduced, outlining what kinds of prison films have been made in different periods of US film history. The aim of this review is to illustrate the range of ways in which prison makes an appearance in film and to suggest some of the ways in which penal realities can come to be reflected in and commented on in film.

Defining an area of study
All of the contributors to the debate on the relationship between prison and film, implicitly or explicitly, see prison growth as a problem. If prison were a perfectly functioning social institution we would have less cause to consider why we have 'prison film' and how the 'prison film' we do have affects people's perceptions and misperceptions of prison. It is possible to study any set of films in a variety of ways and for a variety of reasons but our study starts with a concern for the ways in which film might influence perceptions of prison and so, indirectly, penal realities. But investigating this could include a consideration of a wide variety of films: from murder mysteries to police procedurals; to family melodramas in which crimes are committed; to 'hood movies', or 'race' social comment movies; to courtroom dramas and miscarriage of justice movies, and so forth. All of these may talk in some way to the processes by which a person or group of people may come to end up serving a prison sentence. Such an approach may well be legitimate and fruitful, although it might also make the study of the relationship between prison and film infinitely large and perhaps lose something of the specificity of enquiring not just about why and how people come to commit crimes but why society is prepared to believe in prison as a response to crime. Rightly or wrongly, the debate about the relationship between prison and film has from the outset narrowed down its focus of concern and, reasoning that we have to start somewhere, has begun from a notion that there is such a thing as a 'prison film'. Depending on our age group and background, common sense and our stock of film knowledge might suggest to us that films

such as *The Birdman of Alcatraz* (1962), *Cool Hand Luke* (1967) and *Brubaker* (1980) all seem to have something in common. All three films are set in and address the subject of, prison. They are—on a simple descriptive definition—'prison films'.

But is this approach adequate, or do we need to give more thought to the definition of the term 'prison film' and its implied close relation—the prison-film genre? Mason (2003b) seems to think that we might—citing Tudor (1995) on the problems of defining and studying genres and suggesting that there is a fundamental problem which arises—because:

> To take a genre such as a western, analyse it, and list its principal characteristics is to beg the question that we must first isolate the body of films that are westerns. But that can only be isolated on the basis of the 'principal characteristic' which can only be discovered from the films themselves after they have been isolated.
>
> (Tudor, 1995: 5 cited in Mason, 2003b)

But this 'circular predicament', as Mason terms it, only arises if we insist, as Tudor seems to do, that we cannot separate out the distinction between a descriptive definition of a prison film and an analytic definition. Tudor's problem, that we have to know the characteristics of films in a genre to identify which films belong to the genre, can be avoided if we adopt a two stage process of first identifying those films which are descriptively prison films, before then going on to consider which of those films have some generic similarities that would justify identifying a prison film genre. However this is not a perfect solution to approaching the analysis; problems still arise and we need to clarify the meaning and usage of our terms.

Strictly speaking the term 'prison film' should include prison film dramas and prison film documentaries. Rafter (2000) considers both dramas and documentaries in her chapter on prison film, although most other contributors try to look more specifically at movies. What is the significance of 'fictional' dramatic representations of prison? Of course the distinction between drama, docu-drama and documentary can itself be made problematic—where does a documentary on the Attica prison uprising stop and its fictional recreation as a movie based on a true story begin—*Attica* (1973), *Attica* (1980) or *Against the Wall* (1994)? This chapter follows the previous literature in looking at fictional prison drama. Whilst accepting that many of these products are attempting to re-tell real world events, the distinction between drama and documentary is maintained. Our first interest is in prison movies (dramas), although it is legitimate to suggest that we might need to pull documentaries into the analysis at a later stage. Here we use the term 'prison movie' to refer to the fictional products that we are interested in, but for convenience the terms 'prison film' and 'prison movie' are used interchangeably, reserving the term 'prison-film documentary' to refer to those non-fiction prison films which we are, for the moment, defining as outside the scope of our study. However the term prison film (or prison movie) is still problematic. What constitutes a prison film/movie? Nellis (1988) takes the term prison movie to refer to:

> a feature film ... [rather than a documentary] ... which is set wholly or mainly in a penal institution, whether for men, women or adolescents or—more loosely—which takes imprisonment and *its consequences* as a primary theme.
>
> (Nellis, 1988: two emphases in the original)

This is a useful starting point for a *descriptive* definition of the films which might come under the category of prison film. It could encompass future set sci-fi prison films and prisons in historical dramas. Including 'imprisonment and its consequences' allows us to bring 'escaped and released prisoner movies' into the analysis, which is possibly reasonable in defining an area of interest, although it raises the issue of why not allow other widenings such as 'going to prison' movies, courtroom dramas, etc. There are other boundary problems. How much of the film need be set in the prison to qualify as 'wholly or mainly'? And similarly what constitutes 'imprisonment and its consequences' being a film's primary theme? The film *American History X* has only some 20 minutes of its action set within a prison and this in flashback, whilst the main character is outside of prison. Although the prison experience is significant to the decision of the main protagonist in the film to reject racism, arguably the primary theme of the film is racism and its rejection, rather imprisonment and its consequences. Similar boundary problems occur with films such as *A Map of the World* and *Freeway* which both feature 20 minute prison segments in films which address more generally the cultural politics of crime. We would have to conclude that the descriptive category of prison film encompasses a core of films which are relatively incontrovertibly prison movies and an ill-defined periphery of films that might qualify at the analyst's discretion.

Perhaps a more serious problem arises when we move from prison film as a descriptive category to considering whether and how prison films operate to influence our ideas about and understandings of prison. Do prison films share some quality which would enable 'prison film' to function as an analytic category? Here it could be suggested that, for analytical purposes, the category 'prison film' may be a 'chaotic conception'—i.e. a category which 'combines the unrelated and divides the indivisible' (Sayer, 1984). Some examples illustrate the point.

The Shawshank Redemption (1994) is set for almost its entirety in a prison and in descriptive terms is incontrovertibly a prison film. Yet in review and comment the film is often described as being 'not really a prison movie'. What people who make this observation are presumably getting at is that, whatever it was that all those old recognisable prison films you might have seen were doing, this particular film, despite its superficial similarities, is not doing the same. We need to take this point seriously. We cannot assume for analytical purposes that all films set in prison are variations of the same thing. For analytical purposes, *The Shawshank Redemption* might have more in common with some non-prison films, for example *It's A Wonderful Life* and may need to be analysed as such (see Kermode, 2003). Another recent film *Undisputed* (2001) tells the story of a heavyweight world champion boxer who is committed to prison, providing the opportunity to stage a boxing match between 'the champ' and the prison's own undefeated champion. Although the film is set 'wholly or mainly' in a prison, it has relatively little in common with films such as *Brubaker* or *The Birdman of Alcatraz*. Is *Undisputed* a boxing movie set in a prison, or a prison movie with a lot of boxing in it?

To an extent these problems revolve round the issue of whether there is such a thing as a prison film *genre*, where the use of genre as an analytic category might be taken to imply not only that a group of films exist which share certain identifiable common characteristics, but also that this shared similarity is significant for our understanding of how these films work and what they do. Rafter (2000) is one analyst who has suggested that such a genre exists and who has identified in some detail both what would appear to be its agreed characteristics and the range of films in which these characteristics manifest themselves—and significant examples in which they do not. Our discussion will now examine her specification of the genre and suggest some criticisms that might be made of her analysis.

Nichole Rafter on the prison-film genre

Nichole Rafter (2000) starts from the premise that film, and in particular Hollywood movies, are an important source of our ideas about crime and criminals. Her book devotes a reasonably substantial chapter to the analysis of prison and execution movies although her overall subject of study is 'the crime film', which she identifies as films that *'focus primarily on crime and its consequences'* [italics in the original]. Her concern is for 'serious movies' that contain the ideas which reflect how society thinks about crime. She excludes from her analysis action-adventure films (*Die Hard* etc.) and crime comedies. The films chosen for analysis are selected on the basis of: critical reputation and audience reaction; whether the film has anything to say about the relationship between crime and society; its significance for film history; or significance for understanding the politics of everyday life in relation to age, gender, ethnicity, 'race', etc. These criteria and her exclusions, Rafter suggests, enable her to:

> discuss the best and most important crime films and avoid the worst and most trivial, the endless stream of ephemera about air-plane hostage situations, cop buddies and babes in prison. (Rafter, 2000: 7)

But whilst these methodological choices have the advantage that they enable the analyst to avoid having to consider every conceivable crime film, they may improve 'manageability' at a cost of reducing 'understanding'. It may be that it is amongst 'the dross' and 'the ephemera' that we find the movies that reveal how film transmits ideas and understandings of crime and prison. Rafter also excludes made-for-TV movies from her analysis. This again is understandable in terms of manageability—it would be difficult to locate and review all of the relevant TV movies—but if we know of one that relates to our films under consideration, why not include it in our analysis? We cannot afford arbitrarily to exclude films which help us understand how things work.

Rafter's general approach to the study of her crime film category is to suggest that the dominant tendency at work within these films is the production of 'escapist fantasies'. These films set up situations in which aspects of the criminal justice system appear to be questioned (for example, police corruption or miscarriages of justice), but then provide a story-line in which the injustices of the system are eventually righted—the bent cop or brutal prison Warden eventually gets his or her comeuppance. Film is providing a simplistic screen resolution to problems that, in the real world, are much more intractable and difficult to solve. Such films do not therefore equip us with the imaginative resources that we need to think about how these problems might be tackled.

Rafter's general approach carries over into her discussion of prison films which she suggests are identifiable by their use of stock characters, scenes, themes and plots. Whereas Cheatwood (1998) has suggested that prison movies need to be periodised to identify how they track penal eras (for example, the Depression era, rehabilitation era, confinement era, and administrative era),

Rafter suggests that no such periodisation is necessary because the same generic characteristics, with few exceptions (one being the representation of the Warden), crop up in prison films of all eras. She seems to be proposing a trans-historical genre based on the same recurring characteristics. These generic characteristics would include stock characters such as: 'the prison innocent'—someone either wrongly imprisoned or incarcerated for a minor or morally justifiable offence, for whom prison might seem an excessive punishment; a stool pigeon—a.k.a 'the Rat' or 'the Snitch'; an experienced convict buddy who usually befriends the prison innocent; a Warden—in earlier films fair and reform-minded, but in later films more megalomaniac, and/or a sadistic chief of guards. Rafter suggests that the stock theme of prison movies is the oppression of the prisoners and their struggle against the tyranny of the authorities. The stock plots of the genre concern the main ways in which these struggles are conducted e.g. through riots and/or escape attempts.

It can be shown that these characteristics recur in any number of prison films from across the history of the genre. The 'prison innocent' makes an appearance in many prison films of the 1930s, but also in films as recent as *The Last Castle* (2001) in which Robert Redford plays a general who has been court-martialled for a morally defensible decision to disobey an order. But the problem with restricting the analysis to identifying the recurring characteristics of the genre (or prison-film clichés) is that it gives the impression of a well-defined and stable genre, with less attention devoted to the in-depth analysis of particular films. But we do need to look at variations within the genre. So for example, *The Birdman of Alcatraz* is a serious attempt at dramatising the life and penal career of one man and a film that was made at a time coincidental with the end point of the events it depicted. In contrast, *Murder in the First* (1995), although superficially similar, is a much more stylised *retrospective* look at, coincidentally, the same prison. Can we understand these films by suggesting that they are basically variants of the same essential thing—'genre-pic' prison movies?

In the analysis provided by Rafter, when the elements of the genre are pulled together to provide an account of what a genre-pic prison film looks like it is to support a characterisation of the prison film not that different from the view expressed by the reviewer of *The Last Castle* cited at the outset of this chapter. A standard prison film involves a 'prison innocent', who at first struggles to survive the environment but who with the help of a convict buddy—or stand-in—rises to a position of prominence and takes on the evil regime achieving an eventual victory. According to Rafter, 'In all these films good triumphs over evil' (2000: 120). Hence prison films which conform to the constraints of the genre are:

> ... essentially fantasies, films which purport to reveal the brutal realities of incarceration while actually offering viewers escape from the miseries of daily life through adventure and heroism. Presenting tales in which justice is miraculously restored after long periods of harsh oppression, prison movies enable us to believe, if only briefly, in a world where long suffering virtue is rewarded. (p. 117)

Or further,

Historically, prison films have taken for granted a clear and stable system of morality. The heroes may be criminals, but they are obviously admirable, the bad guys are abominable and the heroes win. Based on comfortable moral verities, standard prison films raise questions about justice in particular cases but do not doubt that justice exists and lies within human reach. Nor do they ask hard questions about the prison system. What they do best is what they do over and over again: set up a situation in which an individual is being punished unfairly, and then develop a plotline in which the balance of justice is restored. (p. 130)

In effect Rafter reduces the prison-film genre to one of its themes, that of 'Justice Restored'. This underlying dynamic is said to be at work across the genre, from *The Big House* (1930) and *The Criminal Code* (1931) up to more recent films including *The Shawshank Redemption* (1994) and *Murder in the First* (1995).

This is, we argue, an over-stylised account of the genre which leads to a dismissive attitude towards films such as *The Birdman of Alcatraz* (1962), *Cool Hand Luke* (1967) and *Brubaker* (1980). These should not be understood and dismissed as 'prison film fantasies'. But here we should note that there is more in Rafter's analysis. She identifies a number of prison films which do not conform to the conventions of the genre. Three elements are identified: an 'Alternative Tradition' of prison films including: *On the Yard* (1979), *Short Eyes* (1979), and *American Me* (1992) (films which lack heroes and avoid happy endings); New Prison Documentaries including: *The Thin Blue Line* (1988), *Through The Wire* (1990), *The Execution Protocol* (1993) and *Aileen Wuornos: the Selling of a Serial Killer* (1992); and finally Self-reflexive Prison Films such as *Weeds* (1987), *Natural Born Killers* (1994) and *Swoon* (1991) (which spoof and lampoon prison films, revealing the artificiality and shallowness of the generic conventions of the traditional prison movie). All in all these three categories are introduced to highlight a contrast between:

genre movies that ... essentially repeat the formulas of the past ... [and] ... critical movies that turn the old conventions inside out, and self-reflexive films that explore new possibilities in representation ... [two tracks] ... one for commercial entertainments and the other for political truth-telling. (p. 137)

And so we end up with the statement by Rafter that started this chapter—that 'feel-good' prison movies are out of place in a mass incarceration society. Hollywood films fail to ask the hard questions about the problem of prison and therefore we need to look outside of Hollywood for films which do. Why Rafter is wrong in her championing of her various alternative traditions over more conventional movies will be explored in greater depth later. Her work captures one element of the Hollywood prison film—that genre movies on the theme of 'Justice Restored' can operate as an 'ideological manipulation' producing films which, although they appear to criticise prison, in fact produce a fantasy resolution to the problem of prison. Rafter might be right in her suggestion that such films allow their viewers to participate vicariously in an armchair revolution against the tyrannical prison authorities whilst, back in the real world, tolerating unprecedentedly high incarceration rates and record prison building. One of the effects of Hollywood prison movies could be to help 'corrode our doubts and worries about the prisons solution' (Matheisen, 2000). But it is not clear that all prison genre movies have this effect. Firstly, not all genre prison movies have a Justice Restored narrative. Many prison movies end in defeat for the prisoners and rather than justice being restored, 'authority is reasserted'. This needs to be incorporated into the analysis. Even for those films which adopt the formula Rafter identifies, we do not have to agree that they have the suggested ideological effect. These films may do something different to what is being suggested, or may do things in addition to what is being suggested. There are a whole range of issues around the representation of prisons and prisoners which are not touched on in the discussion offered. Reducing the prison film to its generic characteristics excludes from the analysis consideration of the changing *mise en scène* of the prison film, changing representations of prisoner subcultures and dangerousness, and so forth.

At the risk of seeming overly critical of the work of one particular analyst, it might be helpful to identify some of the deficiencies in Rafter's account in order to help point the way towards where we should be going. As has already been suggested, the analysis presented reduces the prison film genre to one of its elements—that of justice restored—overlooking the equally important dynamic of authority reasserted. The analysis in effect divides prison movies into a dichotomous categorisation: prison film fantasies and an alternative tradition (admittedly with some variations). But the alternative tradition category is in danger of becoming a catch-all for anything which does not fit the justice restored model and arguably the analysis does not understand the significance of these alternative tradition films or the way in which they interact with prison 'genre-pics'—this is discussed below in relation to the film *American Me*. As already mentioned, the discussion fails to periodise the genre so that when the same characteristics appear in films in different time periods they are held to mean essentially the same thing. This overstates the homogeneity of the genre and fails to distinguish between distinctly different uses of the same 'generic formula' (for example, *The Big House* (1930) v. *Murder in the First* (1995) or *The Last Castle* (2001).

Virtually all of the films considered by Rafter address the male experience of prison. Whilst footnotes to the analysis bemoan the lack of attention given to research on the history of women's prison film, the analysis airbrushes women out of the picture, failing to consider women's prison films which fit the criteria for inclusion (see, for example, *Anne Vickers* (1933), *Ladies They Talk About* (1933) and *Caged* (1950)). Excluding women from the analysis leads to overstating the extent to which the prison film is a masculine/masculinist phenomena.

Moving to the issue of explanation, Rafter's account supplies an inadequate explanation for the existence of the genre, particularly because it fails to provide any theory or account of: the role of prison in US society; how prison is legitimated; and how prisons change. Without providing some suggestions as to how prisons change over time, it is not possible to suggest whether or not prison film contributes to or hinders penal reform. The need to do this is implied by the claim of the analysis to be investigating the ideological significance of the genre. But relating the prison film to contemporary penal realities would require us to expand the range of films under consideration. In particular, the exclusion of film 'ephemera' from the discussion amounts to a deliberate neglect of films that need to be included if the analysis is to be able to appreciate the full ramifications of the prison film. Action adventure films set in prison, such as *An Innocent Man* (1989) (Wilson, 1993) and sci-fi prison films, e.g. *Escape from New York* (1981) (Cheatwood, 1998) need to be considered. Although the discussion seeks to understand actual or potential transformations of the prison film, in its concentration on identifying an unchanging genre the argument fails to understand and appreciate the significance of *The Shawshank Redemption,* which is paradoxically referred to both as a self-reflexive text, knowingly nostalgic for the conventions of the prison film genre and at the same time as being a 'traditional prison film'. Finally, the limitation of the remit to films of US origin, whilst understandable in terms of practicalities and prioritisation, misses an opportunity to refine and develop the analysis. In our discussion below we attempt to develop the significance of these points.

'Justice restored' or 'authority reasserted'?

Do prison movies allow the eventual triumph of the prisoners? A moment's thought would immediately suggest that they generally do not. At most, prison movies might allow the 'prison innocent' to clear his or her name, gain a reprieve, or endure a sentence. Successfully overthrowing a corrupt and oppressive regime occurs far less often. Is it true that in genre prison films the 'prison innocent' hero treads a well-worn path from initial suffering, through to eventual triumph? There is no doubt that some prison films use this motif. Rafter (2000) mentions *The Big House* (1930), *The Criminal Code* (1931), *Each Dawn I Die* (1939) and the later examples, *The Shawshank Redemption* (1994) and *Murder in the First* (1995). The more recent and completely formulaic *The Last Castle* (2001) also follows this model and there are certainly more examples that could be given here. But in a sense, if Hollywood films have heroes and happy endings then it is perhaps not surprising that (some) prison films also have heroes and happy endings. What perhaps is surprising is the extent to which the prison film gives us a hero who we have been encouraged to believe in, but who in the end either lets us down, or is allowed by the film only to 'snatch defeat from the jaws of victory'.

We can suggest examples in support of this theme. In *Riot in Cellblock 11* (1954), the rioters briefly seize control of the prison and put to the authorities their demands for improvements in conditions. When their list of demands is printed in the newspapers the rioters believe they have won and negotiate a peaceful end to the riot, in return for an agreement of no victimisation. But the film ends with the leader of the riot/negotiations being told that the state governor has blocked the agreed reforms and welched on the no recriminations agreement, with the result that they will have another 30 years added to their sentences (Nellis, 1982: 26). In *The Birdman of Alcatraz* (1962), Burt Lancaster as Robert Stroud endures 52 years in prison, with 46 of them spent in solitary confinement. The film ends with Stroud landing on the quayside of San Francisco Bay in the process of eventually being transferred from Alcatraz to a prison hospital, at a time when he was too old for the transfer to make any difference and Stroud in fact died shortly after the transfer. To suggest that this is a justice restored ending would be a travesty given that the film makes it quite clear that the penal authorities kept Stroud incarcerated long after he was rehabilitated and never had any intention of allowing his release, whatever he did. The film could equally be identified as operating in the manner of 'injustice revealed'.

One of the all-time classics of the prison film genre is *Cool Hand Luke* (1967), in which Luke dies at the end of the film, having been shot by 'the man with no eyes', at the end of his third unsuccessful escape bid. Again Luke, like Stroud, pays a high price for maintaining his individuality. A 'sassy and truculent hero' he may be, but if we believe in him, he (or the films makers) will have let us down by the end of the movie. Some prison movies have more ambiguous endings. In *Brubaker* (1980), for example, Robert Redford stars as the reforming Warden who discovers corruption and wrong-doing in the Arkansas prison farm. But his attempts to reform it and challenge corruption fail and he is sacked/resigns from his job. As the new Warden speaks to the assembled inmates signalling a return to the old regime, he is met with a surprise show of resistance from the prisoners. This ending and film warrant greater discussion than space permits here (see Nellis, 1982 and further discussion in *Chapters* 4 and 8).

Clearly Burt Lancaster, Paul Newman and Robert Redford, amongst many others, did not see a happy ending where good triumphs over evil and moral order is restored. These films do not illustrate a theme of justice restored but rather one of authority reasserted. This theme extends itself to prison films set outside prison. For example, one all-time classic 'prison movie' is *The Defiant Ones* (1958) (and see *Chapter 9* for further discussion). This is an 'escaped prisoner movie' set entirely outside of prison. When the prison van that is transporting them goes off the road and crashes, chained together cons Sidney Poitier and Tony Curtis make a break for freedom. The remainder of the film is about the manhunt to track them down. The determination of Curtis and Poitier not to be caught and returned to prison, and their attitude towards their crimes and the appropriateness of prison as a response to them, clearly mark this out as a prison movie. By the end of the film we, the viewers, are rooting for Curtis and Poitier to get away and jump that train ride to freedom. Again they, or more correctly the film's makers, let us down as the two escapees manage only to 'snatch defeat from the jaws of victory', leaving the calm patient sheriff who has been leading the manhunt simply to walk up to them and arrest them. The inevitability of the law requires that the prisoners cannot be allowed to win.

One more example will perhaps suffice, this time from the released prisoner movie *Straight Time* (1978). Small-time crook Dustin Hoffman is released on parole from prison, obtains a job, finds a girlfriend and tries to go straight. The film starts by being pretty much on Hoffman's side. His apparently genuine attempt to go straight is made more difficult by his bully boy probation officer who is on his back looking for any minor breach of his conditions of parole so as to be able send him back to prison. Labelling and self-fulfilling prophecy take over and soon Hoffman has returned to a life of crime. But his crime spree does not last long and by the end of the film he has accepted the inevitable, ditched his girlfriend and, as the closing titles tell us, was caught soon afterwards and returned to prison. But the film sells Hoffman short. Whilst at first it is sympathetic to his plight, Hoffman's character is blown off course too easily and embarks on an inept crime spree too readily. It is hard not to conclude that his return to offending was fairly inevitable. Whether the message is that criminals are incorrigible offenders, or that prison makes criminals thus is not entirely clear. The fact remains that the film does not have a happy ending.

So, are we to re-assign Sidney Poitier, Tony Curtis, Burt Lancaster, Paul Newman, Robert Redford and Dustin Hoffman to the category of Alternative Tradition prison movies, or are we to conclude that there is more going on in the prison film genre than a simple formula of justice restored? We suggest that there is a notion of 'authority reasserted' at work in the prison film genre. But what is the significance of this theme? The films encourage us to identify with the prisoners and in our hearts we want them to win. But with our head, when they lose, we perhaps accept that this is the way it must be. The 'authority reasserted' ending could be a way of cultivating respect for and acceptance of authority, or even for abuses of authority. But, alternatively these endings could exemplify the theme of 'authority reasserted *at a cost*'. The prisoners lose, but we witness the lengths that the authorities were prepared to go to in order to bring about this defeat. But, we would suggest, it is not possible to discern what is going on here just by looking at the films themselves. We have to look outside of the films to the times and context in which they were made and are viewed to get a sense of what's really going on.

FILM ERAS AND PENAL ERAS

Nichole Rafter rejects the idea that the prison film genre needs to be periodised. In her analysis it appears as a more or less explicitly timeless entity, with some minor qualifiers. A genre-pic prison movie is a genre-pic prison movie whenever it happens. We do not need to investigate the differences between 1930s and 1990s genre-pics, as these are essentially the same. The difference is between genre-pics and the various alternatives, not between films within the genre itself. There are two problems with this proposition. Firstly, it is a mistake to think that because the same generic convention occurs in films in different time periods the genre itself has stayed the same. So, for example, the analysis below will go on to suggest that we cannot assume that a 'prison-innocent' in a 1930s movie is the same as one in a 1990s movie. Secondly, the category 'prison film' is bigger than the category 'prison-film genre'. Rafter's alternative tradition prison movies start to emerge from the 1970s but we need to know why this was. And did it reflect a change in film trends or a change in penal realities?

Cheatwood (1998) argues that the stock characters of the prison film take on different inflections in different eras. In particular, the inflections of these characters reflect the degree of optimism about the possibility of reforming criminals and the prisons that house them. So, for example, over time the character of the Warden has shifted from being fair and reform-minded to being more megalomaniac. Similarly, the hero of the prison film has evolved from being a regular guy square-John, to a more tough-guy hero. But the question is, can we track changes in the prison film (genre) over time? And if we can, do they relate to changes in penal realities? Our view is that we need to try to do both. How is it possible to understand what prison films were doing in any particular period without having some account of what was going on in the world of penal affairs? Does prison film conceal and mystify prison? Or is it an indirect way of commenting on the system and a means of disseminating ideas and understandings about the need for change? Without providing some account of penal realities and how they change we cannot even begin to answer these kinds of questions. In *Chapter 2* a periodisation of the British prison film was introduced and illustrated in *Table 2.1*. The periodisation advanced for the UK has some similarities and some differences to that advanced by Cheatwood for the US, as shown in *Table 3.1*.

Table 3.1: *Relative periodisation of UK and USA prison films*

The UK (*Chapter* 2 this volume)		The US (Cheatwood, 1998)	
1930s	Pre-war restriction	1930s	Depression era
	Post-war optimism	1942–62	Rehabilitation era
	Retreat from optimism	1963- 80	Confinement
Late 1970s/ early 1980s	Concern	1981–present day	Admistrative era
New millenium	Nostalgia		

For the British prison film the periodisation works because: there is a relatively small number of identifiable films that need to be considered; it is possible to identify the formal and informal social pressures that constrained prison film-making—particularly for the earlier periods; the film-makers deploy a small number of representational strategies (mainly serious drama, comedy, social realism, Brit-pic); and finally there is a reconstructable account of penal history possible across the period (see *Chapter 2*). For the US, we can immediately see that there are more films to be considered, illustrating a greater variety of film styles, sub-genres and representational strategies. Some prison movies are contemporary, and some are retrospective, but to different extents and in different ways. Lastly, penal realities are more complicated in the US, which has a much larger prison population experiencing a wider variety of conditions in different states, with varying degrees of punitiveness and penality (see Beckett and Western, 2001; Garland, 2001; Donziger, 1996). All this makes developing a workable periodisation difficult, and indeed perhaps impossible. But we need to *try* to see if such a periodisation can be developed.

The 1930s
The left hand side of *Table 3.1* is discussed in detail in *Chapter 2*. But we will recap in order to contrast it with the periodisation advanced by Cheatwood. Firstly, there would appear to be major differences between the two countries during the 1930s. In Britain this was a time of restriction; few prison films were made and the central government tightly monitored the flow of information out of penal institutions. Film-makers were discouraged from making films about prison. At that time conditions in some prisons, such as penal servitude and corporal punishment, were out of step with more progressive institutions symbolised by the newly emerging open prisons. In the US the situation appears to have been quite different. The Depression era was the hey day of the prison film, with an estimated 60 or more US prison films made in that decade (Nellis, 1988: 3; Querry, 1975). This probably reflected the lack of central control of the penal system and the fact that prison Wardens had much more autonomy. There is ample evidence to suggest that reform-minded Wardens were a major source of material for prison films (Nellis, 1982). At this time Wardens needed to be reform-minded as many prisons still ran on regimes inherited from the previous

century. So for example, one philosophy of 'correction' advocated by Elam Lynds, the one time controller of Auburn Prison in New York state, was that 'in order to reform a criminal you must first break his spirit' (cited in Crowther, 1989: 9). Hence Lynds supported prison regimes based on a silent system, prolonged solitary confinement and whippings for minor infringements of discipline. Such regimes were never accepted by prisoners. Auburn Prison and also Dannemora Prison in New York state were affected by rioting in 1929, the year before the release of *The Big House* (1930) generally regarded as being the first prison movie talkie of any significance.

The 1930s were a period of intense debate about penal reform and new ideas about criminology were being developed and popularised. This is seen particularly in women's prison drama, including *Ann Vickers* (1933), *Ladies of the Big House* (1931) and *Ladies They Talk About* (1933). These films are important social documents which cast some light on how penal thinking was developing and it is not adequate to dismiss them as being merely 'B' movies about 'babes-behind-bars'. Indeed the films raised questions about the nature of crime and delinquency and whether delinquents could be diverted from crime by appropriate interventions.

The post-war prison movie
For the UK we identified in *Chapter 2* an era of post-war optimism, which for the US Cheatwood dubs the 'era of rehabilitation'. In the UK this was marked by a growth in the number of prison films produced and in films illustrating new welfare state thinking, as applied to crime and deviance. For the US the timing was slightly different. Because prison film developed earlier in the US, the post-war period sees a fall in the number of such films being made, although some 32 prison films were made in the 1940s (and perhaps 20 in the 1950s) (Nellis, 1982). It is obviously not possible to locate and view 52 prison films to establish their characteristics in this period. Our discussion needs to be illustrative. Firstly, a shift in thinking in the films towards a 'medical model' of penal intervention can be seen in women's prison drama. (See, for example, Morey (1995) on *Caged* (1950), *Women's Prison* (1955), *Girls in Prison* (1956) and *House of Women* (1962).) In these films the figure of the prison doctor or psychiatrist invariably makes an appearance, although the films differ in the extent to which they are optimistic about the extent to which prisons could reform their charges. The basic storyline of *Caged* involves the prison innocent Marie Allen entering prison, having committed a minor crime, and emerging from it a hardened con. *Caged* is generally reckoned by most commentators to fall somewhere between women's prison drama and *film noir*, although it has all of the elements that appear in more clichéd and formulaic women-in-prison movies. It could be conceded that in the US by the 1950s the women's prison drama movie was already moving away from serious drama towards a campy, clichéd formula that would later develop into the 'exploitation' sub-genre (see Morey, 1995).

But was optimism about reform of prisoners or penal institutions present in terms of male prison films in this period? Again a comprehensive survey is not possible but some illustrative films can be mentioned. Firstly, *My Six Convicts* (1952) was a light comedy based on a book by Donald P. Wilson about his experiences as a prison psychiatrist. The story of the film follows a group of convicts who are test cases for a psychiatrist developing new ideas about rehabilitation. When an escape bid by one of the cons turns nasty, the others rally round to save the day and to justify the faith their prison psychiatrist has shown in them. Another less well known, but perhaps in some ways more interesting film, is *Unchained* (1955). This film, about an open prison in Chino, California, was based on a book by its Warden called *Prisoners Are People*. The film advanced an optimistic view that open prisons based on trust can be an effective way of encouraging reform and rehabilitation. Perhaps the most ironic thing about *Unchained* is that it is little heard of and is not even generally remembered or acknowledged as being the source of one of the most popular songs of all time. *Unchained Melody*, which in the US/UK has been a number one hit on four occasions for four different artists, was specifically written and recorded as the theme song for the film. Although musicologists have studied the lyrical and musical structure of this piece extensively, they have generally failed to mention in their analysis that the song originated as the theme for a prison movie.

The mild optimism of *Unchained* and *My Six Convicts* was perhaps overshadowed by the 1951–3 wave of riots that affected US prisons, events reflected in films such as *Riot in Cell Block 11* (1954). It could be suggested that the ending of this film fits a model of authority reasserted, although it is 'authority reasserted *at a cost*'. It splices together newsreel footage of the 1951-53 prison unrest with dramatic action. The film showed the prisoners to have had a grievance and the (reasonable) riot leaders to have been betrayed by political treachery. Despite its ending the film disseminates the view that all is not well with US penal institutions and advocates reform. Riot also showed up in *Inside the Walls of Folsom Prison* (1951). The contemporary story of the film concerns the efforts of a reform-minded Warden to reform the prison, whilst running alongside this in flashback is the story of a riot that took place 30 years previously. The flashback riot occurs because of the sadistic regime of the earlier prison Warden and ends with the wholesale slaughter of the cons (Crowther, 1989: 15). Both films seem to carry the message that reform is necessary.

Some years later, but still within (if just on the border of) Cheatwood's rehabilitation era, we have *The Birdman of Alcatraz* (1962). As noted previously this was released in the year that Robert Stroud was transferred from Alcatraz to prison hospital. The film, which follows Stroud through 50 or more years of incarceration, most of which were spent in solitary confinement, is a swingeing critique of the failure of US prisons to rehabilitate their charges. The centrepiece is a confrontation towards the end between an ageing Warden called Shoemaker (Karl Malden) and an ageing Robert Stroud (Burt Lancaster). Shoemaker tells Stroud that American prisons are getting better, that leg irons and ball and chain have been abolished and educational programmes introduced. Stroud tells Shoemaker that his prison is a failure—more than half of the people discharged from it will come back again and, argues Stroud, no amount of reform can change the basic flaw of corrections, that penal theory does not know or understand how or why individuals come to rehabilitate themselves. *Birdman* stands neatly on the cusp of a change between two eras. It condemns penal history and proposes regimes more geared towards rehabilitation, just at a time when Stroud is able to see that this 'new model' of rehabilitation will work no better than the old (see also Nellis, 1982 for a similar discussion). *Birdman* is probably the great prison film of the post-war period. To dismiss it as a 'prison film fantasy' is just ridiculous.

A retreat from optimism (the 1960s and 1970s)
In Britain this period reflected a retreat from optimism. Depictions of prison in film become less positive about the possibilities for the reform and rehabilitation of either prisoners or penal institutions. In the US Cheatwood calls this era the period of 'containment'. But after *Birdman* in 1962 the 1960s produced few memorable US prison films. *Cool Hand Luke* (1967) is the one film that most people would remember, but that was set in 1948, harking back to an earlier period in penal history. It is possible to argue that *Luke* was an exercise in 'bashing the South', portraying it as backward and bigoted. Its relationship to the then contemporary penal realities and its influence on people's understanding of prison then and now is more difficult to discern. But it could be suggested that in being set in the past it distances 'the infernal prison' (Nellis, 1988: 3). If 'the prison of which we should be ashamed' happened in the past, then the fact that society can now put this up on screen and show it to us might be taken to imply that this is a problem that has already been solved—penal reform has already taken place. In this way, films like *Luke* can act as a kind of 'repressive tolerance' (Nellis, 1988). They imply that democratic processes and criticism work, whilst ignoring the current penal realities and the problems that they create. An alternative reading of this film is discussed in the next chapter.

Two years after *Luke* came *Riot* (1969) starring Gene Hackman and Jim Brown. This is probably the 'tipping point' of US prison film. Firstly, unlike the previously discussed riot films of the 1950s, in *Riot* the disturbance is planned as cover for an escape attempt not as part of a protest for reform. Whilst of course prison films have featured riots serving as cover for escapes before, this particular film marks a change in the way in which prison subculture is represented. The staged riot gets out of hand and the inmate controlled prison descends into decadence. The prisoners set up a homosexual brothel and a court to try other inmates for their 'crimes' against the inmate code and thus the film marked the beginning of a shift towards a more predatory prison. Although it could be suggested that *Riot* eerily anticipated the Attica uprising of 1971, in which inmates and hostages died as the National Guard retook the prison, Crowther (1989: 17) suggests that in the film the use of force by the authorities to put down the riot is constructed as being justified. Why prison shifted to being represented as a meaner environment at this time is not clear. Was it a reflection of changing penal realities and the way that they were perceived? Or was it simply a product of changing film trends following the ending of the US Motion Picture Production Code in the mid-1960s?

The themes of homosexuality and predatory behaviour in prison were continued in the US/Canadian production *Fortune and Men's Eyes* (1971). The 1970s saw other 'left-leaning' Hollywood prison or prison-related-films including *Steelyard Blues* (1973) the story of an ex-con, a prostitute and a psychiatric patient who renovate a flying-boat so as to be able to escape to a place 'where there are no jails' (Nellis, 1982: 36). Other films of the period included the TV Movies (TVMs) *The Glasshouse* (1972) and *The Jericho Mile* (1979). The first told the story of how a newly arrived inmate and then guard come to discover the extent of corruption and complicity between the prison authorities and the inmate 'top-dog'. The film ends on a typical 1970s downbeat note, that even if news of the corruption could be got out no one would be listening. *The Jericho Mile* told the story of an inmate athlete who trains for and qualifies to run at the Olympics but turns down the opportunity to go. The decade also saw the emergence of the 'blaxploitation' prison film, with James Fanuka's *Penetentiary* (1979) and its sequels. An allusion to black power was contained in the film *Brothers* (1977) fictiously modelled on the prison experience of George Jackson. Also important are two films discussed by Rafter (2000): *On the Yard* (1979) and *Short Eyes* (1979). But the suggestion that can be made is that at this time genre-pics were relatively weak and various alternative traditions or 'left Hollywood' were growing stronger. The Burt Reynolds' vehicle *The Longest Yard* (1975; UK title *The Mean Machine*), *Escape from Alcatraz* (1979) and the US/UK production *Midnight Express* (1978) (featuring the escape of a young American convicted of drug-smuggling from a Turkish prison), were the three main straightforward prison-film genre-pics of the 1970s. During this period cinematic prisons became more multi-racial and their makers less optimistic about their potential for change.

What about women's experience of prison? The 1970s seemed to address the serious issues of prison in the masculine gender. There are few, if any, examples of serious women's prison drama in this period—although this is a judgement that might change if we were to research made for TV movies. As far as film is concerned, the 1970s is remembered as being characterised by a series of 'babes-behind-bars', 'exploitation' movies that are sometimes termed the women-in-prison sub-genre (e.g. *The Big Doll House*). Nellis (1982: 24) has described this cycle of films as 'titillatingly sexist, superficially political and sickeningly sadistic'. Clowers (2001), talking about a similar set of films from later periods, suggests that their formulaic storylines bear no relationship at all to the realities of women's correctional facilities and that they contribute to the public's misperception of prisons and prisoners (Clowers, 2001: 25).

Whether the time is right for a revaluation of the exploitation prison movie is unclear. The 'blaxploitation' movies of the same era were at one time held in similar low esteem. So the story goes, desperate to boost falling audiences Hollywood, or near Hollywood producers served up to black and white audiences a cartoonish slice of ghetto-life. Tough, gun-toting women in such movies were held to be merely superficial male fantasy symbols. But 'blaxploitation' has recently been reappraised with some of the films now being seen as 'black genre' films. They did feature black casts and settings and did tell stories from a black perspective, about relationships with the police, urban decay and drugs. Often the films provided an indictment of white society, although the seriousness of this critique was decried because of the low-budget formula the films adopted. Actress Pam Grier, rediscovered by Tarantino in *Jackie Brown*, is the link between the two genres, starring in both the 'blaxploitation' classic *Coffey* (1973) and the previously mentioned *The Big Doll House*.

Having said this, just because 'blaxploitation' has been revisited does not mean to say that 'exploitation' has to be revisited also—the two 'ploitations may be quite different. One film from the 1970s that at the time was at first seen as an exploitation movie but is now regarded as a minor classic is *Jackson County Jail*

(1976). It tells the story of a Los Angeles advertising executive, who quits her job and unfaithful lover and sets out to drive across country. On the way she is assaulted and robbed by hitch-hikers, seeks refuge in a bar and is assaulted again. When the police are called she is arrested and thrown in gaol on a charge of vagrancy and then raped by the deputy supervising the gaol. Killing him in self-defence she is forced to go on the run with her cell-mate, a murderer awaiting extradition. The film ends with the usual 1970s pessimism. The other out-of-prison lovers-on-the run film from this time is *The Sugarland Express* (1973), Stephen Spielberg's cinematic directorial debut.

We do need to ask why the 1970s produced the type of prison film that they did. As Cheatwood has suggested, corrections had moved into an era of containment. The prison population was rising, slowly at first, and then more rapidly from the middle of the decade (Matheisen, 2000). The prison uprising at Attica in 1971, in which 29 inmates and ten of their hostages died when the National Guard were ordered to retake the prison, was followed by another vicious prison riot at Santa Fe, New Mexico in 1980, that demonstrated prison was not working, a sentiment reflected in films of the time. The Attica uprising was recorded in the film documentary *Attica* (1973), chanted by the crowds supporting the bank robbers in the hold-up gone wrong movie *Dog Day Afternoon* (1975) and appeared in TVM version in *Attica* (1980) (and then later remade again as a TV movie in *Against the Wall* (1994)). The 1980 Santa Fe, New Mexico riot does not appear to have made it into (Hollywood) film form—had something changed?

The 1980s and 1990s
The first prison film of the 1980s (but perhaps better described as 'the last of the 1970s') was *Brubaker* (discussed in the next chapter). After this, the 1980s produced a diverse range of prison films, with no real strong contenders for the status of genre classics. The post-apocalyptic sci-fi prison made an appearance in *Escape from New York* (1981). Here the problems of managing the prison have been abandoned. Manhattan has been walled off and become a post-apocalyptic containment zone. Later films included *An Innocent Man* (1989) starring Tom Selleck. This is a significant film for our analysis. In it prison innocent Tom Selleck becomes the object of attention by a predatory gang, on his entry into a Californian maximum security prison. From the outset Selleck is warned by his fellow inmates that he will have to kill the man who is harassing him if he is to survive his prison term. At first our prison innocent cannot believe that this is the case but later realises that it is literally true. Accordingly he plans and executes the murder of the leader of the gang, tormenting him in order to avoid the highly unpleasant plans that they have in store for him coming to fruition. Keeping your head down and doing your time is not an option in this type of prison. In *An Innocent Man* the prison has become a racially-divided, kill-or-be-killed environment. Other action-adventure prison films of around the same period are populated with a *mise en scène* of hardened convicts, sporting facial or whole-body tattoos and built bodies. The films *Lock-up* (1989) and *Death Warrant* (1990) utilised this imagery (see Wilson (1993)) and *Runaway Train* (1985) and the TVM *Convict Cowboy* (1985) are also relevant here.

As already mentioned, Cheatwood (1998) suggests that the prison film has been characterised by a decline in the reform-minded Warden and a shift in the character of the hero, from regular-guy square-John, to tough-guy. In *An Innocent Man* the Warden has disappeared altogether and is never seen throughout the whole of the film. In a way, the same could be said for the in-prison sequence of the film *American History X* (1998). Throughout the whole of this sequence the prison authorities are never seen. Their presence in the prison environment is negligible, apart from providing totally basic custodial tasks such as the morning unlocking of cells. Gangs run the prison apparently without intervention from the authorities. Some might argue that films like these reflected the fact that the US prison had changed and become a meaner environment. Equally they could be seen as a form of myth-making that turns prison into a 'cool' symbol. The once stigmatised ex-con is now the prison-savvy urban 'gangsta'. However, it should be noted that there are problems in attempting to characterise films in the 1990s. In addition to the examples discussed the decade also produced films like *The Shawshank Redemption* (1994) and *Brokedown Palace* (1999), both of which are discussed in some detail in the next chapter. Any discussion of the prison film needs to be able to locate these examples within its framework. We will return to the problems of periodisation and chronology below but here we might just briefly consider if there is any relationship between the films (or at least some of them) and penal realities.

Film and US penal realities

In Cheatwood's last era—the administrative era, from the 1980s to 1999—the problem for the penal authorities was managing the prison population that arose out of punitive punishment and the race to mass incarceration. In 1970 US incarceration stood at something around 180 per 100,000 of population. By 1985 it had risen to just under 320 per 100,000—by way of comparison for the same year the figure for the UK was something just under 100 per 100,000. Prison growth is expensive and money spent on prisons is money that is not spent on schools, hospitals, and parks, etc. (see Donziger, 1996 for a fuller discussion of these issues). How this prison growth was legitimated and the role that film and TV may have played in the process is obviously a big question. There is now an enormous literature on fear of crime and the demonisation of criminals (see for example Sarat, 2001; Garland, 2001). In America it has been suggested that the media promulgates a continuous stream of imagery of crime. Highlighting acts of mindless, senseless violence, committed by dangerous, unredeemable criminals, the media re-enforces punitive attitudes towards crime and does little to disseminate alternatives to prison and so fuels the expansion of the prison-industrial-complex (Sarat, 2001; Garland, 2001). But what role did/does prison imagery play in this process and what role might Hollywood film play?

The rise of the 'super-max'
One place to start might be the 'story' of the super-max (or the super-maximum security facility) (King, 1999b). So this 'story' goes, at the same time as America's prisons became fuller, with more people serving longer sentences, they also became more racially mixed and, for a variety of reasons, more violent and predatory environments. One version of this story has it that inmates serving

long sentences, particularly those serving life-without-possibility-for-parole, have few incentives to display good behaviour. Such prisoners, it is suggested, can and do attack correctional officers and fellow inmates with impunity. From the 1980s this idea of dangerous, predatory and disruptive prisoners who could not be controlled by normal correctional means came to be dubbed, first by penal authorities and then by the media—'the worst of the worst'. Following this it was suggested that a new kind of super-secure maximum security prison would need to be built to house them.

The 'counter-story' to this suggests that the notion that the prison system was in danger of being overrun by dangerous and predatory inmates in need of draconian methods of control and restraint was and is a nonsense. The use of super-max prisons, where prisoners can be kept more-or-less permanently locked up, with little or no opportunities for association or programmes for rehabilitation, is a strategy to discipline prisoners and maintain control of an overstretched and overcrowded penal system. Demonising prisoners through a discourse of 'the worst of the worst' suited penal authorities, deflecting onto prisoners the blame for problems within the system.

It could also be suggested that super-max prisons had other benefits for the penal system. The meteoric rise in the US prison population required an expansion in the correctional facilities available, but rightly believing that there would be little appetite amongst fiscally conservative suburban Americans for building costly penal facilities for low-tariff minor offenders, politicians and prison administrators sought to convince the public that there was a need for a new kind of facility. Once they were convinced that a new category of facilities was necessary the expansion of super-max capacity took place—to the benefit of prison administrators, prison builders and operators (and their investors) and politicians wishing to be seen to be tough on crime. Inmates from former maximum security facilities could then be funnelled up into super-max (often on arbitrary and subjective assignment criteria) and low-tariff offenders moved up into the facilities vacated. Critics of super-max prisons would argue that what is wrong with all this is that there is little evidence that such facilities were necessary. Further, the regimes imposed in them have been subject to extensive critique and are regarded by many, including organizations such as Amnesty International, as constituting an abuse of human rights (Human Rights Watch, 2000).

The story of 'the rise and rise of super-max' (King, 1999b) may be worth telling. Arguably film played a role in disseminating the understandings and sentiments necessary to legitimate such developments. The prison-related film *Con Air* (1997) explicitly articulates a 'worst-of-the worst' discourse as a group of super-criminals are transported by plane to a super-max facility (see O'Sullivan, 2001). In this and other action-adventure 'prison-films'/prison-in-films of the late 1980s and 1990s *mise en scène* and iconography is probably more important than narrative. The look of the convicts and prisons, and even the screen persona of the stars who feature in them (for example Nicholas Cage and Ving Rhames) are distinctively different from the earlier classic post-war prison films featuring the likes of Paul Newman, Burt Lancaster, Tony Curtis, Sidney Poitier and so forth. There may be something in the argument that Hollywood disseminated a screen imagery that resonated with and helped legitimate the discourses which underpinned the expansion of correctional facilities, although it would be difficult to document this empirically.

But the importance of super-max facilities—which cater for less than two per cent of the inmate population of state and federal prisons (King, 1999: 163) (and an even smaller percentage of the figure for total inmates if the number of people in county gaols is added in) should not be overstated. More inmates are housed in county gaols than in maximum security facilities and the main expansion of the prison population has taken place amongst low-tariff offenders, serving short sentences of less than a year in county gaols, and non-violent offenders serving more than a year in minimum and medium security state penitentiaries (see Donziger, 1996). In Texas, problems of overcrowding in some county gaols have become so severe that overflow facilities have been created by erecting rows of tents, pitched in a field in an arrangement that looks somewhat similar to a refugee or army camp. As is well-known, prison film has a bias towards showing long-term, high-tariff offenders in maximum security facilities. The reality is that the majority of prisoners in the US and the main area of prison growth are low-tariff offenders housed in minimum security facilities. Until Hollywood makes a 'tent-city prison-movie' it will be guilty of portraying 'a skewed and selective representation of prisons and prisoners' (Walmsley, 2000). Although both Donziger (1996) and Wacquant (2001) suggest that prisons really have become more dangerous and predatory environments and that this extends to even low security facilities and county gaols, we would propose that there is a need to examine critically the notion of 'dangerousness' and a need not to reproduce uncritically the idea that prisons are beset by the problem of controlling a 'worst-of-the-worst' disruptive inmate population.

With regard to the representation of prison in film, Hollywood's sin here is probably one of omission as much as commission. Viewers of action-adventure or sci-fi prison movies may not literally believe the portrayal of prison and prisoners depicted in them (although there may be a residual plausibility), but equally these films would not give their viewers the imaginative apparatus necessary to appreciate the value of alternatives to custodial sentencing. Still less do they encourage a sentiment that society can and should shift towards a restorative model of justice (see for example Nellis (2003) on electronic monitoring in the films *187* (1994) and *He Got Game* (1998) and the alternatives discussed in *Chapter 9*).

So, is it possible to establish a relationship between film and penal realities? It is perhaps interesting to note that in the mid-1980s to late 1990s the UK experienced a lull in the production of prison movies and certainly produced no equivalents to the *An Innocent Man* style of movie. The production of prison film only picked up again from 2000, and then with the post-*Shawshank Redemption* Brit-pic prison movie (*Chapter 2*). Yet across this time period the UK prison population rose to an all-time high and is predicted to continue rising. And in the US, where presumably everyone consumes the same Hollywood cinema, there are massive interstate differences in incarceration rates, from North Dakota (112 per 100,000 in 1997–8), to Minnesota (113) and Maine (124) to Texas (717), Louisiana (672) and Oklahoma (617) (Beckett and Western, 2001:40). This suggests that attempting to establish a direct relationship between film representation and prison numbers is not what we should be trying to do. We need to be wary about attempting to draw too tight a connection between media representation and penal realities. But this observation is intended as a warning against over-simplistic and deterministic interpretations of the analysis being proposed here. The general point remains, which is that we should attempt to develop an analysis of how prison film (narratives and imagery) relates to penal realities. We do need a history of 'the prison film' and the 'prison-film genre'. We do need to recognise shifts within the category of prison film, for example, away from pure genre movies towards action-adventure and sci-fi prison films, and to investigate their changing iconography and relate these to real world debates about crime, criminals and prison.

By the 1990s pure prison movies/prison-film genre-pics had become fairly rare. The prison film sub-genres and the appearance of prison in other genres become of more significance. Mason suggests that the 1990s saw 'a re-emergence of the prison film, both in production terms and in popularity' (2003:14), but bases this mainly on *The Shawshank Redemption* (arguably not a prison film at all), and is able to mention *Murder in the First* (1995), the UK film *In the Name of the Father* (1994) and *Dead Man Walking* (1995). If we count death-penalty movies as prison films then the 1990s possibly did see a revival as, in addition to *Dead Man Walking*, there are probably another six or so Hollywood productions with celebrity stars or directors that could be pulled into the frame. But if we believe death-penalty movies constitute their own sub-category with their own generic themes and conventions (see Sarat, 2001; O'Sullivan, 2003 and *Chapter 4* of this volume) then the 1990s still looks pretty sparse for 'pure prison movies'. Rather we see a fragmentation and dispersal of the range of films we need to consider. The relevant range includes: *Death Warrant* (1990) (the Jean Claude van Damme cop-action-adventure prison movie); *Escape from LA* (1996) (a Kurt Russell 'sci-fi' prison movie); *American Me* (1992) (a barrio-prison-gangster movie) (Denzin, 2001), *Con Air* (1997) (again a 'cop-action-adventure movie') (King, 1999) (in which this time the hard-body 'cop' is an about-to-be-released time-served convict) (Nicholas Cage)); the black prison film comedy/parody *Life* (1999), and the miscarriage of justice bio-pic *The Hurricane* (1999).

Significant representations of prison also occur in: the Spike Lee directed bio-pic *Malcom X* (1992); *American History X* (1998) (a white gang-hood-prison movie); *Face-off* (1997) (a futuristic 'cop-action-adventure movie'); and *A Map of the World* (1999) (a family melodrama addressing the cultural politics of revenge). If we added in made-for-TV movies and straight-to-video/DVD movies we would multiply the numbers in each category.

Coming into the new millennium prison films continue to be made: the Steve Buscimi directed *Animal Factory* (2000); and Cheryle Dunn's *Stranger Inside* (2001) on life in a women's state penitentiary gained critical success around the film festivals. The 2002 film *The Yards* is a released prisoner movie and Spike Lee's *25th Hour* (2002) is arguably a going-to-prison movie, as is the earlier film *Slam* (1998), which deserves a mention for its critique of the impact of mass incarceration on black 'inner-city' populations. (*Slam* and Spike Lee's *He Got Game* (1998) are discussed in *Chapter 9*). Again in 2001, Ving Rhames and Wesley Snipes star in *Undisputed*, a boxing-match-in-a-prison movie, which has very little to say about prison, but which attaches to the film nevertheless the iconography of the cinematic version of what a maximum-security prison is like.

All of these films in some way raise interesting questions about prison and the way it is represented in film. Some of them address US penal realities directly, others more indirectly. Relatively few conform to the Rafter model of justice restored, and even those that do conform in a fairly knowing way (*Shawshank*, *Murder in the First*). In Rafter's approach some of the films identified above would not even make it into the analysis. Those that did would either have to fit into a more or less unchanging model of justice restored, or become by default 'alternative tradition'. This is not very satisfactory. It defines the genre in terms of only one version of it, and misses the point that her alternative tradition films should be considered to be part of the prison film 'genre' as a whole, to the extent that they help contribute to the ways in which prison films are read and understood. In any case, if the alternative tradition fills up with more entries than the main genre then how can we call it alternative tradition?

PERIODISATION, CHRONOLOGY AND GENRE

If we wish to examine the relationship between prison-film and penal realities one place to start would be to develop a periodisation. This Cheatwood (1998) has done with his four-stage model of the Depression era, the rehabilitation era, the containment era and the administrative era illustrated in *Table 3.1*. Mason (2003b) rejects Cheatwood's periodisation by finding two exceptions to it. *Cool Hand Luke* is from the 1960s and belongs to Cheatwoods 'containment era', but as Mason points out, that film refers back to an earlier period of penal history and could be seen as owing more to the 1930s chain gang movies than the confinement era. Secondly, Mason notes that Cheatwood himself sees *The Shawshank Redemption* as an anomaly within his model. The story-line in the film, where the character Red who is guilty of committing a crime and eventually confronts this and recognises that he has done wrong, is more characteristic of the 'rehabilitation era'. On the basis of these two anomalies Cheatwood's periodisation is rejected as being 'half-baked'. This seems a bit harsh. We might argue that to reject the periodisation would require a fairly systematic survey of all the films produced in a given era, or a representative sample of them. If most of the films fit the suggested characteristics of the dominant tendency then the periodisation works, notwithstanding some exceptions and anomalies. In short Mason (2003b) has not gone far enough to be in a position to say if Cheatwood's (1998) periodisation is half-baked or not.

In *Chapter 2* a periodisation of British prison film was introduced which we believe works. The prison films of the 1950s were different from those of the 1970s. The periodisation is not refuted by finding a film that does not fit the suggested model, or by giving a suggested alternative reading for any given film within it. It is perhaps worth making the point that periodisation does not have to imply that all films in a particular period were the same; periodisation is the start of the analysis not the end. If we have a periodisation that 'works' then we can start looking for anomalies, suggesting alternative readings for particular films, examining differences between films, and so on. No periodisation will answer every analytic question thrown at it. The value of a periodisation is its ability to suggest relevant questions for investigation. We need also to note that there is a difference between periodising 'the prison film' (what kind of films were made, when and how they related to penal realities) and periodising the genre—have the conventions changed, does the meaning of them change over time?

Despite these problems we cannot leave Rafter's notion of a timeless genre unchallenged. Mason (2003b) rejects Cheatwood's periodisation of the prison film but calls instead for a chronology. Mason seems to advance something like a natural history for the genre, although he starts from Cheatwood's Depression era. Mason suggests that it is no accident that the 1930s were the hey-day of the prison film, with some 60 or more such films being made (Mason, 2003b; Nellis, 1988; Querry, 1973). Prison film in this era resonated with the concerns of recession-racked America. The prison film was a form of protest cinema, which articulated the grievances of 'the little man' against 'the system'. Mason is in implicit debate with Rafter on this point. Whereas Mason sees the films as articulating a critique of prison, coming to symbolise the system that was the source of despair in 1930s America, Rafter sees them as an ideological manipulation where the prison innocent enjoying triumph over the system represents a fantasy resolution to the problem of prison. But the thrust of Mason's argument is that in the early 1930s the prison film genre was newly emerging and novel (despite Rafter's comments on its pre-history in the silent era) and the formula not yet clichéd. The figure of the prison innocent allowed the films to encourage viewer empathy with the criminal and, as Nellis (1982) suggests, one of the themes of films of this period is that some convicts are fundamentally decent people, regular guys who have temporarily gone of the rails. The films need to be understood in the context of the sentiments that would have been current in Depression era America.

Nellis and Rafter: Differing views of *The Big House*
In relation to this it is instructive to contrast the view of *The Big House* (1930) offered by Nellis (1982) with Rafter's view of the same film. Rafter's (2000) account never really discusses this film, but only uses it to distil the characteristics that for her identify the genre. Her discussion of the film reduces it to a genric formula, although this is presumably one that viewers in the 1930s would not yet be familiar with, unless we grant the unlikely proposition that genre was already fully worked out in the silent era. Rafter's description of the film is as follows:

> *The Big House* (1930), one of the first prison films with a sound track, revolves around three convicts: Butch, an older, hardened criminal who is experienced in the ways of the prison; Kent, a yellow-bellied snitch; and Morgan, the handsome middle-class hero who never squeals and is a loyal friend to Butch. It turns out that Morgan did nothing worse than commit forgery—once. He escapes long enough to fall in love with Kent's sister, only to be recaptured and returned, broken hearted. When a riot breaks out, Butch and Kent die, but Morgan halts the violence single-handedly, an act for which he is rewarded with his freedom. At the movie's close he leaves the prison to marry Kent's sister and live 'abroad', where he can start over as an honest man. Two other characters also play important roles in *The Big House*: The warden, who is wise, tough and fair ('If you've got grievances', he tells the prisoners, 'come to me …

I'm running this show, and I'm ready for you'); and a 'rat,' who sneaks around gathering information for the administration. (2000: 117-8)

Here is Nellis's description of the same film:

> *The Big House* is a serious movie. It conveys the tense, explosive atmosphere of prison life and studiously avoids the suggestion of automatic camaraderie among convicts, which many prison films overplay. The basic story is simple enough: Wallace Beery, a Hill regular [the film was directed by George Hill], plays a convict baron whose megalomania finally sparks a riot, but woven into this are criticism of the official ineptitude which allows reformed men to stay in prison, old cons to corrupt younger ones, and the prison population in general to have so much time on their hands that making each other's lives miserable is the cons' only pastime. This theme, the failure of prison to rehabilitate, together with the scenes of admission to prison and solitary confinement have become integral to the narrative and iconography of subsequent prison films, and have helped give *The Big House* its status of minor classic. (1982: 15)

Nellis is not denying that there is a prison film genre, nor suggesting that we cannot identify recurring stock scenes or that *The Big House* is not a founding instance of the genre. But his account of the film is strikingly different from Rafter's. Rafter reduces *The Big House* to its generic conventions, which in reality only emerged subsequent to the production and screening of the film itself. Nellis gives a slightly different account of what the film is about, emphasising more the impression of prison one might gain from watching the film. Of course no two analysts will ever produce identical accounts, but Rafter's description is skewed by her concern to identify an unchanging prison film genre which she is applying retrospectively and therefore with hindsight.

Genre development: Novelty, convention, exhaustion
Mason's (2003b) approach to prison film is better, suggesting that the genre has gone through a process of natural development. Following, or perhaps adapting slightly, his argument we could suggest a three stage model of novelty, generic convention and exhaustion.

Firstly, when a genre first emerges it is 'novel'. Viewers are not necessarily aware of its conventions, and things that later come to be seen as purely conventional may have particular meaning in the early development of the genre. In the case of the prison film the prison innocent originally functioned to gain sympathy for the criminal; to suggest that anyone could come to be imprisoned either falsely, or for a minor mistake or understandable wrongdoing; and may also have suggested that criminals come to offend for different reasons, and that some may be capable of rehabilitation. Scenes of entry into prison, which now have become stock, may have been intended to convey, and even succeeded in conveying, the shock of reception into prison. Intentional cruelty by the guards, or harsh punishment, may similarly have been intended to present the audience with new ideas about what prisons are like.

As the genre develops the conventions come to be applied formulaically and the audience begins to recognise them as such. The appearance of stock characters, or stock scenes tell us that we are watching a prison movie and this alerts us to how we are meant to understand what is happening on screen. So, for example, in the 1974 film *Mean Machine* (US: *The Longest Yard*), Burt Reynolds plays an ex-pro football star who has fallen from grace and is admitted to a Florida prison. At his induction interview in the Warden's office he is informed that he will use his skills and experience to coach the prison football team. When Reynolds attempts to decline this offer the chief correctional officer delivers a vicious dig in the stomach with his night-stick causing Reynolds to double-up in pain. We the viewer laugh! Why? Because we know were watching a prison movie, and that in a prison movie the hero has to endure indignities before eventually triumphing over them. We may already be anticipating that the officer who struck the blow will receive his comeuppance before the end of the film. The conventions of the prison movie which were intended to carry meaning in the early days of the genre, now only carry the meaning that we are watching a reassuringly predictable genre film.

Next we suggest, genres go into decline when they reach a period of exhaustion—when the conventions become so well-known that they cannot be taken even half seriously. Today attempts to use stock scenes that were once meant to convey menace now just become laughable. In the 2001 film *Undisputed*—the boxing-match-in-a-prison movie—the cons in the dining hall start becoming aggressive, banging their spoons and threatening to riot. The corrections officer on duty turns to his partner nearby and asks: 'What's wrong with these guys, have they been watching too many prison movies?' Once a genre moves into exhaustion it begins to take on the form of parody.

Similarly, the women's prison film could be seen as having moved through a series of stages, at first producing serious drama (*Anne Vickers* (1933), *Caged*, 1950), but then as the conventions crystallised and became more well known, serious women's prison drama became formulaic women-in-prison/girls reformatory movies (*House of Women* (1962)), which became exploitation movies (*Big Dolls House* (1971)), and finally parodies of exploitation movies (*Girls in Prison* (1994)).

All of these films may utilise the same conventions, but are doing different things. But this is not only true as we move across inflections of the genre, but also when comparing films in the parent genre across time. By the time of the arrival of *Murder in the First* (1995), whatever its pretence to be taken seriously, we know that we are watching a formulaic prison movie. It does not matter how sadistic the Warden/guards/stay in solitary confinement appear to be, we take these to be the kind of things we would expect. But, we cannot assume that the way we watch *Murder in the First* now is the way that cinema audiences in 1930 watched *The Big House*.

The problems of genre
Appealing though a model of genres moving through natural progression of novelty, convention and then exhaustion is, like any other model one could propose in film studies it immediately generates more questions than it answers. Film reality is obviously more complicated than a straightforward specification of the model would suggest. One way that genres can extend their life is through transforming themselves and mutating into new sub-genres. We could develop a more complicated picture than a single pure genre undergoing a process of sequential development. If, however, we stick with the simple model for the

moment, there are still a number of questions that we can ask. Firstly, how are we to understand this chronology? Is it a series of successive stages? Do all, or at least most, of the films produced within a genre at any one time conform to the same stage of genre development? This would seem not to be the case. The phases of novelty and convention may overlap, at which point some producers will be following the conventions of the genre in an entirely formulaic way, having no intention other than to make a predictable and easy to watch genre-movie, whilst at the same time other producers may be working within the constraints of the genre, but striving to keep their approach to it novel and challenging for the audience. Hence we have a distinction between films which have no intention other than to conform to the genre and films which intend to use it to convey ideas and understandings, in this case about prison.

Following on from this we can pose the question: is the exhaustion of a genre inevitable, or can producers find ways of breathing new life into it? Can they update or develop the ways in which the conventions of the genre are represented in order to prolong their ability to carry meaning? A related and perhaps more serious question is whether convention and exhaustion are retrospective. Is it that films in the prison film genre which were originally intended to be novel/meaningful, and to avoid being formulaic, later come to be seen as 'just a prison movie'?

Related to this is the question of when exactly a genre shifts from being novel to being conventional—a close thing to call. Even when watching it today it is not too difficult to see *The Birdman of Alcatraz* (1962) as a serious attempt at dramatising the life of one person's penal career in order to make some more general points about the nature of prison. By contrast *Cool Hand Luke*, only five years later, seems intended to have been made as a prison film. Luke's rebellion against authority, the representation of the corrections officer in the form of 'the man with no eyes', and dialogue such as 'it seems like what we've got here is a failure to communicate', along with a host of other features including sweatboxes, road gangs, escapes, and so forth, are all telling us, and would have told us at the time, that we should be realising that we are watching a prison film. The problem then becomes that as more of such movies accumulate over time and become part of our cinematic knowledge, then even serious drama like *The Birdman of Alcatraz* come to be seen as 'just another prison movie'. This tendency of the genre to destroy itself has been commented on before, particularly by Nellis (1982) who perhaps phrases the issue slightly differently. Commenting on why prison movies have failed to contribute to creating a climate more conducive to penal reform he suggests:

> Many prison movies are made in deliberate bad faith, utilising the horrors of imprisonment only for their dramatic potential and indifferent to any wider significance which they have. There is rarely any question of them having influence, despite their ostensibly subversive stance. The difficulties which arise in relation to genuinely critical prison movies are then dealt with by redefining them simply as more sophisticated examples of the cheap exploitation movies, higher class entertainment but sensational nonetheless. It is not that they are taken seriously and tolerated, for this would have implications for social action, but rather that their seriousness is repudiated by deliberate comparison with their inauthentic counterparts (Nellis, 1982: 44).

Nellis seems to be implying that there is a real distinction between prison films made in 'bad faith' merely for entertainment purposes, and those made in 'good faith', possessing a serious critical purpose. These two kinds of prison film exist, and we would be able to tell the difference between them, if it were not for the processes which (mis)associate the one with the other and fail to make the relevant distinctions between them. In this view 'the dross' destroys 'quality'. But the situation is more complicated than that and we need to consider the alternative proposition that even if only 'good faith', serious purpose, critical prison movies were made, would the genre still destroy itself through accumulation and excess?

We can develop this issue by referring back to Rafter's discussion of genre-pics and her alternative tradition. Rafter (2000) identifies that tradition as consisting of prison movies which reject heroes and happy endings. She includes in this tradition *On the Yard* (1979), *Short Eyes* (1979) and *American Me* (1992) although most likely a good number of other films could be pulled into it if we considered a fuller filmography of prison movies from the 1970s and later.

One problem with distinguishing genre-pics from alternative tradition is that the distinction works best if the two sets of films are watched by different audiences. But if audiences watch films from both traditions, then the films in each tradition help to condition the ways in which each are watched. Rafter's alternative tradition prison film *On The Yard* is still a prison film and contains a lot of similarities with more conventional genre-pics. Many of its ideas about relations between corrections officers and inmates, and about inmate subculture itself, are recognisably similar to depictions in more conventional prison films. At the end of the day, *On The Yard* is a film about the awfulness of prison. It shows that bad things happen (an inmate dies as a result of a punishment beating by a fellow con that went too far), and so (in)directly contributes to the view that bad things happen in prison movies because that is what prison movies are about. It is indeterminate whether someone watching *On The Yard* on late night TV would see it as a 'good faith' prison movie, or 'just another prison movie', albeit one departing from the traditional formula a little more than usual.

The point can be developed by considering another of Rafter's alternative tradition films—*American Me* (1992). This film tells the story of Latino/Chicano gangs inside and outside of prison in Los Angeles, from the time of the Zoot Suit Riots (1942) to the present day. The story follows its main protagonist, Santana, from his drift into gangs at a young age, through to a stay in a juvenile facility during which he kills one of his peers, and so graduates to 'State Pen' on reaching the relevant age. As a result Santana spends most of his life in prison, although part of the film is set during the period when he is out and back in the neighbourhood. Santana begins to think about settling down and getting out of the gang-life but an unlucky drugs bust, for carrying dope that is not even his, lands him back in prison where he is killed by members of his own gang.

Rafter (2000:131–2) produces a perfectly reasonable reading of this film suggesting that Santana is not a hero, nor even an anti-hero but a non-hero. She rightly accords the film a serious purpose, in that its writer, director and star, Edward James Olmos, intended the film to be a critique of gangs and the 'gangsta' lifestyle. Judged on its own the film works reasonably well in this respect. The final scene where Santana meets his unhappy end, but also the scene where Santana is arrested by a patrol cop—the pull that returns him to prison, underwrite the argument that Santana's gangster power is mythic, non-existent and not worth having. Rafter praises the film as not just criticising the prison but the society that creates the prison and for dealing with complex social problems which are not amenable to simple solutions and which cannot be accurately represented or resolved by a happy-ever-after ending.

But the meaning of the film changes depending on which tradition we relate it to. So Denzin (2001) for example, locates the same film in relation to a cycle of other barrio-prison-gangster movies that appear at around the same time (e.g. *Bound by Honor* (alternative title *Blood In ... Blood Out*) (1993)). These films in turn relate to the 'hood movie cycle' *Boys 'n the Hood* (1991), *Colors* (1988), *To Live and Die in LA* (1985) and *Menace To Society* (1993).

These 'hood movies' all suffer from the problem that, whatever their intentions, they tend to reproduce and disseminate the imagery they wish to critique. Films which seek to critique 'the gangsta', in the end just trade on and circulate 'gangsta cool'. *Bound by Honor (Blood in ... Blood Out)* is a three hour epic with a similar storyline to *American Me*. Rafter notes the existence of this film in a footnote recognising this similarity and suggests that it also is an alternative tradition prison movie. But most of the people who see *American Me* and *Bound by Honor* do not connect them with 1970s prison movies that they have not seen and have probably never even heard of. They relate the films to each other and to other gang-related movies. Amongst the contributors to IMDb debate rages as to whether *American Me* or *Bound by Honor* is the greatest barrio-prison-gang-related movie ever. Contributions on *Bound by Honor* seem to be roughly divided between 'greatest movie ever made' to 'completely over-rated, cheap exploitation crap'. Opinions on *American Me* are similarly divided. What we have here is possibly a kind of variation on Nellis's theme of 'the dross' destroying the 'quality'. A film with serious purpose is undermined by a chain of associations with other films. But perhaps more than that, *American Me* undermines itself. In displaying prison as a turf for racially-divided gang-warfare, a kill-or-be-killed environment, complete with predatory behaviour in the form of obligatory male rape, the film is inviting its audience to revel in the awfulness of prison. Just another 'way cool movie' to argue over and compare with other gang-prison movies. If prison and 'the gangsta' have become connoted as 'cool', it matters little that Santana is not a hero, nor even an anti-hero; a non-hero will do just as well to satisfy a kid in Belgium watching a film made in and about America.

CONCLUSION

What we now seem to have arrived at is the proposition that the prison film genre is fragmenting. The number of 'pure prison movies' is declining, the number of sub-genres increasing, and prison is making an appearance in a wide range of other genres. It might be suggested that this is how it has always been. 'The prison film is notoriously difficult to define' (Mason, 2003b), and has always stretched from *Jailhouse Rock* to *Six Against the Rock* taking in *The Man in the Iron Mask* along the way. There may be an element of truth in this, although as will be argued in the next chapter there is some significance in the fanning out of the representations of prison appearing in films such as *Freeway* (1996), *A Map of the*

World (1999) and *Brokedown Palace* (1999). We need to recognise that the boundaries of genres are inevitably 'fuzzy'. Some films within the prison-film 'genre' draw meaning from chains of association with films outside the genre. We need to be methodologically alert to the idea that we cannot draw too tight boundaries around our area of study but, rather, must be prepared to pull other films into the analysis where appropriate.

But does all this matter? If a film is just a film and if no one confuses fictitious cinematic prisons with real ones, why do we need to analyse prison film? In a sense the basis for an answer to this has already been laid above. In the 1930s reform-minded Wardens tried to get made films that showed that prison reform was desirable and necessary. In the 1950s a wave of riots flared across US prisons. Films recorded the occurrence of these riots and commented on them. The riots and the representation of them suggested that prison was not working. In the 1970s issues of race, homosexuality and corruption in prison were all represented in film as were events like the Attica uprising. It is not unreasonable to suggest that over time film has told the story of prison, albeit in a manner mediated by the constraints of dramatic representation and of genre. But, was anyone listening? Has the prison film contributed to creating a climate more conducive to penal reform? And, can we reconcile the proposition that it has done so with the current realities of an expanded penal state and the rise of mass incarceration? The next chapter retraces our steps a little and returns first to the 'pure prison movie'—films where prison is the setting and the subject of the film. We need to consider how we explain the existence of such films and how they inform our ideas about prison. We will then be in a position to understand the penal reform functions of the prison film and know why we should defend rather than criticise Hollywood.

The filmography for this chapter appears at the end of Chapter 4.

CHAPTER 4

Tracking the US Penal State: In Defence of Hollywood

If one could total up all the hours of screen time that have been devoted to imprisonment, all the years of effort that have been put into making prison films, and if one could count all the people that had seen them, one might be tempted to wonder if it had all been worth it.

(Nellis, 1982: 44)

The degree of civilization in a society can be judged by entering its prisons.

(Dostoevsky)

The prison populations of both the UK and the US currently stand at an all time high. The penal systems in the two countries are quite different, and the UK's level of incarceration in no way approaches that of the US. Nevertheless the two countries do face similar policy choices—either to allow the trend towards imprisoning ever great numbers of people to continue, or to develop alternatives. If we are to have an informed debate on these political choices the public need to be equipped with the necessary imaginative metaphors to appreciate 'the pains of confinement' and 'the irrationality of prison'. They also need models and metaphors that would enable them to engage with the ideas of 'restorative justice'. In Western society there is a bias towards prison which skews the debate and requires countering (Mathiesen, 2000). In Britain and Europe prison regimes have improved in the post-war period but these improvements have generally been accompanied by a growth in the prison population. In the US there is a high degree of variation in the penal realities of different states, nonetheless taken as a whole the country exemplifies a trend towards an expanded penal state. Penal reform organizations now have two goals: to improve where possible the conditions inside prison and to oppose and, if possible, reverse prison growth. But can mainstream popular film assist in this process or does film contribute little or nothing to penal reform?

The strategy in this chapter will be to reject the notion that prison film has contributed little to penal reform. If prison film can be shown to have contributed to such reform in the past, then there is every possibility that it can again in the future. Whilst previous theorists have been sceptical as to the value of Hollywood cinema as a source of change and have seen prison film as an ideological manipulation—a way of deluding us that we 'know prison' when we in fact do not—this chapter will suggest an alternative position: that the classic 'pure prison movie' carried out several important penal reform functions which have helped to diffuse the sentiments and dispositions needed to signal when penal reform is necessary. In the current period, the situation is more complicated because we have a greater variety of ways of representing prison, with much more uncertain effects. But our general argument is that we need more prison movies not fewer if film is to make a positive contribution to public appreciation of the relevant issues.

EXPLAINING THE PRISON FILM GENRE

Before turning to consider some of the different ways in which prison makes an appearance in contemporary popular cinema, we need to revisit a question that has troubled previous prison film theorists. Why does the genre exist? Why do we have prison films? The discussion here will again focus on Rafter (2000), because she has most recently identified a systematic set of explanations for the existence of 'the prison film'. Some of her points concur or disagree with other contributions to the debate which we will pull in where appropriate. Finally, an alternative approach to explaining why the prison film exists and what ideological work it does will be introduced.

Rafter: Why the prison film exists
Nichole Rafter (2000; 123–8), identifies various attractions which might account for the fascination we apparently have with prison film and the pleasures that we derive from it. The prison film offers us: opportunities to identify with perfect men; fantasies of sex and of rebellion; opportunities to participate vicariously in perfect friendships; and it makes claims to authenticity so as to provide us with insight into a secret world. We also need to consider the implications of Rafter's overall argument that the 'prison-film genre' operates on the basis of a model of 'justice restored' producing only escapist prison fantasies. What are the implications of this argument for our overall understanding of the genre?

Let us first consider the proposition that prison film offers us 'sassy truculent heroes' who stroll around the yard without an apparent care in the world. This seems to be a weak argument. Many of the heroes of prison films are flawed and not just in Rafter's alternative tradition. In the mainstream genre the heroes often let us down. Escapes are foiled, riot leaders betrayed, years of confinement are endured but at a very high personal cost. Rafter overstates the triumph of the prison innocent and is probably overly influenced by *The Shawshank Redemption*, which arguably does not even belong in the genre proper anyway, but is a second degree inflection of it (see the discussion below). The argument that prison film is popular because it offers fantasies about sex would seem to be similarly poor. Rafter refers to the 'women-in-prison/babes-behind-bars movie' as illustrating this point although this has little relevance to the sample of prison films she has discussed which overwhelmingly concern the male experience of prison. For male prison movies Rafter suggests that the friendship between the prison innocent and his convict buddy often carries a homo-erotic subtext and hints at a physical intimacy between men. There is some truth to the idea that male prison films are explorations of masculinity. There is also a possibility that some characters in prison films may be overtly heterosexual but 'surreptitiously gay' (Wood, 1986). But Rafter would need to explore further to establish for how many and which sections of the audience these characters are 'working', for her to establish this as a general reason for the popularity of prison movies. In any case the idea that prison films carry this male-male homo-erotic subtext is possibly in conflict with her next suggestion, that prison films give us an opportunity to participate in 'perfect friendships'.

Prison films invariably include an enduring friendship—usually, but not always, between the prison innocent and his older, more experienced buddy. Rafter is quite right to identify this as a characteristic of the genre. It certainly is a recurring motif which, once pointed out, can be seen operating across a whole variety of prison films. Even if we exclude *The Shawshank Redemption*'s knowingly hyperbolic portrayal of this convention, it is an important theme which occurs both in the genre proper and in Rafter's alternative tradition. It is also something that is quite specific to prison films and in a way ideally suited to them. Men developing enduring *platonic* same sex friendships, under conditions of adversity is not really a strong recurring feature of any other genre. But to what extent does it explain the attractions of the genre? What makes us think that viewers want to watch this kind of thing? Why does not this motif show up in other kinds of films? And would not heterosexual males prefer to see their screen heroes 'save the world' and 'get the girl'? We need to think a bit more about this as a convention of the genre and what it meant when the genre was novel. The relationship carries connotations of cross-class identification and, as Rafter implicitly recognises, is part of the manner in which middle-class prisoners can be reorientated to see themselves as part of the oppressed group (the inmates), rather than to identify with the prison authorities. This convention also shows up in women's prison drama, and again the significance of it there needs to be analysed. As is argued elsewhere in this book, the experience of the middle-class prisoner who is unexpectedly incarcerated has particular significance for our understanding of the legitimacy of prison. We could develop an extensive discussion of the functions of the 'perfect friendship' convention within the genre, but the extent to which it contributes to an explanation for the existence of the prison film is more doubtful.

Next we can consider the proposition that the fascination with prison film is that it gives us an opportunity to look inside a 'secret world' that we do not usually see. Rafter suggests that roughly half of prison films claim to be based on some real life experience or true story. And of course even those which are more straightforward works of dramatic fiction still make some claim to authenticity in the ways in which prisons and prisoners are portrayed. We gain our knowledge of prison, its routines, slang and inmate subculture from prison film. But, argues Rafter, this claim to authenticity is bogus. The artificiality of the medium and the conventions of the genre prevent it from telling 'the true story of prison'. There is obviously a degree of truth in what is being said here, and an argument has been developed elsewhere in this book that one of the effects of prison film may be to encourage us to think that we 'know prison' when in fact we do not. But this judgement can be a little one sided, particularly when combined with Rafter's overall assessment of the genre as providing only escapist fantasies. This then relates to the argument that prison film allows us to 'participate in fantasies of rebellion'. We side with the prisoners and feel happy when they win. Sometimes they lose and we might feel a little sadder, but nevertheless accept that perhaps this is the way it must be. But this dismisses Hollywood genre prison films as having nothing to say about prison and providing us with no information that might inform our understanding of penal issues. In short, Hollywood for entertainment, the alternative tradition(s) for 'truth-telling'. But, can we afford to write off Hollywood? And is it true that Hollywood films like *Brubaker* (1980) contributed nothing to people's understanding?

Prison film politics: Aiding or retarding penal reform?
Other writers have expressed different views on the ideology and politics of the prison film. Mason (2003b) supports the idea that in the 1930s the prison film was a form of protest cinema. It was only when the genre became clichéd and formulaic that it ceased to serve this purpose. This suggests all kinds of questions about whether the era of mass incarceration has not also produced protest cinema and if so is it only to be found in the alternative traditions, or also in more populist versions. Nellis (1982; 1988) has a slightly different position, granting that some prison films have had an intention of being protest cinema, but seeing problems with the way that the genre as a whole functions to reaffirm the legitimacy of prison.

The Nellis argument
Nellis advances a view of the prison film quite different to Rafter's, emphasising more the model that has been referred to in the previous chapter as 'authority reasserted'. He outlines his view thus:

> Although an element of protest certainly informs some of them, a case can readily be made for interpreting *the majority* of American prison films as a subtle form of propaganda, an entertaining way of circulating fearful, almost infernal images of intractable inmate violence (the corruption of (relative) innocents, rape, murder) and awesome state power (the thwarting of jail breaks, the suppression of riots, executions, prolonged solitary confinement) to the widest possible population, in the interests of spreading deterrent ideas. (Nellis, 1988: emphasis in the original)

Although there are some useful ideas in this statement (infernal imagery, displays of 'awesome state power'), pulling the items together to make up an argument about subtle propaganda in the interests of spreading deterrent ideas seems strange and out of step with the rest of Nellis's own work (1982). Firstly, why should the screen representations of demonstrations of 'awesome state power' spread 'deterrent ideas', rather than serve to question and undermine the legitimacy of the state? On the suppression of riots, Nellis's (1982: 25–6) reading of *Riot in Cell Block 11* is much more open than the summary of the theoretical position would suggest. It is quite easy to see this film as 'authority reasserted *at a cost*'. The film puts up 'on screen' that the rioters had grievances that even the Warden could see, but they were sold down the river by the machinations of the political system. Film representations of riots are one way in which the memory of such events is kept alive in the culture. Do they not signal the message that 'prison is not working' and demonstrate a loss of legitimacy?

Similarly, it is strange to see executions featuring in Nellis's statement as elsewhere he has consistently argued that screen representations of capital punishment have been part of the campaign against the evils of the death penalty. Nellis cites *I Want to Live* (1958) approvingly, describing its ending as 'one of the most powerful statements against capital punishment ever seen on screen' (1982: 25), crediting it with helping to carry forward the campaign against capital punishment in the US. Elsewhere he has championed the UK death-penalty movies *Yield to the Night* (1956) (US *Blonde Sinner*) and *Now Barabbas* [*Was a Robber*] (1948) (see Nellis, 1993; 1988).

There is generally a contradiction at work in the writings of Nellis on prison film. On the one hand his reading of individual films is always guided by a close attention to their historical context and origins. Nellis (1982; 1988; 1993) is always keen to show the extent to which prison film originates from experiences within the penal system and reflects the real world debates and issues of its context, albeit in a refracted and mediated manner. Yet in his theoretical assessment, the argument usually comes back to the proposition that prison film has failed to create a climate conducive to penal reform. Nellis (1982) suggests that prison movies have contributed very little to penal reform, an assertion echoed by Mason (2003b). But this claim is based on relatively little, and indeed is arrived at by way of a slippage from, first a suggestion that it is difficult to establish the penal reform effects of any prison film, through then wondering out loud rhetorically if the effort devoted to prison film had been worth it, to finally stating outright that prison film has indeed contributed little to penal reform. But what is this based on? In his research on prison film Nellis is always alert to collecting whatever information is available on how particular films were viewed and received by the public; which films became talking points, in newspapers and review; which films were taken up by penal reformers as being illustrative of their cause. But for his assessment of the penal reform impact of the US prison movie this all comes down to one film—*I am a Fugitive from a Chain Gang* (1932).

Based on a true story, *Fugitive* was very popular and highly acclaimed. It would appear to be the only film that has had sufficient impact on public debate to generate identifiable real world penal reform, in this case in the shape of a proposal to replace the Georgia chain gang and to phase out stocks and sweatboxes. But Nellis (1982) argues that these proposals came some five years after the film, were slow to be implemented and, when they were put into effect this was because, independent of the film, newspapers in the north wished to embarrass the south. Nellis reports that not until 1943, some eleven years after *Fugitive*, did a new state governor finally abolish the wearing of stripes, shackles and leg irons, and pardon Robert Burns—the escaped convict who had been the subject of the film (Nellis, 1982: 14–15). Here, and also discussed in Mason (2003b), the example of *Fugitive* becomes reduced to being the only concrete evidence of a film having a penal reform effect, but in fact having less impact than is sometimes realised, taking longer to operate and only succeeding because there were other pressures at work to bring about change! Hence, pessimism about the role of prison film in penal reform. But this approach would seem to be setting a very high threshold. Who would expect one film to have a unilateral and direct effect on penal realities independent of other pressures? Surely the task of the film is to disseminate the idea that reform is necessary, not single-handedly to bring it about independent of other social forces? Is this approach expecting to find too direct a link between prison film and practical change? More thought needs to be given to how we establish whether film can contribute to the 'climate' within which penal reform is debated.

On the enduring and recurring unpopularity of the prison film

The contributors to the debate on prison film reviewed above tend to argue from an assumption that the prison film enjoys some form of recurring popularity. They tend, implicitly or explicitly, to start from a standpoint that the prison film is popular and that it is this popularity that needs explaining. The explanations advanced then tend to revolve around some kind of idea that we, the viewer have a 'desire to see prison'. For Rafter the genre 'offers the inside scoop, a window onto the inaccessible but riveting world of prison' (2000: 127). But is prison riveting? Mason offers a similar view:

> Perhaps most appealing to the audience is [that] the prison film opens up the world of the prison. The audience have the opportunity to share in the criminal world, to move in circles of illegality from the safety of their cinema seats. This viewer-experience is positively encouraged by the film: the audience is locked up with the inmates, hears the escape plan, talks to the officers and exercises in the yard. It is perhaps in this that the real appeal of prison film lies. (2003: 295)

Finally, Nellis (1982; 1988) has always strived to fit the prison film into the 'big picture', at times wondering if it is 'a strategy of repressive tolerance', or alternatively 'a means of spreading deterrent ideas', and perhaps seeing a social explanation for the prison film as a means of cultivating respect for authority and bolstering the legitimacy of the prison. But at the end of the day even Nellis falls back on a demand-led, 'desire to see' explanation. Following an extensive survey of US prison film—from *Manslaughter* (1922) to *Brubaker* (1980), he concludes:

> Ultimately, it matters little that prison movies are so uninformative about prison life, or that their commitment to reform has not been taken seriously. Authenticity and inspiration ought never to have been expected of them, and where they occurred they were merely a bonus. For all their vaunted social criticism the majority of prison movies are invigorated by forces which engage the psyche rather than the conscience, and if we can glean from our deep emotional reactions to them a better understanding of why we both *fear and adore confinement*, and trace out its implications for society, all well and good. (Nellis, 1982: 48 our emphasis)

In the final analysis Nellis asserts that Western culture has a 'fascination with confinement', which in turn explains our fascination with prison film. This again is a demand-led, 'desire to see' type of explanation.

However, the thing that is wrong with all these arguments is that they assert that the prison film has a popularity which requires explanation. Coincidentally, (or perhaps not) Rafter, Mason and Nellis also all assume or assert, implicitly or explicitly, that the (Hollywood) prison film has contributed little or nothing to penal reform. Both arguments need to be rejected. If we can establish the recurring unpopularity of the prison film and suggest why and how it contributes to reform, then we can see such film as it should be seen—a reflection of prison's demand to speak to us, not of our desire to see prison.

There seems to be some agreement that the hey-day of the US prison movie was the 1930s when some 60 or more such movies were made (Querry, 1973). Nellis suggests that the number of prison movies made fell during the 1940s, with perhaps 32 films being produced, and again in the 1950s and 1960s. The last of these decades probably produced fewer than 15 prison movies, depending on what we are prepared to count. Nellis (1982) suggests that it only produced two memorable ones, *Luke* and *Birdman*. The 1970s saw something of a revival. Nellis (1982) suggests that perhaps some 15 prison films were made, but a fuller filmography might get the figure nearer to 20 that could legitimately be counted. In the 1980s and 1990s problems of definition become more serious. Fewer 'pure prison movies' (set in a prison, taking prison as their subject) were made and the numbers depend on how we might count sci-fi prison films, where prison is to an extent just a stand-in for a post-apocalyptic action-adventure film. Nevertheless even including films which are not really prison movies in the same sense as *The Big House*, *Birdman*, or *Luke* we still would not get more than 20 mainstream cinema release prison films to a decade.

Where does all this get us? Well, firstly it tells us that the prison film is not big box-office business. To take the much vaunted hey-day of the 1930s, when prison film resonated with the problems and sentiments of Depression era America, the figure of 60 movies sounds a lot, but if we divide by 10 we come down to six movies a year—including 'A' and 'B' features. This is at a time when the Hollywood studio system was churning out some 500 movies a year. After that we rapidly get down to decades where not more than 20 prison films were made, or two a year. If we were to restrict ourselves to memorable, smash hit, post-war 'pure prison movies', the list does not total more than a handful— *Birdman*, *Luke*, *Midnight Express*, etc., and of course the main argument for a continuing popularity of the prison film *The Shawshank Redemption* (1994)—which we discuss below. But how does prison film fare in terms of box-office gross? The Internet Movie Database supplies a table of the top grossing movies of all time at the worldwide box office. The list is unadjusted for inflation, which skews it towards the present, although *The Jungle Book* (1967) still makes it into the top 200. It is a reasonable guide to what did good box-office business over the last 15–20 years. Looking down the list for January 2002, the first entry for anything that could remotely be called a prison film is the concentration camp film *Schindler's List* at number 82. The next entry that could conceivably count, is the death-penalty movie *The Green Mile* at 121. Other items of interest include *Face-off*, a film with a 15 minute in-prison sequence in it at number 148 and *Con Air*— the transporting prisoners action-adventure movie at 170. There is no other entry in the top 200 that could possibly count, leading to the conclusion that, aside from the questionable exception of *Shawshank*, there are no 'pure prison movies' in the top 200 all time highest grossing films at the box-office.

It might be argued, quite rightly, that this list is (i) biased because it is unadjusted for inflation and (ii) includes loads of summer blockbuster hits that lots of people went to see but nobody really cares about. A list of people's all time favourite movies might be a better indicator of the esteem in which movies are held. Again Internet Movie Database supplies a list of the (voted for) top 250 films of all time. It pulls in films going back as far as the 1930s, although none from the 1920s make it. How does prison film do? Well, straight in at number two is the prison movie that is not a prison movie, *The Shawshank Redemption*. But apart from that what else? Running down the list the already mentioned *Schindler's List* is at number four. The next possible entry comes in at number 48, the prisoner of war movie *The Bridge on the River Kwai*. The next conceivable entry is at number 68—the prisoner of war movie *The Great Escape*. At 71 is the

UK film *A Clockwork Orange*. The previously mentioned death-penalty movie *The Green Mile* is at 120. The first 'genuine article' prison movie comes in at 122—*Cool Hand Luke*. At 229 is *Oh Brother Where Art Thou?*, arguably an escaped prisoner movie. No other prison film appears in the top 250, leaving *Cool Hand Luke* as arguably the only genuine 'pure prison movie' to make the list. It is perhaps worth mentioning that *One Flew Over The Cuckoo's Nest* (1975) comes in at number 11, but also that a little known early 1950s British disaster movie *The Day The Earth Stood Still* (1951) entered at 170. *Cool Hand Luke* is the only real prison film to beat this not particularly significant film in the top 250 favourite films of all time. All the other prison films ever made come below it.

The conclusions to be drawn from all this are: there are not that many prison movies made; the ones that are made do not do particularly good box-office business; and do not rate that highly in people's figuring of all time favourite movies. The 'popularity' of the prison film has been overstated. Cinema goers have to be dragged kicking and screaming into cinemas to watch a prison movie, and indeed will not go unless the producers sweeten the experience with something else: Hollywood feel-good formula (gets the girl with a happy ending), comedy (*Mean Machine* (1974) (aka *The Longest Yard*), masculine action-adventure (*Con Air*), 1960s cool (*Cool Hand Luke*), 1990s cool (gangsta-prison films), etc. There is no desire to see prison. Even the best prison movies are no more than cult movies—they have no mass popular appeal. If you asked the average member of the public to name the stars and titles of five post-war prison films, they would most likely struggle.

PENAL REFORM AND PRISON FILM

We need to dispense with the view that the prison film is popular in order to avoid thinking that it exists because 'we' have a 'desire to see prison'. We do not. *It* has had a desire to speak to us, but how loud is its voice? And is anybody listening? One problem with Nellis's (1982) argument that the prison film has not been conducive to penal reform is that it is not based on any systematic account of penal reform in the US, or the changing American prison. Without such an account how is it possible to know if penal reform has taken place, to what extent, and when, etc? Without this, how can we identify the forces behind penal reform and the role that film might have played in the process? In our judgement as to whether the US prison film contributes to, or hinders, penal reform comes down to one key question. Has the American prison got better or worse? The problem here is that the US prison population is a sizeable entity, housed in a range of different institutions, in states with very different penal cultures. And, of course, the question of whether the American prison has got 'better' would beg the question of what constitutes 'better'/what is progress? In order to develop the necessary account we would need to have an official history of the American prison, recording the major changes to penal regimes and an accompanying set of experiential accounts of how prisoners experienced these regimes, across the relevant time periods. Is it possible to construct such an account? Does one already exist?

The 'improving prison' or the 'predatory prison'?

It might be suspected that if asked whether the American prison was getting 'better' or 'worse' many academic penologists and criminologists might be tempted to answer 'worse'. The impact of mass incarceration, the spread of 'truth in sentencing' and mandatory minimum sentences, and the use of Life Without Opportunity for Parole as a substitute for the death penalty, all add up to more people serving longer sentences in prisons which it is suggested are becoming more predatory, more racially-divided and racked by various kinds of abuse. The trends identified also imply a rise in women's imprisonment which, given women's role in society with their greater responsibility for childcare and domestic arrangements, may be more problematic than men's. It could also be suggested that women in correctional facilities with mixed-sex staff (or even single-sex staff) may face particular risks of abuse.

What we are constructing here is a notion of 'the predatory penitentiary'. Such an entity may well exist within the US penal system and—to the extent that it does—it is a problem which needs addressing. But we should be wary of caricaturing the entire US penal system as being affected by problems that may only bear on some institutions within it. The notion of the predatory prison has to an extent been constructed around the perceived problems of managing long-term offenders in maximum security facilities, yet most offenders are held in county gaol or minimum/medium secure penitentiaries. We need to be careful not to think of the entire US system in terms of an image derived from one part of it. Wacquant argues that prisons really have become more predatory and that aggressive 'street culture' has replaced the previous, more stable 'criminal code' and that these changes affect the lower-tariff institutions as much if not more than the maximum security penitentiary. But surprisingly, Wacquant (2001: 98) argues that it is this growth of dangerousness that accounts for the proliferation of super-max facilities. Alternatively, King (1999) devotes more attention to suggesting that the construction of 'the worst of the worst' is a misrepresentation of even the relatively small proportion of the inmate population to whom the designation might be applied. We need to ask to what extent US correctional facilities do actually reproduce the problems of 'the predatory prison' or to what extent 'dangerousness' is 'a media-led myth about maximum security life' (Clowers, 2001).

Theories of penal change

As we do not have a fully worked out account of US penal realities, and as any such account would be a contested one, let us pose the question in the hypothetical. To the question of whether the American prison is improving there are, in a sense, two possible answers (if we abstract: the problem of local variation and people who want to sit on the fence and put in lots of qualifiers). Either it has got better or it has not. If the answer is that it has, we need to know why? What forces might have brought about the change? If the answer is no, we need to know why not? Concerning the first approach we can suggest that prisons get better when the standards in them become known, or are believed, to lag behind the standards society deems socially acceptable. At the end of *Chapter 2* we considered how Thomas Mathiesen (2000) has addressed the irrationality of prison and enquired how, given this irrationality, prison as an institution can survive.

How then might prison change? We might suggest that it changes through a process of counter-denial. It loses its legitimacy when the processes of denial and concealment are overcome and thus when counter-denial creates the space to 'speak the truth about prison'. This truth is that the pains of confinement are always worse than the public would imagine them to be and, that there is an irrationality to prison as an institution which systematically fails to achieve its stated goals. Who then are most aware of the prisons fiasco? The answer is two groups: prisoners, and the staff who work within the corrections industry. It is from these groups that first-hand accounts of prison and its irrationalities can come. There are problems with both sources. Prison staff can have an interest in denying the prisons fiasco and operating as sources of concealment. Prisoners lack voice, in as much as they lack the means of communication—they do not run their own radio stations, publish their own newspapers, or have the resources or opportunity to make films suitable for full cinematic release—and to the extent that they remain a marginalised, stigmatised group accounts of their experience of prison may be discredited when put into the public sphere. Nevertheless prisoners produce poetry, writing and autobiography in an attempt to communicate their accounts of their experience of prison. But as important as these products are, the market for them is limited and unless they are picked up and translated into some popular form they will generally not reach a mass audience.

Rafter (2000) has observed that 50 per cent of prison films claim to be in some way based on a true story. Nellis (1982; 1988; 1993) has patiently researched the extent to which prison film has been based on the work of people with insider knowledge of the penal system. Particularly in the 1920s and 1930s reform-minded Wardens, who saw the media as being important to their ability to bring about change in penal regimes, were a major source of screenplay ideas, acted as consultants on films, made their prisons available to film makers who wanted to use them and on occasion even appeared in the films themselves. Not surprisingly these films often featured reform-minded Wardens. As the prison film develops we find examples of films that have been based on books by people who have 'done time'. There is little point in listing all of the prison films that have such connections because it is already agreed that it is some 50 per cent of the total. It might be objected that whatever the origins and intentions of these products, when they enter into the realm of being dramatised in film, then the artificiality of the medium, the constraints of genre, processes of formal and informal censorship and regulation, commercial pressures, and popular tastes and demand take over to produce the escapist fantasies with their bogus claims to authenticity that Rafter (2000) has complained about. But how do we know that these claims are bogus unless we look at some specific examples? Can film speak the truth about prison?

Film and penal change
Both Rafter (2000) and Nellis (1982; 1988), in slightly different ways and from slightly different perspectives, conclude that prison film carries little significant penal reform information. One of the reasons why they might say this is because

they are academic criminologists whose level of knowledge of criminal justice processes, criminological ideas and theories, and penal realities is greater than that of the average member of the public. Their judgement is also influenced by their understanding of film and their expectations of it. But we need to ask—what level of information does a film need to carry and convey? And how does it operate to do this? The public generally lack an awareness and appreciation of 'the pains of imprisonment'. As such they lack both factual information about what goes on inside prisons, and may also lack the models and metaphors necessary to make sense of whatever information they do have. In the absence of prison film, the level of public awareness of prison would be worse than it currently is. To take an example, if asked: 'Is corporal punishment still practised in US prisons today and if it is how should we feel about it?'—how would the average member of the public respond and what imaginative resources would they have to draw on to make sense of the question? Arguably, their answer to this question will involve film knowledge, as will be shown in the discussion of the issue developed below—but first we need to identify the penal reform functions of the prison film.

Prison film works in several ways and has a number of functions in relation to penal reform. Some of these functions (and examples of films demonstrating them in operation) are already recognised by some commentators, particularly Nellis (1982), although the overall effect and significance of them is usually decried. The functions could be identified as follows. Prison film has:

i) a *revelatory* function—bringing to light practices which are or should be disapproved of;
ii) a *benchmarking* function—helping to set standards of decency for what is and what is not acceptable practice in prisons;
iii) a *defence* of gains function—attempting to combat backsliding by penal authorities on gains established by i) and ii) above;
iv) a *'news'/memory* function—spreading the news that certain events happened and keeping alive a memory of them; and
v) a *humanising/empathy* function—representing prisoners as people, in an attempt to counter processes of depersonalisation and dehumanisation.

Examples can be suggested of prison films which attempt to carry out all five functions. *The Birdman of Alcatraz, Brubaker,* and *Cool Hand Luke* would be three good case studies in this regard. Equally there may be some prison films which do not attempt to address any of these functions at all and *Escape From New York* (1981) might be a candidate here. To the extent that *Escape* expresses the view that there is nothing more that can be done with prisoners than to wall them off in one part of the city and leave them to fight it out amongst themselves, the film might be said to carry an anti-penal reform message, although even here other readings of the film and its effects are possible. Although our three suggested case study films come from the more 'acclaimed' end of the prison movie spectrum we should not think that the penal reform functions identified can only be carried out by pure prison movies, or serious drama. It is quite possible that some of the movies that Rafter might dismiss as being 'ephemera' and of those

Nellis might dismiss as 'bad faith', actually serve to carry forward some of these functions and do so in ways that other films could not. Made for TV movies may be important in this respect and even borderline exploitation movies. We can illustrate how film discharges these functions by considering the example of the use of corporal punishment in adult male prisons.

Film, corporal punishment and prison
Is corporal punishment used in adult male US correctional facilities? If the practice has died out, when did it die out and why? Oshinsky (1996) suggests that from around the 1900s the use of corporal punishment as a judicial sentence began to die out in Southern states. However the beating of prisoners with leather straps (or 'paddling') within correctional facilities in Arkansas, Texas, Florida and Louisiana was common and generally known about and accepted by the public. On prison farms in Mississippi, prisoners could be whipped for fighting, stealing, showing disrespect to an officer, or failing to meet work quotas. Most serious of all was the offence of escape, or attempted escape which could carry an unlimited whipping (Oshinsky, 1996). In 1951 five long term prisoners at Colorado's Cannon City prison made an unsuccessful escape attempt. They were marched into the prison gymnasium and 'paddled' in turns by the Warden and prison guards. The *Denver Post* decried the action and the Governor hurried to the prison to investigate. The Warden defended the use of corporal punishment, arguing that it was an effective method of discipline in 'a language the men understood'. Public opinion was not so happy about the affair and the Governor and State Prison Board moved to outlaw flogging in the prison (*Time Magazine*, 30 July 1951). In 1967 the Arkansas State Governor fired the superintendent and three wardens at one of the state's prison farms as a response to reports that random beatings of inmates with a strap was one of the abuses known to be occurring there. Subsequent events at the prison are reported on in the film *Brubaker*, discussed below.

In more recent times in the US there have been suggestions that corporal punishment should be brought back as an alternative to prison. Rather than build and run expensive prisons, why not offer convicted offenders the option of corporal punishment? It is cheaper and quicker! It has also been suggested that corporal punishment for prisoners should be re-introduced as an effective form of discipline. These proposals have not received a great deal of support. Where reports have arisen that correctional officers have used corporal punishment on inmates in recent times, these are regarded as instances of abuse and have led to discipline or dismissal of all guards, or law suits by prisoners for compensation.

Although the discussion above is not a comprehensive treatment, it does suggest that a process of penal reform has occurred. Whereas at one time it was a known and accepted practice to administer harsh physical beatings to prisoners as a form of discipline, this is no longer acceptable. If relatively mild physical punishment, even when inflicted in the form of 'horseplay', is regarded as an abuse for which a corrections officer might loose his or her job, what has happened for this change to come about? Cavadino and Dignan's (1996) radical pluralist model of the penal crisis might be relevant here. According to these authors, prison (and therefore the practices within it to the extent that they are known about and understood) needs to attempt to maintain legitimacy with three groups: prisoners, prison staff and the public (including politicians and officials). Where serious deficits of legitimacy arise in one or more of these groups problems will occur. With regard to corporal punishment it is not clear to what extent prisoners ever accepted this as legitimate, rather than an oppression which they endured because they were powerless to change it. Prison staff clearly seem to have supported the practice at one time but have perhaps now moved towards acknowledging its unacceptability, although attitudes within staff groups may differ. Finally, the public generally do not approve of the practice and there is little real support for its re-introduction. What has happened to bring about these changes? Public opinion seems to have been important. The public needed to know of the use of such practices and come to perceive them as being something that was unacceptable. What role might film have played in this?

The position being advanced here is not that representations in prison films (unilaterally and on their own) work to bring about penal reform. Rather, as Nellis (1982) has pointed out, prison film works best alongside other media. But prison film can be a way in which certain ideas, sentiments and dispositions relevant to penal reform can be circulated. Prison films may have had the capacity to become 'talking points', the focus of public debate and so have helped to raise certain issues in the public's mind. But the role of film is not so much the transmission of 'factual' information that can be derived from other sources, it is more to provide the audience with imaginative resources to appreciate the issues. Film can also have a role in circulating a sentiment, or understanding that something is wrong, as much as to advance formal rational argument, which may be better developed elsewhere.

In the 1900s corporal punishment was accepted on some prison farms (and indeed was still being practised as late as 1968), although in 1951 in some states it was seen as being unacceptable. Our aim here is not to give a comprehensive account but an illustrative one. The discussion will focus on two films—*I Am a Fugitive From a Chain Gang* (1932) and *Brubaker* (1980).

I am a Fugitive from a Chain Gang
Firstly, *I am a Fugitive from a Chain Gang* (1932) detailed abuses of leased labour in the Georgia chain gangs. In one scene a prisoner is shown receiving corporal punishment. Or rather the film never shows the beating but only the other inmates, as they look on in horror. Some might argue that such scenes in prison films have become so common that it is now possible to find examples of parodies of this scene. But we cannot assume that this depiction was viewed with amusement in 1932. The public appear to have taken it quite seriously and the film became a focus for debate and, in combination with pressures from northern newspapers, it led to some changes in Georgian penal practices.

Notwithstanding Nellis's suggestion that the penal reform impact of the film was overstated, the argument advanced here is that the film should be seen as an exercise in revelation, benchmarking, defence, and humanisation. The film *revealed* practices that may not have been known about even in Georgia and certainly not in the rest of the US. It is generally agreed that the film succeeded in inviting support for the convicts and opposition to some of the practices on the chain gangs. In expressing a disapproval of certain practices and garnering public support for this disapproval, the film is operating as an exercise in *benchmarking*. It is signalling to penal authorities what the limits to the acceptable prison are. Retrospectively, *Chain Gang* can act as means of *defending* any gains that were achieved. If the film details practices that were deemed to be unacceptable in 1932, then where such practices occur much later on those responsible for them may feel they need to be conducted in secret or concealed. The film can succeed in this effect because it involves a process of *humanisation*. Rather than road gang convicts being seen as a depersonalised mass of chained and uniformed felons, it brings to life the individual character of one particular member of the chain gang. Finally, the choice of Hollywood star Paul Muni to play the lead role is significant in as much as the public find it easier and more agreeable to identify with the screen representation of the convict than real-life convicts. As more people go to see prison films than undertake prison visiting, the fact that the heroes of prison films look like movie stars should be seen as an advantage not a criticism—dramatic representations can help to create *empathy*.

On appraising the impact of the film it matters little that change was not as quick as might have been hoped for, and not as complete. Change still occurred. It does matter to some extent that chain gangs continued and were re-packaged as County Public Work Camps. But what this shows is that film cannot entirely insure against processes of concealment, or backsliding by penal authorities. This does not invalidate the role of film in penal reform. Rather it demands more films—to do more revelatory work.

Cool Hand Luke is significant here. It has been criticised for being retrospective: a film made in the 1960s about a past era. As intimated in the previous chapter, in setting 'the prison of which we should be ashamed' in the past, the film could be accused of encouraging complacency and misperception. The film almost implies that 'prisons today are not as bad as that'—penal reform has already taken place. An alternative view would be that *Luke* is still acting as a benchmark. It tells penal authorities that their standards must either exceed this or be concealed. As we know from *Brubaker* later, not all prisons were exceeding these standards, some were out of step, and so in 1967, the same year as *Luke* appeared, the superintendent of the Arkansas prison farm was sacked and a new reforming Warden appointed. It is not being suggested that one event, the cinematic success of *Cool Hand Luke*, caused the other event—the appointment of a reform-minded Warden. Rather, *Luke* is acting as a barometer of social acceptance and sentiment at the time. For people who are interested in the regional dimension of these issues it probably is significant that the film was seen as an exercise in 'bashing the South' just as much as *Chain Gang* was.

Brubaker
Starring Robert Redford, *Brubaker* (1980) continues a story started by *Fugitive* and taken up by *Luke*. It is a fictionalised version based on a 'real life' account in a book by Thomas Murton of his attempts to reform the Arkansas prison farm. In the film version, but not in real life, Redford as the reforming Warden checks into the prison that he is about to take control of in the guise of an inmate, to see for himself the extent of the problem that he is about to take on. Arguably the key scene comes early on in the film when the newly arrived inmates ('new fish') are bunking down shortly after reception. There is an air of nervous excitement. The

men seem reasonably happy, if a little nervous about their arrival in a penal institution. The guards and trusties then appear and select a man from the group, apparently at random, informing him that he has committed a breach of discipline. He is taken to the end of the bunking room and beaten with a leather strap, whilst the other men look on. The whole atmosphere changes in an instant. The men fall silent as it dawns on them what they are in for: harsh, arbitrary and intimidatory punishment which they are powerless to resist. The scene is done in all seriousness and is very different from equivalent scenes in more clichéd prison movies. The beating is witnessed by the new Warden who now has an insider's view of the nature of the problem, a view which we incidentally share.

Brubaker appeared in 1980, having been made at the end of the 1970s. It addresses events that occurred in 1967/8, the account of which was published in book form in 1970 (Murton and Hyams). But how are we to appraise the significance of the film? It is usually discussed in terms of its ending. Redford/Brubaker attempts to reform the prison but meets with very little cooperation either from the staff, or even the prisoners. Increasingly he discovers more abuses in the prison, eventually culminating in the discovery of a field of decomposed remains, which are assumed to be prisoners who have been beaten and murdered. Brubaker calls for a full investigation which the authorities try to close down. Eventually he is given an ultimatum: stop stirring up trouble or be sacked. Realising that the official investigation will be a cover-up, Brubaker resigns/is sacked. This ending to the film represents the liberal's dilemma—work within the system to achieve small change, or try for real change and be rejected by it. Redford chooses rejection: seen as confirming pessimism about penal reform, although Nellis (1982) suggests that the film:

> ... remains faithful to the essential political lessons that he [Thomas Murton] learned, viz, that the state government which appointed him did not really want prison reform, but only a semblance of it, and that no amount of personal integrity and individual effort will succeed against a corrupt and complacent administration. In emphasising this the film undermined the myth of warden autonomy which earlier prison films helped to create and ensured that henceforth prison reform must be seen in a wider political context, and never taken for granted, even among those who claim to promote it. (Nellis, 1982: 42)

But this apparently favourable judgement on *Brubaker* as telling a story that was worth telling does not stop Nellis from proceeding to conclude that prison film carries very little real information about prisons and has contributed little to penal reform.

Discussions of *Brubaker* usually imply that the film ends with the reforming Warden choosing to resign/be sacked rather than collude with a cover-up. But the scene where Brubaker walks out of the official enquiry in disgust is not the end of the film. It ends with him returning to the prison to clear his office and collect his belongings. As he loads these into his estate car the men of the prison are assembled in the yard, armed trusties and guards looking on, as the new Warden speaks to the men. His speech informs them in no uncertain terms that the prison is going to return to the old regime and they will work in the fields or be punished with the strap. Things will return to how they were and everyone will have the certainty of knowing what the rules are and of knowing their place. At first the men listen in silence until one of them, a trusty, starts to slow handclap. Someone else joins in and then others. As Redford drives away the whole group are slow-handclapping the new Warden in a surprise show of defiance. The old regime has lost its legitimacy, with the prisoners (including the trusties who are part staff/part prisoner), and by implication with us the viewers/the public.

There is a great deal more that could be said about this film. *Brubaker* could be analysed in the terms suggested by Mathiesen (2000) (processes of concealment and denial/counter denial work), Cavadino and Dignan (1996) (radical pluralist perspective on the penal crisis) or possibly Pratt (1999) utilising Norbert Elias on the civilising process as applied to prison. It can also be analysed in terms of: revelation, benchmarking, defence, 'news'/memory, and humanisation/empathy. The film is not entirely without its problems. Although the corporal punishment scene is done well, as the film progresses the crimes of the regime become more fantastic, before finally culminating in the discovery of bodies. The film is in danger of being seen as an exercise in excess, even though it actually represents a toned down version of events that were said to have happened within the prison!

It is possible that *Brubaker* could come to be seen as 'just another prison movie'. Nevertheless, the representation of prison that it portrays remains in our shared culture and so arguably it can still function in the manner suggested. The film reveals that as late as 1968, and possibly later, there were practices in US prisons that many people might have thought would have died out long before. This acts as a benchmark which suggests that—to the extent these or equivalent practices still exist elsewhere—they need to be changed or concealed. The film condemns those people who would advocate a return to corporal punishment in penal institutions. Lastly it humanises the prisoners and allows us to have empathy with them, and this has a racial dimension which could be developed in a fuller analysis (see Oshinsky, 1996).

FILM, PRISON AND CRIME IN CONTEMPORARY AMERICA

Brubaker is a Hollywood movie. It has a slightly flawed hero and an ambiguous ending. *Birdman* and *Luke* are also Hollywood movies, which have ambiguous if not unhappy endings. Hollywood never has been solely obsessed with justice restored narratives with happy endings. *Birdman*, *Luke* and *Brubaker* all contributed, directly or indirectly to penal reform. It may be objected that at most they reformed the prison not the society but that is a much bigger debate. And some people might still argue that prison has not improved but has only concealed its old abuses better or invented new ones. What we hope we have established is that film operates by diffusing sentiments as part of a process whereby what was acceptable at one point in time can come to be seen as unacceptable at another point of time. In short film has contributed to the penal reform debate.

How we should set in context the 'gains' made by penal reform is beyond the scope of this chapter. But in terms of our interest in film we cannot leave the analysis here. We need to ask if there are any prison films which do not contribute to penal reform in these terms, or which are positively harmful to it. The completely formulaic films *The Last Castle* (2001) and *Murder in the First* (1995) might be candidates here. What do they reveal? What do they benchmark? One might be tempted to say, nothing that has not already been revealed and benchmarked before. But still these films contain ideas about crimes and criminals and in humanising their inmates they suggest that prisoners are not incorrigible offenders who commit evil crimes of their own free will. Even a film as lightweight as *The Last Castle* (Redford again) cannot be dismissed as simply not worthy of analysis.

If we move out of the conventional prison movie into some more modern prison-related films, these become more difficult to analyse because they depict contradictory accounts. Films like *Con Air* (1997) and *American History X* (1998) could be accused of circulating notions harmful to penal reform. They directly or indirectly reproduce ideas about racially-divided, predatory prisons populated by hardened convicts. The *mise en scène* of these films may serve to legitimate notions of 'the worst of the worst', or reproduce 'myths about maximum security life' (e.g. the absence of inmate relations of support and organization). But even here the picture is more complicated than would first seem. We see storylines of reform and redemption (the Nicholas Cage character in *Con Air* is a time-served convict who returns to grace; in *American History X* there are redeeming relationships between Derek and his African-American prison workmate, and Derek, Danny and Doctor Sweeney). Reading these texts is difficult because they are complex and contradictory. The same could be said of films like *American Me* (1992), which although portraying the predatory prison as a testing ground for cool masculinity, suggests that people who have gone through processes of degradation still have potential to change. The film indicts society for its lack of vision in not being able to break the cycle of degradation.

What all this suggests is that we need to do *empirical work* on how these films are received, understood and used. We also need to think about what influences the way people understand film. It may then be possible to develop strategies of film education (conceived of in a non-elitist way) to explore with the public how they understand and consume prison film. These arguments are developed later in this book. What is being suggested is that film representations of prison and prisoners can humanise offenders and lay the ground for questioning some of the irrationalities involved. Against this it might be suggested that a reality check is needed and that, whatever popular cinema may or may not have contributed to penal reform, the reality is two million people incarcerated and six million in contact with the criminal justice system (Bureau of Justice Statistics, 2002). The US is well into its prison binge, and when not binging on prison the penal system is binging on having people out on probation or parole. What kind of films are necessary here to deal with this situation and what impact can they have?

Film and the four stories of US penal realities
It might be suggested that there are four stories that need to be told in and about the American penal system. The first is the story of super-max. Although this accounts for less than two per cent of the inmate population, and is in volume terms a relatively small issue, as long as there is *prima facie* evidence that super-max constitutes an abuse of human rights then the experiential accounts of

prisoners held in super-max units need to be documented and relayed in sympathetic form to the widest possible audience. We should not rule out the possibility that this could be done in a Hollywood movie with a happy ending, starring whoever is the current next-big-thing male movie star. But more likely accounts of super-max may be relayed better by 'new documentaries' or independent film (for example Australia's *Ghosts ... of the Civil Dead* (1988)). We also need to appraise the film and TV prison drama that we do have for its ability and willingness either to address or to avoid the issue.

The second story is the story of the two million people incarcerated. They may be located in vastly different institutions and enjoy vastly different experiences, suggesting that a range of films would be necessary. For all of these people the pains of confinement are likely to be in some way greater than uninformed sections of the public might think or accept. Their story needs to be told in films which close the gap between dramatic perceptions of prison and the reality. This does not mean that prison films have to be realistic. It does mean that they should not seek to conceal or deny the pains of incarceration or the irrationality of prison as an institution which, whilst claiming to reform its charges, often only acts to confirm them in their patterns of offending behaviour. This could be done in anything from Hollywood blockbusters starring Julia Roberts to low budget made for TV movies.

Next we need to consider the four million people who are 'under correctional supervision' on probation and parole (Bureau of Justice Statistics, 2002). What is this experience like? Should we rejoice at the number of people 'enjoying' non-custodial sentences? Should we increase the number of people under such supervision in preference to prison? What are their experiences, what is their trajectory?

The last story that needs to be told is that of the Death Row inmate. To an extent this is one that Hollywood has already told and told well—see O'Sullivan (2003) for a defence of *Dead Man Walking* (1995), *Last Dance* (1996), *True Crime* (1999) and *The Green Mile* (1999). Those who oppose the death penalty might wish to see more Hollywood movies on the subject, particularly films that deal even-handedly, but not unsympathetically, with Death Row inmates and their crimes (a criterion that might add *The Chamber* (1996) to the above list). If these films are not made then by default the cultural ground will be ceded to those who make films which portray Death Row inmates as manipulative devious psychopaths (*Just Cause* (1995), *Witness to the Execution* (1994 TVM)). But more than this, as Life Without the Possibility of Parole is substituted for death, we need films that document the experiences of these inmates. We also need to look for the films that endorse a cultural politics of punitiveness that supports such sentencing. This would include locating and critiquing films such as *In the Bedroom* (2001), which asserts that the failure of the law to meet the desire of victims for revenge implies that victims should take their own revenge. We should also identify the films which attempt to counter this regressive cultural politics, for example *A Map of the World* (1999), below.

The real answer is that we need more prison movies. We need movies set in maximum security facilities. We need prison movies set in county gaols. We need more 'going-to-prison movies' (*Slam* (1998), *25th Hour* (2002)) and more 'just-got-out-of-prison movies' (*He Got Game* (1998), *The Yards* (2000)). Prison film does and should include everyone from Spike Lee to Sharon Stone. Such films are not particularly popular and difficult to get made. In a sense, whenever anyone succeeds in getting a prison film, or prison-related film made it should be regarded as a triumph.

Nellis (1982) has raised the issue that prison movies made in 'bad faith' might destroy the impact of those made in 'good faith'. Two points are worth noting here. Firstly, how do we identify these supposedly 'bad faith' movies? There is an argument to be made that it is sometimes amongst the films that some analysts would describe as 'dross and ephemera' that valuable work is done. The made for TV movies and straight-to-video/DVD films may have an unrecognised value. Our suggestion is that if any prison film scores any points on the criteria of revelation, benchmarking, defence, news/memory or humanisation/empathy then it should be regarded as worthy of being made.

It may be possible to encourage 'good faith' prison movies to reposition the 'bad'. The meaning of movies is not fixed, but depends on the context within which they are viewed. Any film can, in principle, be repositioned to mean its opposite. A film that is constructed to endorse the idea that punishment is and should be about retribution and revenge, can be used to reveal the bankruptcy of that position. What cultural interventions can reposition films? Can a whole 'sub-genre' of prison films (gangsta-cool) be repositioned by one three minute music video? Alternatively if we look at a 'prison film', or a 'released from prison film' and see a message in it that we do not like, rather than wish that the film had not been made we should critique it and attempt to influence the manner in which it is consumed. This can be done through film criticism, or film education, or through the production or championing of 'answer films'. In music an answer record *must* follow the record it answers. Hank Thompson needed to have recorded and released 'The Wild Side of Life' for Kitty Wells to write and record 'It Wasn't God Who Made Honky-Tonk Angels'. In film, the same is not true: an 'answer film' can be made in advance of the film it answers.

What we are suggesting is that the 'meanings' of films are not fixed or given and this implies that we may be able to intervene to answer, or counter those films which might be judged harmful to our cause. This requires that we can identify such films—and 'reading' films is becoming more difficult, as producers deliberately construct texts that are open to alternative interpretations and that deploy more subtle representational strategies. To an extent Hollywood has moved away from making films on the model of narrative realism that characterised classic Hollywood cinema (Bordwell, 1985), although narrative realist films still exist and can play a role in exploring contemporary social issues (Ryan and Kellner, 1990). The next section will examine the operation of some specific examples.

REPRESENTATIONS OF PRISON IN FILM

This section looks at some examples of representation of prison in film. There is no single way to represent prison. Films do not necessarily have to be realistic. In a sense they never can be. So prison films can approximate reality, or reject realism and in varying degrees be surreal or abstract.

The Shawshank Redemption: or *'This prison movie is not a prison movie'*
It would be quite possible to spend years researching *The Shawshank Redemption* (1994) and only begin to scratch the surface of what could profitably be written and said about this film. We need to restrict ourselves to making only a few key points. Firstly, the film is set almost entirely within a prison. On the descriptive definition advanced in this book it is a prison film. But, once we move from descriptive to analytic definition, the status of *Shawshank* becomes suspect. Rafter (2000) simply looks at the film and sees that the conventions of the genre are present and concludes that this must therefore be a prison movie. However, we need to be able to show not only that the conventions are present, but that locating the film as a prison movie explains what it is, what it does, and how it works.

It requires relatively little critical effort to see that the *'Shawshank* as prison movie theory' fails. *Shawshank* has relatively little in common with *Luke, Birdman* or *Brubaker*. These three films are all directly or indirectly dramatisations of real world stories of prison—*Birdman* and *Brubaker* for obvious reasons, and *Luke* because the book that it was based on was written by an ex-convict who had worked in the County Public Work Camps. *Shawshank* is an adaptation of a Stephen King novella, which King was in part motivated to write out of his memories of 1940s/1950s prison movies (Kermode, 2003). A recent monograph on the film (Kermode, 2003) mentions—in passing—the prison movie tradition, but recognises the film as a powerful form of therapy before going on to assess it as (i) a modern day Gospel parable; (ii) an allegory on US political history (Warden Norton as a stand-in for Richard Nixon); and (iii) a tribute to the power of Hollywood cinema and its ability to take people out of their humdrum existences. The film could also just as easily be analysed in terms of its relationship to Frank Capra's *It's A Wonderful Life*.

All of the above approaches to the film are at least as valid as calling it a prison movie in analytic terms simply because it looks like one in descriptive terms. The film is the second most popular of all time (IMDb) when, as already explained earlier, the only other 'pure prison movie' in the top 250 is *Cool Hand Luke* at position 122. Frank Darabont, the director, receives a constant stream of fan mail thanking him for having made the film and reporting that *Shawshank* helped the writer get through a difficult divorce, bereavement, personal crisis and so forth. Tim Robbins reports that people come up to him every day to tell him that they love his film and have seen it 20, 30 or 40 times. No other prison film evokes this kind of response (Robbins and Darabont as cited in Kermode, 2003). Citing *The Shawshank Redemption* as evidence for the continuing/recurring popularity of the prison film is like citing *The X-files* as evidence for the recurring popularity of the police procedural. The reception accorded the film and the esteem in which it is held suggest that it has exceeded its status of being a mere prison movie.

If we turn to the film itself then we might suggest that simply to note the number of times the conventions of the prison film genre (or prison film clichés) appear in it provides only a fairly impoverished analysis. Nichole Rafter (2000: 134–5) spots that the film deploys the conventions knowingly but dismisses this as being merely an exercise in cinematic nostalgia. She still proceeds to identify it as a traditional prison movie which fits her model of justice restored. The film does indeed 'fit' the conventions of the genre, or more accurately displays them in such a hyperbolic manner that the prison film theorist can simply check them off from *Shawshank* and forget having to do the analysis for themselves. The friendship between Red and Andy is the most perfect of perfect friendships, the new fish are the newest of new fish, the first beating comes right on cue, and so on and so forth. Rafter (2000: 120) has referred to the sequence where Andy escapes, cleans out the Warden's safe, the money from the bank accounts and brings about the demise of Warden Norton and Captain Hadley as 'the most fulsome revenge sequence' in the history of the prison movie. Taking this sequence as a whole it occupies a reasonable amount of screen time—perhaps 12-and-a-half minutes. But most of this time is devoted to the discovery of Andy's disappearance, the discovery that his disappearance is an escape and his method of escape. The part of the sequence that runs from Andy arriving at the bank to make a withdrawal, through to Warden Norton committing suicide is very compressed and takes not much more than two-and-a-half minutes in a film of 142 minute. The comeuppance sequence is quite short and just flashes by. If *Shawshank* was a 'for real' prison movie this sequence would have been played at normal pace and the movie would have ended with Andy receiving some kind of public vindication. As it happens the revenge sequence is not the end and Andy's escape is not the end, or the point of the film and we have to wait a while until Red breaks parole to join Andy on a beach by the Pacific—'a warm place that has no memory'.

Although Rafter(2000) suggests that *Shawshank* fits the model of a prison film this is because she is overly influenced by the justice restored version of it. In reality the genre has never quite looked like this and prisoners lose as often as they win. In having both Andy and Red achieve redemption the film does subvert the conventions of the prison film genre. The relevant prison film to compare *Shawshank* with is *The Defiant Ones* (1958), where a comparison of the final scene of each movie would be instructive (see above and *Chapter 9*).

We could make three points about the ending to *Shawshank*. Firstly, it is an 'outlaw ending'. Andy never receives public acknowledgment of his innocence and lives outside of the law, as does Red when he breaks his parole. Secondly, it is an ending without women. It is very unusual to see a Hollywood film which ends uniting two heterosexual men. Butch Cassidy and the Sundance Kid die at the end of the movie, and at the end of most cop-action male buddy movies one of the partners returns to his wife/girlfriend. This 'ending without women' is entirely intentional, as there are any number of devices by which a 'love interest' can be sneaked into a prison movie including, for example, the prison vet (*Convict Cowboy* (1995)); the prison dentist (Julia Ormond in *Captives* (1994); the organizer of a fan club (*The Birdman of Alcatraz* (1962); the Warden's daughter (more than one 1930s/1940s prison movie), etc. Finally, the film ends outside of the US.

It is just too simple to see *Shawshank* as simply a prison movie. It can equally be seen as: a tale of hope triumphing over adversity; a homage to Hollywood cinema; a male recovery movie; a critique and rejection of the American dream; a parody of a prison movie or a meta-prison movie; or an adaptation of a Stephen King novella. Nevertheless, some might argue that as the film is set for virtually its entirety in a prison, do we not have to enquire how the film represented prisons and prisoners? This may be true, but the question is what yardstick do we assess it by? Given the film's obviously fabular nature it is not really claiming to have represented a real world prison. It is an attempt to recreate (and subvert?) an already existing cinematic prison. Does it then make any sense to compare *Shawshank* to current US penal realities and find it wanting? As one reviewer at the time put it:

> Well-crafted, well-acted, and utterly bogus, Frank Darabont's feel-good prison movie represents a creepy height of denial, escapism and easy sentimentality, dodging every real issue of crime and punishment with a hopelessly gimmicky, shamelessly manipulative story.
>
> Read a paper and see how an epidemic of underclass neglect and crime has produced a boom in prison construction, an army of brown and black prisoners, and a profusion of elect-me-I'll-lock-em-up crime bills. Comes now a movie (adapted from a Stephen King novella) from another, simpler planet.
>
> (Mankin, 1994, IMDb Usenet Reviews)

This review seems to be implying that, rather than having *The Shawshank Redemption*, the era needed a film that more directly reflected the then existing penal realities, that is to say—racially-discriminatory mass incarceration. But the problem is that we know what happens when Hollywood tries to do this. We end up with the racially-divided, kill-or-be-killed maximum security prison as seen in *An Innocent Man* (1989) or *Bound by Honor* (1993). This skews the focus of attention away from the real areas of growth of the US penal system and does nothing to cultivate a more sympathetic or rounded understanding of prisoners and their problems. *Shawshank* is preferable. It should not be taken as a literal description of prisons and prisoners, nor even a first order dramatic representation of them. It is a comment on a comment.

Prior to *Shawshank* the trend in US prison movies at the end of the 1980s and at the beginning of the 1990s was towards violent, action-adventure films, set in maximum security prisons populated by hard-core convicts (Wilson, 1993). Cinema was developing a representation of a 'kill-or-be killed' prison. *Shawshank* made an unwitting intervention against this trend postulating an alternative direction for the prison movie. We could see it as giving film-makers permission to make slower paced prison films which had no need for masculinist action-adventure elements. Prisoners can be represented as human, mutually supportive and capable of reform and rehabilitation. In the UK we can see examples of film-makers picking up this challenge in the Brit-pic prison movies *Greenfingers* (2000) and *Tomorrow La Scala* (2002), which have a feel to them unlike either the US or UK prison films that came before them. However, the US has not seen a glut of post-*Shawshank* prison movies, with only the minor prison-in-a-teen-movie effort *Brokedown Palace* (1999), entering as a possible contender. But we should not underestimate the long-term power of *Shawshank*. Now nearly ten years after its initial release it remains a massive 'sleeper influence' on popular culture. The visible signs of its impact in changing the ways in which we think about and see the world will be slow to emerge and take a long time to come to full fruition. The real test of the film will come when the 12-14-year-olds who have watched the film in the years since its release become the film-makers of tomorrow.

Brokedown Palace
Before leaving this topic we should comment on *Brokedown Palace* (1999). This was a relatively minor, low-mid budget, teen-movie. It stars Claire Daines (*Romeo and Juliet*) and Kate Beckinsale (*The Last Days of Disco; Pearl Harbour*), and might be known to a younger audience but probably would not mean much to older film fans. The film tells the story of two American girls who go on a holiday of a lifetime to Thailand, but are duped into attempting to smuggle drugs out of that country. They are arrested at the airport, tried and sentenced to a 33 year gaol term in the Brokedown Palace (a prison). The girls and their supporters believe that they are innocent and that their trial was a show-trial. Efforts are made to obtain an appeal and then a pardon. But the girls become frustrated at the prospect of 33 years in prison for a crime that they did not commit and so, in desperation, attempt to escape. Their escape is unsuccessful and as a result they then face the prospect of having another 15 years added to their sentence.

As described so far, this film may sound like an (in)justice abroad movie along the lines of *Return to Paradise* (1998) or the earlier *Midnight Express* (1978), comparisons which have certainly been made. But it deftly avoids the pitfalls associated with those films. Although about 50 per cent or so of the action takes place during the time the girls are in prison, we see little of it. The prison and its regime is sketched in impressionistic terms. One scene establishes that the prison has a 'snitch' and in the same scene one of the girls receives a relatively minor punishment. Apart from this the female staff appear to be strict but not unkind. One of the girls begins to learn the Thai language and manners. The surprise ending comes when the girls' appeals fail and then their arranged pardons also fall through. At this stage one of them makes the decision to [con]'fess-up' to the crime and ends up volunteering to do her and her friend's sentence. The film ends with the girl who has chosen to stay in the prison standing in the mass ranks of prisoners. The camera picks her out smiling serenely, whilst her voice-over tells us that although she hopes her friends keep working to get her out she does not regret what she did. It was the right decision, probably the best decision she has ever made.

The ending to *Brokedown Palace* neatly inverts the ending of *Midnight Express* (triumphant escape from the 'third world' hell-hole). The prison in *Brokedown Palace* is neither an 'infernal prison' nor a 'sanitised prison', it's just a normal prison. Arguably if this film did nothing else other than to exist as a counterpoint to the harm done by the earlier injustice abroad movie *Return to Paradise*, (America criticising Malaysia on its record on the death penalty) then the film would have been worth making. But, given that the argument of our discussion above has been informed by a Mathiesen inspired perspective that the public underestimates the pains of imprisonment and that we need to reduce the public's misperception of prison, to give a moderate seal of approval to an 'I'm happy to be here in prison even if I have got a 96 year sentence hanging over my head' movie, might seem counter-intuitive. But this just goes to show that issues of representation are never quite as straightforward as they might seem.

Stranger Inside v. A Map of the World
People of colour are under-represented in Hollywood and over-represented in prison. White Hollywood tends to make films with white stars and although black players appear in white prison movies, Hollywood has not recently, if ever, made a prison movie from a black perspective which deals with the black experience of incarceration (outside of bio-pics and depending perhaps on what you think of *Life* (1999)). Arguably this matters because if the same people always get to make the same films this excludes alternative perspectives that need to get a hearing. If prison is a complex and contested reality, then to get a good understanding of it we need to see it represented from a range of perspectives so that we have a greater range of imaginative resources to draw on. We should welcome prison films from black/Latino perspectives, and so on.

The made for TV movie *Stranger Inside* (2001) was directed by African-American Cheryl Dunn and featured a black main cast. It tells the story of Treasure, who having spent much of her life in a series of juvenile correctional facilities, at the age of 21 is graduating to State Penitentiary. There she hopes to find the woman she believes to be her mother, a long-term prisoner called Brownie. They meet and attempt bonding for a while, before tensions between Brownie's role of 'top dog' in the inmate culture, and Treasure's expectations of her as a mother, force them apart. The film has an inconclusive ending with Treasure moving on to another institution, a little tougher and a little wiser, but really no better off.

How does the film represent a women's state penitentiary? The inmates are divided into racially demarcated gangs, with some crossing of race lines but little real inter-racial support or solidarity. The culture is survival of the fittest. You need to be able to defend yourself and 'hang tough'. Correctional officers bring drugs into the prison and have sex with inmates; inmates have sex with inmates. Originating as a TV movie with HBO but later shown at the independent film festivals, the film seems to have been well received and is invariably praised and regarded favourably in reviews—'Gritty', Realistic', 'Brutal but fascinating'.

In *A Map of the World* (1999) Sigourney Weaver plays Alice Goodwin who lives on a Wisconsin dairy farm with her husband and family and works as a school nurse. Her neighbour and best friend is Teresa (Julianne Moore). Their children play together. One day whilst Teresa's children are visiting, the youngest wanders off to play alone and drowns in the pond. Teresa is distraught because she has lost her child and Alice because she thinks the accident was her fault. The two remain friends although the incident puts a palpable tension between them. Alice also finds that the townspeople begin to shun her a little because of the incident. Shortly afterwards, one of the children at the school where Alice works accuses her of abuse. Other children come forward to make similar allegations. To her surprise the allegations are investigated and the case goes to court, where she is remanded to the county gaol to await full trial. The back-to-back incidents of the drowning and the abuse allegations put a lot of strain on all concerned as friends start to desert the Goodwins. Eventually when the case goes to court Teresa has to take the stand to testify that Alice has looked after her children often, without ever having any problems or giving cause for concern. The incident of the drowning comes up, but Teresa sticks to her story that it was an accident that was not anyone's fault and not relevant to her judgement that she would still trust Alice with her children. Boosted by her friend's testimony Alice keeps herself together enough to defend the case and, thanks to some good work by her lawyer who is able to cast doubt on both the original abuse allegation and the 'copycat' allegations, beats the abuse charge.

A Map of the World could be described as a family melodrama which comments on the cultural politics of revenge. Of interest for our purposes is the relatively short middle section of the film during which Alice is remanded in the county gaol. How is the county gaol portrayed? It is racially mixed, appearing to be roughly divided between a disparate group of white women and a group of young black women. The women spend most of their time in the association area watching and commenting on day-time TV. The black women are generally shown as intelligent, articulate and confident. Although there are tensions within the group there are also instances of mutual support. Alice/Weaver does not mix well with her fellow inmates, although eventually comes to be 'in awe of them'. The one significant episode of violence during her stay in gaol arises when she self-injures herself.

The county gaol section of *A Map of the World* is like a little mini-prison movie within a movie. In it Alice/Weaver is 'the prison innocent'. She has been falsely accused and is not worldly-wise to surviving a penal institution. She survives her short stay on remand and eventually goes on to win in court. So is this a triumph of the prison innocent/justice restored narrative? Not really—although Alice clearing her name in court does demonstrate a certain degree of faith in the law. The point of this section, if there is one, is a theme well known to students of women's prison drama—'middle-class' woman goes to prison, meets women from other different backgrounds and emerges wiser for the experience. After the prison section the film runs on a little. *A Map of the World* stands in implicit debate with *Stranger Inside* as two different ways of representing women's experience of imprisonment.

The death penalty in 1990s Hollywood cinema

The 1990s saw the production and release of at least five mainstream and popular 'death penalty movies' made by, or featuring household name stars and/or directors. The films that are clearly part of this cycle are *Dead Man Walking* (1995), *Last Dance* (1996), *The Chamber* (1996), *The Green Mile* (1999) and *True Crime* (1999). Other films from the same period which now show up in TV screenings are *Just Cause* (1995) (starring Sean Connery/Lawrence Fishburne) and *Letters from a Killer* (1998) (starring Patrick Swayze), and also relevant to our analysis, a made for TV movie *Witness to the Execution* (1994).

But why should Hollywood take up the issue of capital punishment? Why did the mid-to-late-1990s see this burst of cinematic attention given to the death penalty? How did these films represent the issue and what impact might they have had on the popular debate about capital punishment? During the 1990s the number of executions carried out within the US had risen steadily, reaching a high of 98 in 1999. This amounts to just under two executions a week in a country which, by the mid-1970s, had come to be *de facto* abolitionist! Austin Sarat (1999; 2001) argues that the death-penalty films of the 1990s tended to reproduce, rather than challenge the notions of criminality that underpin a belief in the death penalty in contemporary America. One of Sarat's main criticisms of the films is that they tend to pose an individualised question—does this particular Death Row inmate deserve to die in this particular instance? This, Sarat believes, detracts from developing a wider analysis of social inequalities inherent in the operation of the death penalty, believing that the films represented a conservative cultural politics of crime.

If we really want an example of a 'conservative' film we should look at *In the Bedroom* (2001) which did advocate a politics of revenge. The films that Sarat singles out for criticism—*Dead Man Walking, Last Dance, The Green Mile* and *True Crime*—featured even-handed and sympathetic portrayals of Death Row inmates. Indeed they advanced a range of arguments against the death penalty, drawn from both the old abolitionism (no one deserves to die) and the new abolitionism (some may deserve to die but we cannot operate the law fairly enough to say who). The films showed that there were Death Row inmates who were put to death who perhaps should not have been (Coffey in the *Green Mile* is innocent; Cindy Liggert in *Last Dance* is rehabilitated and only denied clemency because of the machinations of the judicial and political system). The death-penalty films identified above undertook the functions of: *narration*: telling the stories of the Death Row inmates; *witnessing*—that there had been a resurgence of use in the death penalty and that this involves injustice; *benchmarking*—arguing that a death penalty is always cruel and unusual whatever the method of execution and should fall below the decency threshold; and *humanisation* and *empathy*. Rather than seeing faceless (or still photographed) Death Row inmates as 'the murdering scum who killed our children' the films turned their Death Row inmates into people with whom it was possible to empathise. These movies were in opposition to films such as *Just Cause* and *Witness to the Execution*, which portrayed Death Row inmates as manipulative, devious liars who would do anything to postpone or avoid justice. The list of functions of narration, witnessing, benchmarking, humanisation and empathy is almost identical to Sarat's (2001) analysis of the significance of the efforts of abolitionist lawyers when they defend their Death Row clients. Given this, it is surprising that he should be so down on Hollywood, which in effect attempted to relay the experiences that he had documented to a wider audience.

The death penalty films of 1990s Hollywood cinema talked about the use of capital punishment in contemporary America. Was anyone listening? From around 2000 public support for capital punishment began to fall as did the number of executions carried out. In January 2003 Governor George Ryan emptied Illinois' death row on leaving office—an action that would have been inconceivable only a few years earlier. There were obviously a number of factors and circumstances behind his decision and it is not being suggested that Governor Ryan watched a Clint Eastwood movie and suddenly decided that the death penalty was wrong. But it presumably must have been easier for him to make the decision if he thought that the tide had turned against the death penalty. The Hollywood death-penalty films of the 1990s (*Just Cause* being the exception) had extensively rehearsed the argument that the death penalty was arbitrary, capricious and therefore immoral. The arguments of the abolitionists were represented in film.

CONCLUSION

Has prison film tracked the US penal state? From *I Am a Fugitive From a Chain Gang* (1932) to *Brubaker* (1980) pure prison movies have acted as relayers of accounts of penal realities. The films acted as prison's voice to the wider society and tracked changing standards of decency. Other films have recorded that particular incidents took place. Prison riots are remembered in film. Whatever message these riot films suggested about the origins of such disturbances, or solutions to them, their mere existence signalled that all was not well within the penal system. It is not really fair to blame film for the growth in prison population. Since World War II most Western societies have demonstrated an increased willingness to incarcerate people. It may be a paradox of penal reform that as the prison becomes reformed, society becomes more willing to use it. Film has had less success in representing the expanded penal state. There are relatively few 'going-to-prison' movies and relatively few 'just-got-out-of-prison' movies. Those that have arisen have done so on the margins of film popularity. Hollywood film has had a fixation with the maximum security prison, whilst still failing adequately to represent the issue of super-max. The resurgence of the use of the death penalty in America was extensively reported and commented on in film. In conclusion then, film—in both its Hollywood form and its independent traditions—has tracked, albeit imperfectly, the US penal state. Film is a way of reporting and commenting on crime, prison and punishment. Sometimes the films which do not appeal to critics, theorists and analysts are the ones that do most good work in this regard. Opponents of prison growth cannot give up on Hollywood. Unless Hollywood makes films which report on and critique the expanding penal state then there is little chance of successfully opposing and reversing it.

FILMOGRAPHY for *Chapters 3* and *4*

1922	Manslaughter
1930	The Big House
1931	The Criminal Code
1932	I am a Fugitive from A Chain Gang
1932	Ladies of the Big House
1933	Ann Vickers
1939	Each Dawn I Die
1947	Brute Force
1950	Caged
1951	Inside the Walls of Folsom Prison
1952	My Six Convicts
1954	Riot in Cellblock 11
1955	Unchained
1955	Women's Prison
1957	Jailhouse Rock
1958	I Want to Live
1958	The Defiant Ones
1962	House of Women
1962	The Birdman of Alcatraz
1967	Cool Hand Luke
1968	Riot
1971	Big Doll House
1971	Fortune and Men's Eyes
1972	Sounder
1972	Steelyard Blues
1972	The Glasshouse (TVM)
1973	Attica (Documentary)
1973	The Sugarland Express
1973	Papillon
1973	Steelyard Blues
1974	The Mean Machine (a.k.a. The Longest Yard)
1976	Jackson County Jail
1976	Leadbelly
1977	Brothers
1978	On the Yard
1978	Midnight Express
1978	Straight Time
1979	Escape from Alcatraz
1979	The Jericho Mile (TVM)
1979	Penitentiary
1979	Short Eyes
1980	Attica (TVM)
1980	Brubaker
1981	Escape from New York
1985	Runaway Train

1987	Six Against the Rock (TVM)		1989	An Innocent Man
1989	Lock Up		1999	The Hurricane
1990	Death Warrant		2000	Animal Factory
1992	American Me		2000	The Yards
1992	Malcolm X		2001	The Last Castle
1993	Bound By Honor		2001	Stranger Inside
1994	Against the Wall		2001	Undisputed
1994	The Shawshank Redemption		2003	25th Hour
1995	Convict Cowboy (TVM)			
1995	Murder in the First			
1996	Escape from LA			
1996	Freeway			
1996	Sleepers			
1997	Con Air			
1997	Face/Off			
1998	American History X			
1998	He got Game			
1998	Slam			
1999	Brokedown Palace			
1999	A Map of the World			
1999	Life			

Death penalty films: 1990s

1993	Last Light (TVM)
1994	Witness to the Execution (TVM)
1995	Dead Man Walking
1995	Just Cause
1996	Last Dance
1996	The Chamber
1998	Letters from a Killer
1999	The Green Mile
1999	True Crime

CHAPTER 5

Origins and Intentions: In Praise of *Bad Girls*

First aired in June 1999, ITV's prime-time women's prison drama *Bad Girls* was, by the end of its second season, regularly gaining audiences of more than eight million viewers. In September 2003, as its fifth season came to a close, it was still achieving audiences of six million viewers, a more than creditable performance for a cult TV show at that stage in its life-cycle. The show is said to be popular across a wide range of age groups but particularly amongst younger viewers, with children as young as eleven either staying up to watch the programme, or videoing for later viewing. Whereas for a generation brought up in the 1970s the BBC situation comedy *Porridge* might be taken as constituting their baseline default televisual representation of prison, for the current generation this role is much more likely to be filled by *Bad Girls*. If televisual representations of prison influence people's implicit understandings of real life prisons and prisoners, then *Bad Girls* is a phenomenon which requires analysis and understanding. What implicit understandings of prisons and prisoners is the show likely to generate? And how might the implicit understanding of the *Bad Girls* generation differ to that of the *Porridge* generation?

Bad Girls is an hour-long, weekly show which depicts the lives of prisoners and staff at the fictitious HMP Larkhall, a women's prison located in south London. As the show is set for virtually its entirety within a women's prison, to call it a 'women's prison drama' would seem to be descriptively accurate and, as will be shown below, the programme does indeed draw eclectically on a variety of previously existing traditions of film and television prison drama. But having said this, in terms of style and structure, the programme equally has a lot in common with other 1990s cult TV series such as *Ally McBeal*, or even *The X-Files*. *Bad Girls* could quite reasonably be described as '*Ally McBeal* behind bars', a tag at least as fitting as the slightly disparaging and no more accurate—'*Brookside* in prison'. In eclectically combining aspects of soap opera, prime-time drama and cult-TV, *Bad Girls* emerges as a multifaceted show which delivers a variety of pleasures to its audience(s).

When we come to try and make sense of the show we need to recognise that no one 'owns' *Bad Girls*—not its fans, nor cultural studies academics and analysts, nor even its writers and producers. Its meaning(s) arise out of the interaction between its fan base and the 'text' which the show's producers provide the fans to work with. Having said this, the present chapter will go on to argue that *Bad Girls* is best understood as a more or less conscious attempt to 'speak the truth about prison'. It attempts to maintain a consistent, critical and informative perspective on prisons and prisoners and deploys a range of strategies to combine viewer pleasure with authorial purpose. The success of the show is, to a large extent, down to the creativity of its writers and producers in establishing and reinforcing synergy between these two aims.

One of the most novel aspects of *Bad Girls* across its first three seasons was the headline featuring of an on/off romantic relationship between Helen Stewart (initially the wing governor and then later in other positions of authority within Larkhall prison), and life-sentenced prisoner Nikki Wade. This in turn has generated some debate about the politics of sexuality at work in the programme (Herman, 2003). Whilst not disagreeing with some of the insights and analysis advanced by Herman, we consider that the novel representations of personal and sexual relations at work within the programme need to be understood in relation to the overall purpose of the show—to deliver a wide range of *inclusive* viewing pleasures, in order to maintain public interest in a dramatic product that seeks to 'speak the truth about prisons and prisoners'.

The success *Bad Girls* had in its first three seasons in achieving these aims enabled it to achieve the status of 'the best prison drama ever' although having said this, the programme is also a comment on the problem of sexual desire, an agenda which runs alongside the penal reform agenda of the show.

CULT TV IN THE 1990S

The prison dramas *Bad Girls* (ITV), *Buried* (C4) and *Oz* (HBO/C4) could all be said to be in some ways instances of 'cult TV', even though they differ significantly and do not qualify as 'cult' in a uniform manner. Nevertheless, it is worth considering the meaning of the term 'cult TV' and exploring some of the strategies used to create these shows in the 1990s. How are such shows constructed, why do they work and what they do? *Bad Girls* shares a number of similarities with *Ally McBeal* and *The X-files*, but has relatively little in common with *Star Trek* or *Dr Who*. So, in what sense is *Bad Girls* 'cult TV' and how might this tag help us to understand the show?

Different TV programmes can come to be considered as 'cult' in different ways. The first and most obvious meaning of the term 'cult' would be its quasi-religious meaning. A cult involves a small band of enthusiastic devotees worshipping their idea of a divine being. Cult TV programmes and cult films can also have similar characteristics. A TV programme or film is produced which at first fails to achieve mainstream success. But a small group of 'worshippers' see some merit in the product that others miss. They attempt to keep the show/film alive. Fans of cult movies call for them to be screened at cinemas—in earlier days as 'midnight movies'. With the advent of video, copies of cult movies come to be circulated between fans, who might perhaps call for such films to be officially re-released and re-promoted. Now it is possible to purchase any number of 'obscure classics' on the internet and to find whole websites devoted to particular films, or (sub)genres of films. In TV, fans of a show that originally flopped can call for its re-commissioning, or for its repeat or re-issue. Over time, the initial enthusiasts may succeed in building a mass base of recognition and support for their championed programme. This 'acquired cult status' is usually suggested to fit the life history of the series *Star Trek*. But not all cult TV programmes follow this pattern. The BBC's children's sci-fi show *Dr Who* was a mass popular hit from the outset and enjoyed an almost unparalleled run of unbroken, regular production. The programme has become cult given the interest amongst fans in revisiting earlier episodes, documenting its history, and assessing the philosophy implicit in the show, and so on. It is this fan activity that defines this mainstream TV success as cult. Science-fiction seems particularly suited to generating these 'interpretive communities' (compare also, *The Prisoner*).

One other current trend in cult TV is the rediscovery of the mainstream products of previous generations. TV shows from the 1970s, such as *The Sweeney* and *The Professionals*, have now become the object of fan activity even though many of the new fans are too young to be able to have seen these programmes when they were originally broadcast. Both of these shows were at the time of their creation regarded as cutting-edge, prime-time TV. *The Sweeney* in particular was seen as being a hard-edged look at real world policing. But these shows now are consumed in a much more ironic manner. They offer their viewers opportunities to laugh at 1970s hairstyles and fashions, and fans wait to see how long the characters can go without uttering one of their now famous catch phrases. Drama that was once taken seriously becomes the subject of new forms of consumption. Retro-cult TV is consumed with a degree of nostalgia, irony and playfulness.

So, TV shows can acquire cult status in a number of ways, and often independent of the original intentions of their producers. But perhaps the most interesting development in TV in the 1990s was the emergence of a host of programmes that seemed to have been made with the aim of achieving cult status in mind. These 'made-as-cult' TV products would include shows such as *The X-files, Ally McBeal, Due South, Northern Exposure* and *The Sopranos*. Again, all these programmes are quite different from each other and also it is not always clear where to draw the line between successful cult TV shows and more mainstream conventional dramas which also generate fan activity. But it is possible to identify some of the characteristics of these 'made-as-cult' products and suggest how they are consumed.

One thing that the 1990s made-as-cult TV shows seemed to share was a tendency to construct present day set fantasy worlds. Made-as-cult TV shows take the real world and change it in some significant respect. They operate from a premise which plays with reality and so allows them to seem fresh and innovative. So for example, *The X-Files* is America 'as if' the people who say they have been abducted by aliens are right, and those who do not believe them are in the wrong. Having FBI agents Mulder and Scully, who are conventional in dress and appearance, investigate the supernatural and the extra-terrestrial, made the *X-Files* into 'a cop show with a twist'. *Ally McBeal* represents the proposition of 'what if' the worst fears and nightmares of an insecure twenty-something that she will never find happiness, contentment or romantic success and that Hollywood and her parents lied about love, marriage and Father Christmas, turned out to be true? In Ally's world the worst possible scenario is the reality and romantic success proves elusive.

The cult TV shows of the 1990s gained success because they seemed fresh and innovative. Starting from interesting premises, producers developed a style of pushing premises to the limit. Always having the characteristic of being 'the absurd done deadpan', producers delighted in how far they could push the fans of their shows without losing them entirely. Story arcs can twist and turn unpredictably and the plausibility of the plots—or the characters behaviour within them—is never an issue. Although always apparently set in a recognisable contemporary real world, the shows rejected the notion that they need in anyway represent it faithfully. In *Ally, The X-files,* and *Due South* we are operating in a chaotic and disordered world, where anything can and does happen.

But does the emergence of the made-as-cult formula have any particular social significance? Why did the 1990s see the emergence of these shows and what if anything is their significance? One cynical view would be to suggest that TV producers simply became adept at manufacturing products that would engage and amuse audiences, who had become too familiar with traditional genres and dramatic structures. When the traditional cop show, in which heroic detectives always solve the case has been seen in all its varieties, then more radical variation is needed simply to keep viewers engaged and amused. The cult TV shows are consumed very much with a degree of playfulness and although they might generate extensive internet discussions pondering their meaning and significance, it could be argued that, at the end of the day, they have no deep meaning, or significance.

But despite their playful and non-serious stance the shows in question do raise issues about the basic beliefs that underpin society. *Ally McBeal* questioned and problematised the idea that romantic success and finding your 'one true love' was the path to happiness. Ally's problem is that she believes life is like a classic Hollywood movie, with true love and Christmases, when in fact it is not. *The X-files* raised questions about the nature of science and knowledge, and of how we know what we know. The show advanced a view of knowledge that privileged direct personal experience over the knowledge of detached objective experts. Alien abductees can quite seriously be seen as a metaphor for any number of survivor groups who complain that their accounts of their experience are not being believed.

Both individually and collectively the made-as-cult successes of the 1990s raised issues not addressed in conventional dramas. They also did this in a style unlike conventional drama. They could be said to be characterised by generic uncertainty and this makes it more difficult to read their meaning and message. Given that the shows quite openly proclaim that they feel no need to approximate slavishly to 'the real world', is there any point in criticising them for their failure do so? One interesting example is the case of the treatment of race and racism in *Ally McBeal*. Throughout its life the show consistently portrayed Ally's world in non-racial terms. Ally enjoyed relationships with several African-American friends or partners, but never once were race or racism raised as an issue. The show was criticised for this on the basis that, much as we might wish for a non-racial America, given that race and racism does exist how can the show justify airbrushing it out of existence? In response to this, the show's creator David E. Kelly simply confirmed that it was an intentional decision that *Ally* would never introduce racism as an issue between the characters and reaffirmed that whilst racism might exist in the real world, it did not and would not in Ally's. The same show again suffered from journalistic comment pondering its gender message. Ally is shown to wear short skirts, fall over a lot, be terminally insecure and hung up about finding Mr Right. On the face of it this would seem to be something of a feminists' nightmare, as Ally does not seem to be an ideal role model for women. But as Ally herself said, she 'ain't no role model' and people who read the show too literally will have problems comprehending why so many women enjoyed it.

One of the key characteristics of the US made-as-cult TV shows was the manner in which they turned their backs on an attempt to comment on reality directly. They engaged in a debate with the myths and beliefs that inform our understanding of reality, rather than with reality itself. TV commented on the ideas that had been purveyed by film and TV from the era of Hollywood cinema to the present. This brings us back to *Bad Girls*. We do not suggest that the series simply took up a model derived from the US cult successes. But the show did take something of the style and structure of cult TV and combine it eclectically with styles and techniques derived from soap opera and prime-time drama. This eclectic mix gives it the same generic uncertainty that characterised the shows discussed above. But, is *Bad Girls* playful or serious, or both? And is this eclectic mix intended to comment on a real world referent—prison in contemporary society? Although the show can be located within the various versions of 'cult TV' advanced above, prison and particularly women's experience of prison, would seem to be an important part of its construction. Arguably, without understanding prison drama and its relationship to its real world referent—prison—we cannot really understand what is going on in *Bad Girls*.

WOMEN'S PRISON DRAMA

Women's prison drama has something of a bad reputation in critical and academic circles. In both film and TV the serious attempts at depicting women's experience of prison that do exist are not taken that seriously by critics, or analysts. In film, women's prison drama is said to be dominated by a genre of women-in-prison (babes-behind-bars) exploitation movies. Attempts at serious prison drama are often seen as unwittingly reproducing the conventions of the exploitation versions of the genre. There are relatively few attempts at serious analysis of women's prison drama (see Morey (1995) on women's prison movies of the 1950s; Nellis (1993) on the life and work of Joan Henry—below, Curthoys and Docker (1989) on *Prisoner Cell Block H*; and Herman (2003) provides some additional references on lesbian scholarship on the women-in-prison genre). To an extent this reaction is understandable. Some of the earlier examples of serious women's prison dramas are difficult to locate and without access to the films it is difficult to assess them. It is probably also the case that the products of serious women's prison drama do share the same generic conventions as clichéd reform schoolgirls genre-pics, exploitation movies and parodies of exploitation movies.

We can specify the problem more clearly by considering Marsha Clowers' (2001) analysis of three examples of women-in-prison-pics and an episode of *Charlie's Angels*. She found that all four items had an almost identical structure. In each a young attractive heroine-to-be is admitted, on questionable grounds, to a correctional facility. Once there she quickly discovers that prisoners within the facility are being abused by other prisoners and staff. The recurring characters are: an evil Warden/chief of guards who organizes, or at least condones the abuse; a predatory prisoner who preys on weaker prisoners and cooperates with the institutional abusers; and a victim who suffers abuse and who at some time will suffer death, or a serious injury which provokes a revolt against the corrupt regime. The heroine organizes and leads the revolution and the film ends with either the prisoners fleeing the institution leaving it in flames, or winning some official battle against the corrupt authorities (Clowers, 2001). Following Clowers, we can suggest that this same formula emerges in out and out exploitation movies, through to an episode of a mainstream 1970s TV series *Charlie's Angels*, and to contemporary made for TV movies which claim to be fact-based dramas commenting on the real world abuse of women within US correctional institutions (for example *Prison of Secrets*). How should we understand these dramatic products? Which of them are attempts to provide a 'voice' to 'allow prison to talk to us', and which are merely commercial products pandering to voyeuristic tastes?

Origins and intentions: *The Weak and the Wicked* **and** *Prisoner Cellblock H*
A key argument advanced by this book is that prison survives because the general public systematically underestimate the awfulness of prison, a quality that in some ways can only really be appreciated by direct personal experience. The public also fail to appreciate the futility of prison as an institution that will as often confirm people in their patterns of offending behaviour as much as it changes them. But how can the public come to be aware of these issues?

One of the main ways in which prison can achieve a 'voice' is when people who have experienced it speak out most often in the form of writing, or undertaking public speaking about their experiences. We have previously suggested that the figure of the middle-class prisoner turned penal reformer is significant in this respect. Saying this is not to disparage the writings or penal reform efforts of working-class ex-prisoners. Rather it is based on an appreciation that middle-class prisoners can experience prison as a slightly more intense consciousness raising experience. After all middle-class people benefit more than working-class people from the existing arrangements of society and their small degree of class privilege encourages them to have faith in the legitimacy of social institutions. The experience of serving a prison sentence is one that can drastically revise such perceptions. But, having experienced prison as a consciousness raising experience does not necessarily imply that the middle-class ex-prisoner will automatically take up the cause of penal reform. Indeed their most rational strategy would be to repudiate, or distance themselves from their status as an 'ex-con' and attempt to regain whatever class privilege and status they had previously enjoyed. The fact that some choose not to do this makes such people significant witnesses to the irrationality of prison.

For a variety of reasons discussed below, women's experience of prison can have a particular significance for raising the issue of the irrationality of prison. Women who have experienced prison can become a force for penal reform, but the problem is how they might best relay their understanding of their experience to the widest audience possible. One example already discussed in *Chapter 2* is the case of Joan Henry. In the early 1950s she had been sentenced to a year's imprisonment for a minor fraud (the film of her experience represents her as being technically innocent but morally guilty). After serving her sentence Henry wrote *Who Lie in Gaol*, a first hand account of her experiences. The book, which caused something of a sensation on its release, became a best-seller and was widely regarded as an authoritative account of women's prison conditions and later became the basis for the film adaptation, *The Weak and the Wicked* for which Henry acted as an advisor.

The film is in some ways faithful to the intentions of the book to give a revelatory account of women's prison conditions, although it toned down the book's representation of the conditions within Holloway Prison (HMP Blackdown in the film). The book for example had claimed that younger prisoners were sexually exploited by older female staff (Nellis, 1993: 45). This does not make it into the film in explicit form, except that in one scene a female prison officer briefly watches a young prisoner before turning away and moving on. This scene could hint at potential predatory behaviour. Other than this, the film provides a kind of template for women's prison drama. There is a fight (a brief scuffle) between the lead protagonist and another prisoner. There is a bathing scene when the women are first inducted. The prison is depicted as strict and the potential for unpleasant prison officers to harass prisoners hinted at. The prisoner culture is indicated to be torn between a tendency towards solidarity and mutual support, and a divisiveness that arises from different backgrounds and personalities in a hostile environment. The film also portrays the potential for genuine supportive friendships to emerge between prisoners. When the lead character, Jean, and her friend, Betty, transfer to The Grange open prison the film suggests a possibility for cross-class sisterhood as the progressive middle-class Governor and Jean combine in their efforts to save Betty going down a path to delinquency. The film certainly contains the idea of a middle-class woman learning from her experience and leaving prison with a changed view of prisons and prisoners.

Interestingly, although *The Weak and the Wicked* is a fairly tame film, which stays well within the bounds of respectability, its publicity highlighted the 'convicts-in-skirts' aspects of the film. The publicity posters suggest a slightly more raunchy examination of the topic of women in prison than the film delivers. But arguably, the film tones down the account given by Henry and should have included more of an examination of the conflict between prisoners and staff and the potential for abusive behaviour. Ironically, more freedom to tell the story of prison as it is would have led to the inclusion of more of the elements which are seen as the clichés of the voyeuristic women-in-prison genre!

This problem of representing prison as it is, producing dramatic products that are seen as clichéd, also affected the later long-running Australian TV women's prison drama *Prisoner Cell Block H*. Curthoys and Docker (1989), chart some of the history of the show and suggest that the idea for a women's prison drama emerged in the Grundy TV company in the late 1970s. At the time Australian prisons had been subject to a degree of unrest and public scrutiny. A Royal Commission had recently reported on prison conditions and feminist and prison activist groups had come together to mount an eventually successful campaign to free Australia's longest serving female prisoner. Against this background, the Grundy network commissioned a women's prison drama to be made. The team developing the show spent nine months researching it, reading the official reports on prison, visiting women's prisons and talking to staff and prisoners. Some interviews with prisoners became the source of storylines. The show was intended to be a serious, realistic examination of prison.

From the research a number of features emerged. Firstly, that the majority of women in prison were not hardened criminals but were there for minor offences such as non-payment of bills, drug-related offences, petty theft and so forth. They were often people who just needed a little bit of help and support to get their life together. Secondly, women prisoners and ex-prisoners interviewed were agreed that unpleasant staff, who would deliberately make life difficult for prisoners, were an aspect of prison life and that women with relatively short sentences could have these lengthened as a result of defending themselves against oppressive officers. The third point made was that sexual activity within women's prisons was relatively common. A variety of lesbian relationships existed amongst prisoners, and also sexual relations between staff and prisoners were a characteristic of prison life. In a bid for realism the programme decided that it would include these aspects of prison life.

Prisoner Cell Block H (more commonly known simply as *Prisoner* in Australia) went on to become a highly successful, long-running show featuring a changing cast of a diverse range of strong women. But it never really enjoyed critical success and rapidly gained a 'so bad it's good' tag. A show which had serious intentions quickly came to be regarded by some as 'unwittingly hilarious'. In the UK *Prisoner* was shown as late night TV and carried a slightly naff 'cult TV' tag. A programme that had intended to give 'voice' to prison, came to be seen as the archetypical camped-up cliché. This matters to the extent that it undercuts the ability of the show to educate and inform.

INTRODUCING *BAD GIRLS*

The discussion below analyses *Bad Girls* seasons 1—3 as it appears on the DVD boxed sets currently available. Season 4 of the programme is also available on DVD and season 5 was being broadcast at the time of writing. The first three seasons are chosen for analysis as they constitute a fairly coherent exposition of the nature of the show and follow its original main story arc from its inception through to some kind of conclusion. The discussion here is based mainly on a viewing of the episodes in question and attempts to provide an analysis of the strategies used by the show in its approach to representing women's experience of prison. It is beyond the scope of this discussion to research systematically the ways in which the viewers of *Bad Girls* receive and consume the product.

Bad Girls is very self-consciously a women's prison drama—in two senses. Firstly, the structure of the programme and the choice of topics for inclusion make it quite clear that show is intended as making some comment on real life experiences of incarceration. The programme attempts to say something about prison. But secondly, the producers and writers seem to be acutely aware that women's prison dramas have been done before, and that they are entering a field littered with baggage. The series develops an original and novel approach to dramatising prison so as to achieve its aim of delivering a wide range of *inclusive* viewing pleasures, to maintain public interest in a dramatic product that seeks to 'speak the truth'.

We have suggested previously that the popularity of prison dramas can be overstated. It is rarely the case that simply 'telling the story of prison' will make an entertaining dramatic product. Prison dramas need to 'bribe' their viewers to engage with any account of the reality of prison and any dramatic product that seeks to 'give voice to prison', must also deliver viewing pleasures. *Bad Girls* is much more explicit than previous prison dramas in its understanding of this pleasure/purpose bargain. It quite unashamedly does a 'deal' with its viewers—we provide you with viewing pleasures in return for which you accept that we have some things we want to say about prisons and prisoners. One of the innovations is to separate out more explicitly the 'entertainment' components of the show from its 'message moments'. At any one time the show will be running storylines intended primarily to engage viewer interest and to 'entertain', and at the same time will include storylines or scenes which are intended to carry a 'message'. This separation of 'entertainment' and 'message' is never total and indeed one of the key achievements of the show has been its ability to make the 'message' elements as entertaining and as engaging as those 'played for fun'

Character-types and the hierarchy of seriousness

Our contention is that *Bad Girls* is, at heart, an incredibly serious show. It is drama with a serious purpose. But its strategy for achieving this purpose is to produce an eclectic mix of the 'cartoonish', 'the camp' and the serious. The show juxtaposes the serious and the 'cartoonish' and this is its main strength. We need first to describe how this strategy of juxtaposition operates and then say how it functions to further the aims of the show. *Bad Girls* works with four basic kinds of character types, although some characters may fall between, or move between these types. We can identify: 'pantomime baddies' (Fenner, Shell) and goodies (the two Julies); 'soap opera players' (Yvonne, Di Barker, Maxi); players in a 'prime-time drama' (Helen Stewart, Nikki Wade); and 'dramatic approximations' (definitely Zandra, possibly Shaz). These character types are distinguished partly by the seriousness with which we are intended to take their behaviour and also their roles within the narrative. All character types interact in a variety of ways and no one type serves only one function. However, we can still identify why the types exist.

Firstly, the characters of Shell and Fenner are easily identifiable as 'pantomime baddies'. Their role as villains is to motivate conflict within the show. *Bad Girls* recognises that a women's prison drama without a predatory 'screw' would not be a women's prison drama. We need to have one, and so a decision is made to play the part to excess. Fenner's consistently over-the-top evilness is not intended as a comment on real world prison officers. Shell (not [Mi]'Chelle') is similarly a pantomime baddie. The conventions of women-in-prison drama demand that there be a predatory bully amongst the prisoners, who collaborates with the authorities. The Shell/Fenner relationship is played mainly for dramatic entertainment, more so than it is intended as a comment on the functioning of real world prisons. Fenner also provides a foil for Helen Stewart—arguably this relationship is also played mainly for 'entertainment' not 'message', although other interpretations of this would be possible. Helen's real adversary within the prison is actually Sylvia Hollamby, whose constant carping and old school approach to prison officer work creates many of the problems Helen has to pick up, and which undermine Helen's reformist intentions.

Hollamby is probably best thought of as being a 'soap opera player'. Her character is played for fun but not quite in the same way as Shell or Fenner.

Sylvia's attitude to her job is intended to carry more meaning than Fenner's deviousness and plotting. Sylvia consistently displays old school attitudes, which lead to the unsympathetic treatment of prisoners and which cause a lot of the problems in the prison (everything from Carol's miscarriage in season one, episode one to the Femi incident which indirectly led to a riot in season three, episode eleven). Sylvia is intended, in a humorous way, to be indicative of one approach to prison officer work that was prevalent in prisons in the past and may still be present today.

The character of Yvonne Atkins is a different kind of 'soap opera player'. Her main function is as a locus for storylines. She is the main instigator of scams and schemes (e.g. babes-behind-bars) and is seen as the 'top dog' of G wing. Her struggles with Renee Williams—whom she kills through anaphylactic shock, the Peckham gang and Fenner are mainly dramatic. They give the viewer a story to follow through the eyes of a character whom they identify with. She also carries meaning in generally being one of the ensemble of players who contribute to the possibility of G wing being a mutually supportive group of prisoners with rich girl Charlotte Myddleton (in season three, episodes nine and ten), carrying a meaning of cross-class, gender solidarity which is intended as a comment on one aspect of women's experience of prison.

The characters of Helen Stewart and Nikki can be identified as players in a 'prime-time drama'. By appearance and behaviour they and their story-arc are connoted as to be taken more seriously than the storylines involving Yvonne (babes-behind-bars, the Renee Williams 'poisoning'). But they are still players in a drama. The Helen/Nikki relationship is intended to provide viewer pleasure. It takes the viewers 'somewhere they have not been before'. It is doubtful that *Bad Girls* is trying to tell us something here—that in women's nicks up and down the country female wing governors are becoming enmeshed in professionally dubious relationships with their life-sentenced prisoners. The Helen/Nikki relationship is a neat subversion of a possible characteristic of the women-in-prison genre. Where previous women's prison dramas (*Cell Block H*) may have had a minor subplot featuring a 'con-lover', 'screw' and prisoner conducting a clandestine relationship fearing discovery, *Bad Girls* takes the minor sub-plot and turns it into the headline main story arc. Although the Helen and Nikki relationship seems to have been a major source of viewer pleasure for fans of the show, the main reason for giving these two players higher status in the hierarchy of seriousness is to allow them to carry 'message', with Nikki acting as articulator of legitimate grievances about the management of the prison and reform-minded Helen attempting to respond to these within the constraints of the authority structure. In season three Helen was allowed some minor victories in being able to demonstrate how a prison should be run. Both Helen and Nikki are dramatic characters who carry message, but are not necessarily intended to be 'realist' depictions of prison staff and prisoners.

The last character type might be termed 'dramatic approximation'. The best example is Zandra although Shaz could possibly qualify in this category too. Zandra carried a major storyline from season one, episode two through too season two, episode nine. Zandra enters Larkhall as a drug addict and briefly succeeds in kicking her habit during the time of her pregnancy. After losing custody of her baby she briefly returns to drugs before again kicking her habit with the support and encouragement of her personal officer Dominic McAlister. Just as she is beginning to get her life back in order it becomes apparent that she has a life threatening illness which eventually proves terminal. Zandra is portrayed as being a minor offender who has taken the fall on a drugs rap for her boyfriend and for whom prison is not really an appropriate response to her problems. Thanks to some good work by Dominic she begins to sort out her life although fate conspires to rob her of her happy ending. Zandra is intended to be a dramatic representation of the kind of person who can come to be (inappropriately) incarcerated in British prisons today. Zandra's story arc contains a degree of dramatic licence (the baby on the roof incident, her terminal brain tumour) however the function of the dramatic representation is not to recreate 'the real' but to generate insight into and empathy with 'the real'. In showing that Zandra's life could have been different, the storyline succeeded in achieving this aim.

So, it is being suggested that: Shell/Fenner and the two Julies; Yvonne/Maxi/Di Barker; Nikki and Helen; and Zandra represent qualitatively different kinds of characters. Most of the other characters fall somewhere between these types, or are difficult to place. Di Barker has been identified as a 'soap opera player' but in her obsessive stalker mode she moves nearer to being a 'pantomime baddie'. And, as has already been suggested, none of these types carries only one function. Nevertheless we still need to recognise that there is a difference between the antics of Fenner (who is to Larkhall as JR was to *Dallas*) and, say, the behaviour of Sylvia Hollamby. With a multitude of different characters, playing different roles and carrying different storylines, each interacting with each other on a number of fronts, *Bad Girls* creates an ongoing eclectic juxtaposition. But how is this put together and why does it work?

The first five minutes and subsequent events in season one, episode one
The very first episode begins with an opening title, 'Bad Girls'. Then the music soundtrack comes in—a re-mix of the Bee Gees' hit 'Staying Alive'. We see women in costume dancing in some kind of disco/nightclub setting. Where are we? In the prison or outside it? Cut to a woman in a room, in some kind of pain and distress. Back to the 'night club' scene. The character we come to know as Denny is dancing in some kind of Wonder Woman costume. The title of the episode comes up: 'Them and Us'. Cut back to the woman in pain, who is seen to be wearing a nightdress and appears to be bleeding. Cut back to Shell in costume, cut back to a hand reaching up, then cut back to Shell (wearing a black wig) and then back to the woman in pain, who sits up alone in a bare room. Back to the opening scene and then the lights come up and the prison officers move in. We are in the prison and have been watching the girls rehearsing for their upcoming fashion show. Some banter ensues as the women are informed that rehearsal is over and its time for 'bang-up'.

As the rehearsal ends and the participants file out we are introduced to several characters: Shell (blond after removing her wig); Rachel and the two Julies who give prison officer Dominic McAlister a mild ribbing as he encourages them back to their cell. Rachel, who has seemed uneasy throughout, is first threatened by Denny on behalf of Shell; and then briefly visited in her cell by the character we come to know as Fenner, apparently the senior prison officer. As the women are ushered back to their cells a prisoner, Nikki, tries to get to Carol (the woman we have previously seen in distress) to check on her, but she is turned back by prison officer Sylvia Hollamby. Carol calls for Nikki and then asks Sylvia for a doctor, informing her that she is bleeding. Sylvia turns down her request for medical assistance. Reassuring fellow prison officer Lorna that there is no problem, she leaves her shift complaining loudly about the lot of a prison officer. Carol miscarries in her cell.

This opening sequence carries an incredible amount of information which we the viewers internalise and appreciate with total ease. Subsequent events confirm and develop our understanding of what we have witnessed. Whilst Helen Stewart, the wing governor in charge of the section of the prison where these events have taken place, is making her way to work, at morning unlock prison officer Dominic McAlister discovers the unconscious body of Carol covered with blood in her cell. Sylvia tries to cover up the event and halts the unlock to organize the evacuation of Carol and a cleaning of the blood covered cell. The two Julies (characters low in the hierarchy of seriousness) are called to clean the cell and they relay news of the tragedy to other prisoners. Cut to Helen Stewart's office, where the wing governor is giving Sylvia a dressing down for allowing the incident to happen. Senior officer Jim Fenner defends Sylvia, referring to the event as being 'just a tragic set of circumstances'. Helen decides to meet with the women on the wing to assure them that she shares their concerns, but the meeting backfires with prisoner Nikki leading a very vocal protest against Helen who, unable to prove Sylvia's negligence, is forced to use Jim's words that the event was 'just a tragic set of circumstances'. The confrontation ends with the fashion show being cancelled and Helen putting Nikki on Rule 43 (now Rule 45)—segregation in the punishment block; an injustice compounding an injustice, given that Helen sympathises with Nikki's concerns and agrees with her version of events.

UNDERSTANDING *BAD GIRLS*

From the very outset *Bad Girls* signalled to its viewers what kind of programme it was and what they could expect to get out of it. It almost immediately identified itself as a women's prison drama and was entirely knowing of the fact that such programmes have been made before and have certain conventions. The rehearsal for the fashion show signalled that in a women's prison drama we can expect elements of 'camp fun'. The ending of the rehearsal and lock-up set up the element of girls in a residential institution attempting to subvert and resist the authorities that run it. Even at this early stage recognisable character types were being introduced as described above—all clichéd conventions of the women-in-prison genre (see Clowers, 2001). But the 'cartoonish' nature of Shell and the inclusion of the 'pantomime goodies'—the two Julies—let us know that we were not meant to take certain aspects too seriously.

This self-deprecating element is easily recognisable, and leads to *Bad Girls* sometimes being referred to as being 'cartoonish'—which in some instances it undoubtedly is. But we need to return immediately to the opening two minutes of the episode where, interspersed with the rehearsal for the fashion show are the cutbacks to Carol miscarrying in her cell. These and subsequent events signal serious purpose and intent. We the viewers are able to see an injustice when Sylvia refuses Carol medical assistance and then later attempts to cover up the outcome. The privileged position we, the viewers, enjoy when we watch this event and subsequent reactions to it clearly aligns us with the preferred interpretation that we have witnessed an injustice. Our knowledge of these events has been set up to make it hard for us to resist that reading. Sylvia's lies and Jim's 'tragic set of circumstances' explanation ring hollow. We align ourselves with the Helen/Nikki view of events. And as even at this early stage Helen and Nikki are represented as being attractive characters that we might want to 'buy into' this makes it difficult for us not to align ourselves with their view of events and the interpretation that we have, in fact, witnessed an injustice. But more than this, the programme has somehow succeeded in raising the question, 'Why do bad things happen in prison and can they be prevented?'

This strategy of eclectic juxtaposition is original to *Bad Girls*, although elements of it can be seen at work in other made-as-cult TV programmes of the 1990s. We might suggest here that there is no particular significance to the fact that it is the two Julies who first become aware of Carol's tragedy and relay the news to Nikki, although it does signal that in *Bad Girls* even 'non-serious' characters can be used to advance serious storylines. It also shows that the two Julies exist as part of a larger unit, the prisoner group, which includes serious characters like Nikki, and the prison which includes Helen. Each of the different character types interact and mesh unproblematically as part of a greater whole and the audience seem to have no problem in accepting the eclectic mix. Indeed, part of the pleasure for the viewer is the fact that they are being offered this novel representational strategy. *Bad Girls* offers its audience the opportunity to watch a parody of a women-in-prison movie, a soap opera and a prime-time drama all at the same time and to utilise the viewing skills appropriate to appreciating each individually and in combination. The programme also retains the ability to surprise its viewers should they begin to take too much for granted or to predict how the storylines might develop.

Prison drama: strategies of representation
To understand why *Bad Girls* opted for its strategy of eclectic juxtaposition and to identify what it achieves we can consider the problems and limitations of other strategies of representing prison as evidenced in the examples of *Porridge* and *Scum*. Whereas the first is a situation comedy, the second seems to have been intended as 'social realist' drama. These two products exhibit complementary deficiencies in their attempts to represent prison. In *Porridge* the situation comedy format is used to generate humour out of the conflict between 'screws' and prisoners. Authority is represented as being pompous and in need of deflating—particularly in the form of senior prison officer McKay. We find it easy to ally ourselves with the attempts of the prisoners to survive the institution and 'get one over' on the authorities. In this way *Porridge* can succeed in generating empathy with the prisoner. We can come to 'care' about what happens to Godbar and to wish him well for his life after he leaves Slade Prison. But because of the style of comedy adopted, it is difficult for *Porridge* to raise serious issues. In one episode early on in the first series Fletcher counsels Godbar that the way to survive a prison stretch is to think of every night of bang-up as

one where, instead of going out uptown, one has simply opted for 'a quite night in'. This theme of 'a quite night in' is returned to throughout the episode during which not much else happens. This arguably is one of the least successful episodes in *Porridge* as it lacks the fizz of the more humorous episodes centred around the contest between Fletcher and senior prison officer Mackay. *Porridge* 'cannot do serious' and though it can create an element of empathy with prisoners, who we might hope will return to a productive life after prison, it cannot give its viewers an idea of prison as a bad place, to be used as a last resort.

Whereas *Porridge* can be funny but not serious, *Scum* is the other way around. Produced in the 1970s, *Scum* attempted to act as a revelatory critique of the state of the borstal system. It showed that borstals were far from perfectly functioning institutions and revealed them as having incompetent and uncaring staff who allowed bullying and male rape and failed to prevent suicide. A lot of the violence in *Scum* is intended to act as a critique of the borstal institution by showing that intimidation and bullying are not an aberration but an intrinsic part of the regime. But, although some of the violence in *Scum* has a purpose and is intended to carry 'message', violence is also the dramatic hook or viewing pleasure that the film offers to its (male) audience. The ability of lead protagonist Carlin to outwit the authorities and subdue his fellow prisoners through skilfully executed violence is the main viewing pleasure of the show (see *Chapters* 2 and 8 for further discussion). In portraying prison as a Darwinian struggle for the 'survival of the fittest', *Scum*'s ability to transmit message is undermined by the fact that anything included to reveal the awfulness of the institution has the potential to become just part of the hostile environment within which the anti-hero main protagonist has to struggle.

Bad Girls avoids the problems associated with these earlier prison dramas. It includes *Porridge* type storylines (making home brew in the prison) and similarly aligns the viewer against authority. But as this is only one aspect of the show it leaves other parts of its eclectic combination free to do other kinds of work. *Bad Girls* is more successful than *Scum* in establishing the illegitimacy and petty injustices of prison. This is partly because of the manner in which it separates out 'message' from entertainment. Scenes and storylines which are intended to connote injustice are clearly flagged up as such and where possible are anchored so as to make alternative interpretations of them difficult (Carol's miscarriage, Dr No No's incompetence, etc.). Like *Scum*, *Bad Girls* has a struggle for the position of 'top dog' within the inmate culture, but we are usually aware of which characters are dispatched as part of the Darwinian struggle for survival, an entertainment storyline (e.g. Renee Williams, Virginia O'Kane) and which characters' deaths or adverse occurrences are intended to carry 'message' (Zandra's medical treatment, Carol's miscarriage).

Whereas virtually all prison dramas rhetorically take the side of the prisoners against the oppression of the authorities, *Bad Girls* is probably the only one ever to uncompromisingly and consistently construct itself from the point of view that (women) prisoners understand and appreciate the irrationality and futility of (women's) prisons more than anyone else. In the first two seasons good prison staff (Helen and Dominic) are repeatedly shown to hand down bad decisions and to unwillingly collude in injustice. This said, as the show developed it allowed Helen to experience a learning process and by its third season became slightly more optimistic about whether prisons can be reformed.

Representing prison and prisoners
Bad Girls can be seen as an attempt to give voice to prisons and prisoners. What did it have to say on their behalf? Is prison a necessary and useful part of the criminal justice system? Who gets sent to prison and why? Is prison necessary to protect society from dangerous criminals? What is the trajectory of people who experience prison—will prison have made a difference to their offending behaviour? *Bad Girls* continually comments on these issues and generally concludes that, as far as women are concerned, for a surprising proportion of prisoners prison is not an appropriate response to their problems, or their offending behaviour. 'I shouldn't be here' is a recurring refrain from some of the prisoners of Larkhall prison. When 'posh bitch', Monica Lyndsey arrives at Larkhall one of the first things she says is just that. By the end of the season she is cleared by the Appeal Court and freed thereby proving her initial assessment to be true. The difference between a prison sentence and freedom is whether the prisoner can be motivated and supported to keep fighting their appeal. The same is true for Nikki Wade, for whom the difference between a discretionary life sentence and being freed by the Court of Appeal is the same need for motivation and support. Although Nikki has committed a fairly serious crime she is not particularly dangerous and if freed would presumably be unlikely to find herself in similar circumstances. Zandra, it appears, is a drug addict who became involved in dealing to support her habit and has apparently taken the fall for her boyfriend on a drugs bust. Although she does eventually come off drugs in prison, her view of prison is that drugs are necessary to survive there and that prison is, therefore, the last place you would want to send someone with a drug habit. Prison is shown to isolate her from the things that could help her to reintegrate into society.

Once in prison there is a tendency for prisoners to be treated in terms of labels. Zandra is labelled a drug addict and is therefore thought to be incapable of any change or progress. When she becomes ill her symptoms are at first ascribed to her history of drug use and even supportive Dominic on occasion fails to believe Zandra when she says that she is 'off the drugs'. Similarly, when mild mannered Barbara Hunt exhibits symptoms of distress, as a result of claustrophobia she is wrongly booked into Larkhall as 'mad Tessa Spall'. Her protests that there has been a mistake fall on deaf ears as she spends a weekend down the block before the mistake is realised and there are any number of other instances when labelling someone turns out to be a self-fulfilling prophecy. Unsympathetic staff attitudes, labelling and inflexibility are shown to create more problems than they solve.

Can prison be reformed? In its first and second seasons *Bad Girls* displayed a fair degree of scepticism as to whether prisons can be improved. Well-intentioned Helen Stewart was on several occasions seen to hand down, or collude with bad decisions because of the constraints on her within the prison culture and authority structure. Helen starts out quite naïve about prison, for example, initially thinking that the problem of drugs in prison can be tackled by trying to halt them coming in—a view which Nikki informs her is just plain ridiculous. Helen's well intentioned efforts to control the supply of drugs are shown only to make the situation worse. In the second season Helen returns to run the lifer's group. She is able to encourage Nikki to take up degree education and to kick-start the appeal process that leads to Nikki's eventual release. Helen reviews the lifer's sentence plans and does useful work with Shaz on confronting her offending behaviour.

In the third season Helen starts to achieve some small victories. She is able to get the incompetent Dr No No sacked, and has a success when she demonstrates that, with appropriate medication, Pam who has spent a long period of time on the psychiatric wing, can return to functioning sufficiently to cope on G wing, and to contemplate an eventual move to an open prison. This is one of the few occasions when Nikki credits Helen with being right, whilst admitting that she, Nikki, was wrong. At around the same time a new Nigerian prisoner, Femi, is struggling to cope in the prison due to her lack of language skills and unsympathetic treatment from prison officers such as Sylvia Hollamby. Although the women of G wing try to support Femi, there is little that they can do to solve the basic problem. After an altercation with Sylvia, Femi is physically 'restrained' by a group of prison officers and sent down the block. This causes a degree of consternation amongst Nikki and some of the other prisoners. Unbeknownst to them, Helen arranges a telephone conferencing interpreting session and is able to begin to resolve the problem. Unfortunately, understanding of Helen's successful intervention does not reach the prisoners in time to head off a protest that turns into a riot. Nevertheless Helen's handling of the incident puts a strong case that providing an appropriate service is the most effective form of prison management. There are other significant incidences in the series when support from prison officers can be seen to make an actual, or potential difference to the lives of prisoners.

One of the other main themes of *Bad Girls* is the idea of a women's prison as potentially providing a mutually supportive inmate culture, which can be a basis of prison as a consciousness raising experience for middle-class women. The Monica storyline in season one is the perfect illustration of this theme. Middle-class Monica 'Posh Bitch' Lyndsay, serves time in prison and comes to realise that most prisoners are ordinary, warm supportive people many of whom are getting a raw deal from society and from the Prison Service. On the steps of the Court of Appeal she says so and later goes on to run a half-way house for women leaving prison. This theme was revisited, perhaps less successfully, in the case of Barbara Hunt and then again in miniature in the Charlotte/Yvonne storyline in season three. The portrayal of G wing, Larkhall as a potentially supportive environment helps to humanise prisoners; it turns 'criminals' into people who have faces and a history, creating empathy between the public and the screen representations of prisoners. One of the key questions arising from *Bad Girls* is whether seeing the consciousness raising effect of prison on Monica, Barbara and Charlotte enables the viewer to participate vicariously in that process. Does televisual representation allow us to gain the 'benefits' of a prison sentence without actually having to serve one? This is a question that could be investigated empirically if the right methodology could be devised. What impact has *Bad Girls* had on the implicit understandings of prisons and prisoners held by its viewers? More particularly we could ask: what careers will the 11-18 year olds who have watched the show since its inception go into? What attitudes will they carry with them?

What we cannot know simply from analysing the text of *Bad Girls* is how its messages about prisons and prisoners were received. It would seem that much of the fan activity around the show centred on the romantic relationship between Helen and Nikki. It is quite possible that many viewers simply 'pocketed the viewing pleasures' that they derived from this and ignored any message that there was in the show about imprisonment. Ideally, to understand the show and its impact we would need to have a better appreciation of its different audiences and what they got out of it.

PERSONAL RELATIONS AND SEXUALITY IN *BAD GIRLS*

Whilst the discussion above has concentrated on *Bad Girls* as a prison drama, others have analysed it more as an intervention into debates about representations of sexuality in TV. We cannot rule out the possibility that there are other, better ways of analysing it. The storyline of the on/off romantic relationship between the apparently heterosexual wing governor Helen Stewart and life-sentenced prisoner Nikki Wade emerged relatively early on in the first season and stayed with the show until the end of the third season. During this time Helen ditches her intended fiancé Sean, has a brief fling with the prison's new senior medical officer—Thomas, in season three—and for the rest of the time conducts a 'will they, won't they' flirtation with Nikki Wade. Viewers who strongly identified with this storyline were rewarded twice during the three seasons. Firstly, when Nikki and Helen spend the night together after Nikki's escape from Larkhall and secondly when the pair are reunited after Nikki's successful appeal against her sentence. As suggested previously Helen and Nikki carry a relatively high degree of seriousness/status and, despite the ensemble cast, did constitute its two main protagonists. The unfolding Helen/Nikki relationship was the main story holding the show together over three seasons.

Didi Herman (2003) has investigated the sexuality at work in *Bad Girls*. She argues that Nikki constituted a lesbian heroine who functioned as the 'moral centre' of the show and that *Bad Girls* constructed a homonormative space within which lesbianism/same-sex desire was valued, normalised and legitimated. Further, it suggested that heterosexuality was almost always shown as being dysfunctional within the programme. It is possible that this argument is not incompatible with the one advanced in the discussion above, that *Bad Girls* sought to deliver a range of viewing pleasures to its audience. The Nikki/Helen storyline was popular and novel. It was included to take the audience 'somewhere that they had not been before' (Chadwick, DVD commentary). It may be that *Bad Girls* emerged when the time was right for this particular innovation in the representation of sexuality. But, having said this, the suggestion that heterosexuality was almost always portrayed as negative might raise the question why this did not alienate large sections of the audience who presumably have some kind of an investment in this form of sexuality. We might also wonder why the (claimed) legitimating of normalised, same-sex relationships appeared and seemed to work in this particular programme, when most other TV shows maintained their various versions of heteronormativity. Should we agree with Herman's (2003) analysis? Did *Bad Girls* normalise and value same-sex desire, whilst problematising heterosexuality?

An alternative reading would be that *Bad Girls* problematised and commented on all forms of sexual desire. Sexual desire is represented as being problematic and is always implicitly contrasted with platonic friendships. Supportive, platonic relationships are always represented as good and valuable, as being non-instrumental and as having the potential to achieve a genuine altruism. Such relationships are not without their problems. Julie J may at times seem too dependent on Julie S, and even platonic friends have their moments of falling out. But G wing as a place of warmth, solidarity and mutual support is built virtually entirely on platonic relationships. Whenever sexual desire is introduced it is represented as a complicating factor. This is as true for Helen and Nikki, as much as it is for the instances of heterosexual desire. Sexual desire is shown to lead to jealousy and possessiveness and to cloud judgement (for example, consider Trish's break-up with Nikki, Nikki's reaction to Dominic's interest in Helen, and so forth). This theme can be shown to operate across a wide range of characters. Unsurprisingly sexual desire is represented as negative when associated with pantomime baddie Jim Fenner, but it is also the case that nice guy Dominic McAlister loses something of his quiet confidence and becomes (mildly) inappropriately pushy when he starts to see Helen as a potential partner. Karen Betts is initially able to see Jim Fenner as an abuser and to ally herself with Helen, but becomes unable to see Fenner's abuse or to support Helen, as her own relationship with him develops. More examples could be provided and elaborated on.

The only possible exception to the disparaging of sexual relationships is the instance of Josh and Crystal, the heterosexual couple who marry in a clandestine wedding in the prison chapel, and enjoy a honeymoon in a linen cupboard. But here it is made clear from the outset that Josh and Crystal's relationship is not motivated by sexual desire. Both come to be genuinely concerned for each other and their relationship is about establishing a degree of trust between them, so that they feel confident to commit themselves to each other. Sex only becomes part of their relationship once they have achieved this. All other sexually expressed desires are seen as problematic, whether heterosexual or same-sex. Denny transfers her affections from Shell to Shaz and back to Shell again fairly easily, raising in Shaz's mind the question of fidelity (or more specifically ownership?). In *Bad Girls* sex is problematic unless expressed within a genuinely caring relationship. The relationship between Helen and Nikki is far too fickle and uncertain, and although the writers rewarded the viewers who had invested in this relationship at certain points, it is certainly not held up as any kind of ideal. The life-time, heterosexual, monogamy expressed within marriage by Josh and Crystal is the ideal presented by the show and it is Josh and Crystal who form its moral centre, not Nikki.

The above discussion raises the question as to how such a conventional, some might even say conservative, view of sexuality emerged in a supposedly feminist tract? One answer might be to return to *Bad Girls* as a women's prison drama. Perhaps the disparaging of sexually motivated relationships is a way of highlighting the value of the non-sexual, cross-class, cross-race, intergenerational mutual support that can characterise G wing. But this does not seem particularly convincing. It would surely be quite possible to represent this whilst allowing consensual same-sex activity to flourish unproblematically, as Herman (2003) suggests it does. There seems to be something more at work here and we need to consider the issue of abuse.

Bad Girls generally represents G wing of Larkhall as being occupied by a diverse range of women who have committed different crimes for different reasons. But on several occasions fairly key characters in the drama come out as having been victims of abuse. Shell, Denny, Shaz and Buki are all revealed to have had an experience of abuse, whether within the family, or within the institutions in which they were placed because of their dysfunctional families. Denny's (implied) experience of abuse within institutions is a pointed comment on the notion of removing children from their families to relocate them in a 'place of safety'. Shell is also worried that her children, who are being looked after by her mother are also at risk of abuse, but again there is little point in instigating social work action to remove them to a 'place of safety', if the place that they go to is not any safer than the one they are leaving. *Bad Girls* provides a consistent comment on the problem of abuse and sees all sexual desire as having a potential to be abusive, again unless expressed within caring relationships. The show is a plea for more caring interpersonal relationships and for higher standards of care in public institutions. If seen in this light we can reject any notion that *Bad Girls* is anti-sex, anti-men, anti-heterosexuality or whatever. It is always careful to demonstrate what it is *for* as much as what it is *against*. It values caring relationships and people who support high standards in public institutions, whatever their sex or sexual preference.

The representation of men in *Bad Girls* has attracted a degree of comment. As it happens, the men who express values endorsed by the show are relatively few and far between, with Dominic carrying the flag in seasons one and two and with Josh overlapping and then taking up the baton in season three. But *Bad Girls* does not exclude heterosexual men from watching the show and deriving pleasure from it, even if it does mainly celebrate cross-class sisterhood. *Bad Girls* is an inclusive form of feminism, both in the substance of the show and in the structure of its viewing pleasures. (Here it would be instructive to compare the viewing pleasures offered by the series with the model of Hollywood cinema analysed by Mulvey (1975)). One of the strengths of the show is its ability to pursue its feminist agenda, whilst at the same time producing a commercial and popular TV show with broad appeal. The novel representation of personal and sexual relations is complementary to its aim of commenting on a serious contemporary issue—the role of prison within the UK criminal justice system.

CONCLUSION

A view is sometimes expressed that the commercial products of popular film and TV are produced in a marketplace where the aim is simply to make money. Profit maximisation is said to lead producers to make products that entertain the greatest number of people and this in turn leads to them producing 'safe' entertainment, which has little or no intention to educate or inform. But in the case of *Bad Girls*, although the show appears to have originated as an idea for a commercial product, its producers seem also to have had a clear intention to educate and inform. It has been argued above that *Bad Girls* struck a conscious deal with its audience. The show undertook to deliver to its viewers a stream of multiple viewing pleasures, in return for which the audience was to understand and accept that the makers also wanted to say something about prisons and prisoners. One of the skills of *Bad Girls* has been to allow these elements to become partially, although never totally, separated. Even during its most blatant 'message' moments the writers keep the main storyline going. This is true in the Monica speech, the Shaz meeting, the Femi incident, and others (see Maureen Chadwick's DVD commentary season one, episode ten for a comment on the first of these). The outcome is a long-running, popular show which gives representation to prison—a relatively secret world which could all too easily come to be seen as 'out of sight and out of mind'.

On an examination of the 'text' of *Bad Girls* it could be argued that the show has probably done more than any other prison drama to advance the cause of penal reform. In terms of its representation of prisons and prisoners, the highlights of the first three series were: the Zandra storyline; Monica and her speech on the steps of the Court of Appeal; Shaz's meeting with the feisty old woman whose husband had died in the food poisoning incident; and Helen's handling of the Femi incident, notwithstanding the protest and riot that followed. *Bad Girls* benchmarked what it did not like about prisons and suggested some ideas about the way that prisons should be run. In principle the real world effects of this could be identified and investigated although some thought would be required to devise an appropriate methodology. *Bad Girls* rescued the women's prison drama from cliché and exhaustion and demonstrated that drama can be entertaining, informative and educational. Although it would require further empirical investigation to substantiate the real world effects of *Bad Girls*, based on a textual reading it seems fair to say that the show achieved an incredible amount in the 39 episodes of its first three seasons. Whether it maintained its standards in seasons four and five would need to be the subject of another discussion. But, on the basis of the evidence reviewed here, to call *Bad Girls* 'the best prison drama ever' is probably to understate its achievements.

CHAPTER 6

Hidden from View: *Buried* and *Ghosts ... of the Civil Dead*

This chapter compares the 1988 Australian film *Ghosts ... of the Civil Dead* (directed by John Hillcoat and hereafter referred to as *Ghosts ...*) with the more recent British, Channel 4 series *Buried* (2003, directed by Kenny Glenaan and Morag McKinnon) which controversially failed to be re-commissioned for a second series. It does so conscious of the reality of the different criminal justice systems and media traditions that these dramatic portrayals of prison relate to, and of the expected audiences that a controversial film and an eight-part mainstream TV series could reasonably be expected to reach. However, whilst these are important qualifications, the comparison between *Buried* and *Ghosts ...* does not seem too forced and there are several platforms on which to base it. For example, *Ghosts ...* was set in 'the near future', in a 'new generation' prison (see below) and we could reasonably argue that 2003 would be the 'near future' from the vantage point of 1988. Similarly, *Buried's* set was based on HMP Woodhill, which is the best and most recent British example of a 'new generation design' and which *Buried's* authors visited as part of their research for the programme. Thus in *Buried* we could claim to see the reality of the future that had been imagined in *Ghosts ....*

Here too it should be noted that the point of comparison is not just to uncover similarities but rather to use two different sources to throw light onto a problem or an argument and to help to reveal a deeper understanding of the issues related to the dramatic portrayal of prisons and prisoners. Thus the contrasting and at times competing media and criminal justice traditions of Australia and of England and Wales offer us an opportunity to test whether prison is viewed, presented or dramatically imagined differently within these traditions. Specifically in this chapter, the comparison facilitates a discussion about how prisoners are imagined and here we should note that both the film and TV series deliberately use titles suggesting that prison hides prisoners from the audience's gaze. *Buried* takes its title from a Jacobean play—'Art thou poor and in prison? Then thou art buried before thou art dead', whilst *Ghosts ...* is from a quote in Jack Henry Abbott's *In the Belly of the Beast* (1982). But when both the institution and the prisoners are revealed, what role is prison seen to play? Is prison presented as helping to rehabilitate its prisoners or is it simply a source and location of their punishment? What relationship is the prison seen to have with the 'outside' world and how does that relationship affect the culture that develops inside? Finally, when the prisoners emerge in front of their audience are we left grateful that they are locked up, or angry at the circumstances?

Throughout the chapter *Ghosts ...* is placed not only within the context of the Australian penal system, but also within an Australian tradition of prison movies. Specifically, references are made to two other films which dealt with similar themes. These are *Stir* (1980, director Stephen Wallace), which dramatises the 'old generation' of New South Wales gaols in the 1970s, and which was written by an ex-offender, and secondly *Chopper* (2000, director Andrew Dominik), which is a dramatic and controversial re-working of the books of Mark 'Chopper' Read and is largely set inside various gaols. The discussion of *Buried* is based on a close reading of the shooting scripts of the eight episodes that made up the series and from the personal involvement of one of the authors of this book with the programme from conception to broadcast. This involvement included briefing the two main authors of the series, providing a range of written materials about prisons, reading scripts in draft and suggesting plot developments. Finally, one of the series' authors, Jimmy Gardner, was interviewed about themes raised (see the *Appendix* to this chapter).

AUSTRALIAN PRISONS, RACE AND NEW GENERATION DESIGN

In 1999, there were 97 prisons and 12 periodic detention centres in Australia and the average daily prison population during 1998-9 was 19,850, of whom some 16 per cent were held in private prisons (Hogg, 2002:3). Of note, *Ghosts ...* is set within a privatised prison, whilst *Buried* is set within a state-run facility, although one of the governors, Russo, talks openly of wanting to move to the private sector. These numbers represent an imprisonment rate of some 148 per 100,000 of the general population: higher than the rate in England and Wales during this period, which was 120 per 100,000 (Flynn, 1998:17). This figure masks differences between state and territory imprisonment rates and thus, for example, the Northern Territory imprisoned at the rate of 458 per 100,000 of the general population—almost three times the national average, whilst the rate in New South Wales was 172 per 100,000. Similarly the indigenous people of Australia are imprisoned at massively disproportionate rates when compared to the general population and in 2000 there were a total of 4,095 indigenous prisoners in Australian prisons, which represented an imprisonment rate of 1,727 per 100,000 of the adult indigenous population (Hogg, 2002: 16). Similarly, black people have always been over-represented in English and Welsh prisons and so, for example, in 1995 17 per cent of all male prisoners and 24 per cent of all female prisoners were black with Afro-Caribbeans being particularly over-represented (Wilson and Ashton, 2001:91). This racial dimension is relatively underdeveloped in all three Australian films (see below) but is at the forefront of *Buried*, not least because the lead character, Lee Kingley, is black.

On census night—30 June 2000, for those prisoners in Australian gaols who had been sentenced—the average aggregate sentence was just under five years and more than half of the prison population had served a prison sentence on a previous occasion (all figures taken from Hogg, 2002). Fewer than half had been sentenced for an offence involving violence or the threat of violence, with homicide accounting for only nine per cent of the sentenced prison population. Even these figures will over-represent more serious and violent offences, as they cannot accommodate those prisoners who in any one year are imprisoned for short terms because they have committed less serious offences. Nonetheless, with the exception of *Stir*, both *Ghosts ...* and *Chopper* concentrate on those who have been convicted of serious and usually violent offences, typically murder or manslaughter, as does *Buried*, although it should be acknowledged that *Buried*'s episodic format did allow for new characters to be introduced and also 'released' back into the community. Hogg (2002: 12) observes, 'the prison population is massively disproportionately male and young', a phenomenon in English gaols too and this is reflected in all three films and also in *Buried* where this gender and age imbalance is obvious. Indeed the many complex ways that 'youth' is used dramatically is of interest and, for example, in *Buried, Stir* and to a lesser extent in *Ghosts ...* young prisoners are emblematic of a naïvety about prison life—despite the empirical reality that more than half of those sentenced have been imprisoned before, but which thus allows exposition and explanation. Similarly youth is seen as something sexually desirable and in *Ghosts ...* also as unpredictable and chaotic and thus dangerous to the status quo.

Reference has previously been made to the fact that *Ghosts ...* and *Buried* are set within 'new generation' prisons and ironically, given the violence that dominates the dramatic narrative in both, this architectural design and its associated management features are seen in reality as helping to contribute to a reduction in prison violence (O'Donnell and Edgar, 1996). The features that are viewed as 'new generation' relate primarily to the podular, as opposed to the more traditional linear design—so as to reduce the number of spaces that cannot be directly supervised by staff. In short, the older generation of gaols were generally rectangular, with corridors leading to either single, but usually multi-occupancy cells arranged at right angles to the corridor. Clearly staff could not see around corners and thus were required to patrol in order to see into cells, although they could only see one or two cells at any one time. 'New generation' prisons are divided into more manageable units, or 'pods' and typically single occupancy cells will be clustered around a common area and a secure staff control booth from which an officer in the booth can observe all prisoner activity. Despite these design features being described and indeed being built into their respective sets, in both *Buried* and *Ghosts ...* cell-sharing is the norm and violence predominates. However, it is also worth noting here that *Ghosts ...* uses the possibilities of architecture more imaginatively and opens, for example, with a long, slow, shot of a barren desert that only gradually reveals a prison deliberately carved into the landscape. Similarly *Ghosts ...* also makes use of CCTV—something that *Buried* ignores completely, both to push forward the narrative and to imply a Foucauldian future where observation and surveillance have become a means for exercising control, or at least a semblance of control. Nonetheless in both *Buried* and *Ghosts ...* the podular design allows the action to take place within a defined space, where the characters are offered few, if any, opportunities to escape each other's or authority's gaze, or indeed that of the viewer. The 'new generation' design is thus one which ensures that a closed world is dramatically revealed, whatever the original intention, or reality of this penal architectural development.

GHOSTS AND *BURIED:* AN OVERVIEW

The narrative of *Ghosts ...* is concerned with the events that lead up to a riot in Central Industrial Prison—'the future of containment'—although the riot is in fact not seen and the film is presented in a pseudo-documentary style with prisoner identification photographs and long intertitle quotes from the 'Report' which clears the penal authorities from any culpability. We are informed that the riot took place on October 25 and thus we are presented with a series of events that attempts to explain how it came about. We are specifically told that Central Industrial Prison houses 'the prison system's most violent, unmanageable and predatory prisoners' but there is little character development and we rarely come to know any of the protagonists in relation to what they have done that led to their incarceration, or why they might have been involved with crime in the first place. The film begins and ends with one of the characters—Wenzil, played by David Field—first entering and then leaving the gaol after the riot and to that extent we see the story of *Ghosts ...* through his eyes.

As Wenzil first enters the gaol we see him naked and being given his prison number—in effect his new administrative identity within Central Industrial Prison, but he is also given more informal advice from a fellow prisoner—'Watch your back and stay sitting down for as long as possible'. As Wenzil begins to orientate himself to his new surroundings, so too the viewer comes to see what he is experiencing and what life is like. In fact, prior to the lock down that precedes the riot, there is initially a great deal of freedom of movement within the unit that Wenzil is located upon, although everything that the prisoners do is constantly monitored through CCTV, the use of which contributes to the documentary style of the film. We see well-organized gangs of prisoners preying on each other and waging a perpetual war against the guards, who also wage war on them and who are initially concerned that Grezner, a 'guard killer', with a police escort, has been placed on the unit. We see one prisoner after another using drugs and watching pornography on TVs in their cells and moving freely from one cell to another. Thus we are introduced to various other characters apart from Wenzil, including Waychek, played by Bogdan Koca (nominated for Best Supporting Actor for his performance in the 1989 Australian Film Institute Awards) who appears to run the informal prisoner economy and to his transvestite lover Lilly, played by Dave Mason.

The early action centres on some petty violence amongst the guards, who we see beating up a handcuffed prisoner and another who carefully tears selected pages from a prisoner's book and burns them. However, it is Wenzil's desire to buy a tattoo, which costs a carton of cigarettes and thus involves him stealing a radio to pay the tattoo artist, who advises him that 'a man looks a bit funny without tattoos, doesn't he?' Wenzil is caught by two prisoner heavies with the stolen radio and badly beaten up in consequence. They also tattoo 'cunt' onto his forehead, which means that for most of the remainder of the film Wenzil wears a bandana around his head.

Gradually the staff begin to remove the freedoms and privileges that the prisoners had been enjoying and so we see them and their cells being searched for drugs and other forms of contraband. Eventually the prisoners are no longer allowed to have TVs in their cells—despite one staff member advising that this will mean that 'You're asking for something to happen'. When two prisoners murder a third—an indigenous prisoner—outdoor recreation is stopped and the prisoners are forced to take their exercise in a locked cage within the unit. The authorities also begin to move into the units for new prisoners, who we are told are 'the psychos, the dregs of the whole system,' and one such psycho, Maynard, played by the singer Nick Cave, enters the unit shouting, 'There goes the neighbourhood—I can see a coon in a cage! Nigger, nigger, nigger!' The new tough, lock down regime means that drugs are harder to come by and that there is virtually nothing to do except play dominoes. Old scores are settled and Waychek, no longer controlling the informal economy, is eventually killed when two prisoners pour glue onto him and set him alight, leaving Lilly defenceless. In these changing circumstances the staff become ever more concerned and one, at breaking point, throws his teacup at the wall crying, 'I'm sick, I'm leaving! It's just a job. You're not supposed to get killed doing your job. I'm leaving. Open the door—I'm out of here.' We later discover that he shoots himself. Similarly the prisoners respond to the new regime by self-harming, lighting cell fires and 30 of them begin a hunger strike.

Towards the end of the film we see a distraught Lilly, no longer able to get access to drugs and without the protection of Waychek, being beaten up and killed by Wenzil—whilst all the time being filmed by the guards on CCTV. The murder of one of his fellow prisoners can be seen as symbolic of the 'progress' that Wenzil has made since coming into gaol. However if Wenzil had hoped that this would have given him some status, he is advised by another prisoner, 'You kill a nobody and it makes you a nobody'. But the murders do not end here. We eventually discover Grezner, the 'guard killer' hanged in his cell. These deaths are but a prelude to the horrific murder of a staff member, who is repeatedly stabbed, and to the riot itself, which is reported on the TV news. As a result 30 prisoners are transferred out of Central Industrial Prison and five—including Wenzil, who had been filmed murdering Lilly—are released back into the community. The film ends with Wenzil leaving an anonymous train station to go home and we watch him standing on the escalator ascending into the world above, as if he is emerging from Hell, as an intertitle montage advises us that the 'Report also recommends that the Bureau of Prisons immediately begin construction of a new super-maximum security facility'. Just in front of Wenzil is a woman and as the credits roll we are left to wonder what he might be about to do to her.

Buried too is concerned with a penal journey and whilst the episodic nature of the programme allows for character development which is not attempted in *Ghosts* … and for new characters to be introduced, in essence the series is concerned with Lee Kingley's progress at fictional HMP Mandrake. In its essentials the main story[1] concerns Kingley, played by Lennie James, who claims that he is (morally) innocent of the offence for which he has just received an eight year sentence—shooting and grievously wounding the man who raped his sister. He spends much of his time trying to re-establish inside prison the reputation that he had on the outside, where he was seen as a hard-working family man. However, inside he is naïve and trusting and at the start is able to survive largely because his brother Troy is a Category A prisoner (the highest security category in the English prison system)—a man with a fearsome reputation who is well-known for attacking staff. Early on Kingley is advised by 'Rollie man', played by Sean McKee, that there is a hierarchy in gaol and that he can rank every prisoner based on how long they are serving, how many times they have been in before

---

[1] For episode outlines see www.theprisonfilmproject.com or www.watersidepress.co.uk

and how hard they are. Rollie man reckons that Lee could make it all the way to number one and in essence over eight episodes we see Lee rising or falling in that hierarchy, or choosing as best he can to opt out of it. Along the way, we are introduced to other characters—including staff members, such as the psychologist Nick Vaughn (played by Stephen Walters), senior officer Steddon (Connor McIntyre) and officer 'DD' played by Jane Hazelgrove—the first strong female character. A particular strength of *Buried* is its attempt to see the drama not just in how the prisoners interact with each other but also how the staff work with each other and prisoners.

Through Lee's ups and downs, the viewer is asked to identify with him, a black man proclaiming his (moral) innocence, and to see prison through his eyes, as fellow prisoners abuse each other, smuggle drugs, or mentally collapse as family relationships get destroyed and the outside world gradually disappears from their view. We are asked to question the rehabilitation on offer—in *Buried's* case a 'drug-free' unit run by Nick Vaughn and which seems to swim against a sea of drugs that are available within the prison and which are, we discover, being smuggled in by a member of staff. Crucially, in viewing the world of HMP Mandrake through Lee's eyes, we are also being asked to identify with his demise—his death at the hands of another prisoner, and in the final scene in episode eight the camera captures Lee's look of helplessness as he clutches at his stomach, blood oozing through his fingers, unable to reach his cell bell to call for assistance whilst his cell-mate slips into a drug induced stupor.

VIEWS OF PRISON AS AN INSTITUTION

Both *Buried* and *Ghosts* ... present prison as a failing institution, although *Buried* is less polemical and more measured in its opposition. For example, *Buried* at least attempts to demonstrate the possibility of rehabilitation through Nick Vaughn's 'drug-free' unit and it is clear through discussions with the writers of that series that they had been impressed in their research with what HMP Grendon, which operates as a therapeutic community, had to offer. Indeed, in talking to Erwin James, a former prisoner who writes for the *Guardian*, Kath Mattock, the series producer described HMP Grendon as 'an interesting place, geared to helping people take responsibility for their actions' (*Guardian*, 19 February 2003) and it is obvious that they wanted some element of the possibility that prisoners could change for the better brought into the series. However, this had to be seen against the backdrop of a penal culture that resisted those changes, for one reason or another and where survival was a daily reality. In this respect even Vaughn's 'drug-free' unit was seen as compromised and Jimmy Gardner, who with Robert Jones wrote six of the eight episodes, suggested that the character Henry was deliberately introduced into episode three to reveal the absurdity of the Prison Service's drug testing programme, which encourages prisoners to 'switch' their drug use from cannabis to heroin. Indeed, *Buried* takes this view to its logical conclusion and shows prisoners being released from HMP Mandrake but being brought back into gaol in later episodes after re-offending.

Ghosts ... is deliberately more polemical and uncompromising and as such no effort is made at all to show prisoners being offered help in any form. Staff and prisoner violence dominate the film and, more than this, the violence is seen as being instigated by the prison authorities so as to justify the building of even more secure prisons. Both in *Buried* and *Ghosts* ... the most obvious failures within the prison are the staff themselves. They are consistently presented as ineffectual, corrupt and violent and even those characters who are seen as decent, such as Steddon in *Buried*, are nonetheless still viewed as incapable of effecting change. *Ghosts* ... uses this to the best advantage by not being too concerned with character development and thus simply presents the staff as archetypes, agents of the state, as much imprisoned by the system as the prisoners themselves. Indeed, this rather Foucauldian analysis is perhaps best exemplified by the fact that in the credits for *Ghosts* ... Simon During is credited as a 'Foucault authority'. *Buried* is again less polemical than *Ghosts* ... and attempts to develop the characters of the staff, revealing them as people with pasts and, sometimes, troubled presents. This is not to imply that *Ghosts* ... does not attempt to present some insight into how the staff might respond to the circumstances that they find themselves in and thus one staff member commits suicide and another repeatedly warns the Governor of the riot that is about to take place—but with little impact.

In this respect *Ghosts* ... is a development from *Stir* (1980), which routinely presents the staff as moronic bullies and boors who beat the prisoners for their own sadistic pleasure. In one scene, for example, the principal officer rips an earring from a prisoner's ear and another deliberately destroys the bread that he finds during a cell search. Indeed, the main narrative drive in *Stir* is the personal inability of China Jackson, played by Bryan Brown, to overcome the bullying and intimidation that he faces at the hands of the guards and the collective inability of the prisoners to effect change in a corrupt regime.

In *Chopper* (2000), played by Eric Bana, the guards are again seen as ineffectual, although not sadistic and violent and somewhat in awe of Chopper himself. This is perhaps best demonstrated by the final scene which has two officers sitting on Chopper's bed discussing a news interview that he had given earlier in the day and which is now being shown on TV. It is clear that the staff feel that they are in the presence of a celebrity and as they leave one apologetically points out that he is going to have to lock the cell door. Chopper waves his hand, as if to say 'Go ahead'.

The staff's main role in *Ghosts* ... and *Chopper* is to be invisible. They are simply not around when the action takes place—despite the design principles of 'new generation' prisons. Prisoners are allowed to create their own world, with their own rules, devoid of staff interference. Chopper is therefore able to stab Keith George repeatedly in the neck at the beginning of the film, set in Pentridge Prison in 1978 and in due course is stabbed himself by his friend Jim. As the attack starts Chopper observes, 'It's a bit early in the morning for kung-fu, isn't it Jim?' So Jim stabs him a second and then a third time. 'What's got into you?' Chopper asks, as Jim stabs him again. Chopper hugs him and so Jim apologises but stabs him again, once more and then again. 'Jim,' suggests Chopper, 'if you keep stabbing me, you're going to kill me'. The point here is the absence of the staff to prevent a long-drawn out attack from taking place, although in passing we should also note the black humour in *Chopper*, which is largely absent from *Ghosts* ... and *Buried*—that humour is apparent even in the opening titles, as images of prison walls flash before the viewer and Frankie Laine sings *Don't*

Fence Me In. This staff absence is all the more confusing in *Ghosts* ... —given that staff sit observing prisoners all day via CCTV cameras and indeed filmed Wenzil's murder of Lilly. The greatest absence is that of the various prisons' Governors and when one does appear in *Ghosts* ... he simply refuses to speak to the prisoners at all.[2] There is a power vacuum that prisoners are keen to fill.

We should also see these films as presenting prison as a 'closed institution', where the culture of the institution develops from what happens inside and is divorced from the world outside. The rules that determine how prisons operate have, at best only a tangential relationship with how things would work outside and as one prisoner observes in *Ghosts* ... 'I've seen people killed over a rumour, a look, or a whisper'. The most dramatic presentation of this culture is the acceptance of situational homosexuality. Thus, Lilly is seen as desirable inside prison and in one very erotic scene slowly and teasingly lies on top of a fellow prisoner and bites his lip. As such the viewer is left in no doubt about Lilly's desirability in gaol, a desirability that would no doubt disappear if encountered by the same prisoner in the community. Indeed in *Stir*, Redfern, an older dominant prisoner explains these fluctuating desires to China. 'After I've fucked them,' he says, 'I can't stand them for being such weak bastards for letting me fuck them'. So too Barry Shiel in *Buried* is quite happy to use Lucas for sexual favours and suggests, reminding us of the debt that Wenzil gets into at the beginning of *Ghosts* ... that he should get some 'tats' to make himself even more desirable. As Lucas leaves Shiel's cell when the reality hits of what is going to be happening to him, Shiel calls out to remind him, 'have a shower before you get up here tomorrow morning'.

VIEWS OF PRISONERS AS PEOPLE

Jimmy Gardner describes that in co-writing *Buried* he was influenced by the cult, American TV series *Oz*, with one key difference:

> When I watched *Oz*, I remember thinking that I was really glad that these people were on the inside, locked up and that I was on the outside. I didn't want people to think that about *Buried*, but rather to see more of the people behind the label 'prisoner'—more of the compassion and the humanity. Not 'them' and 'us''. (Interview with Jimmy Gardner, *Appendix* to this chapter)

In this respect, far more than in *Ghosts* ... , *Buried* succeeds in presenting prisoners as people who—in different circumstances—the viewer could quite happily meet in the pub, or have as neighbours. The characters in *Buried* are like us, except that they have been imprisoned and react as we might to the nature and circumstances of their incarceration. As such, they talk and behave as we all do about wives and girlfriends, letters from home, and visits. There are photographs of loved ones posted on cell walls—and it was Lee's mistaken belief that Kappa had been secretly masturbating over a stolen photograph of Lee's daughter Amelia that led to his murder. Characters are slowly but surely immersed into the prison world, thoughts of home and of leaving gaol gradually

---

[2] This theme is taken up in the next chapter.

surrender to institutionalisation, dependency and survival. Dreadful acts then become almost normal and forgivable.

Unlike *Buried*, *Ghosts* ... does not allow its characters a past but rather keeps them firmly in the present. They are only what we see before us and as such each violent incident in which they engage merely serves to distance them further and further from the viewer, or at least what the viewer would like to think of himself or herself. The characters become alien—'them' not 'us'. In this sense the viewer of *Ghosts* ... becomes placed in the same position as the guards who watch the prisoners on CCTV, only the viewer's role is not to police and control but rather more akin to someone visiting a zoo. Thus we marvel at what we see because it is exotic and different, albeit safely caged and at a distance. Even Wenzil, the only character who is given a future, as he ascends the escalator in the train station at the end of the film, leaves the viewer merely anxious and fearful as to what he might be about to do.

In *Stir* the prisoners are always presented as badly treated and abused by their sadistic guards. It is easy to be on their 'side', although the colour here is so lacking in shade as to render this identification meaningless. *Chopper*—largely through the character of Chopper himself—is much more ambiguous and the viewer is never quite certain what is true and what is imagined. As Chopper explains, when questioned by one of his guards as to whether what he has just said in a TV interview is accurate, 'Never let the truth get in the way of a good yarn'. The viewer here is being asked to suspend disbelief too and go along with the thrill of the 'yarn' that is being spun; to enjoy the moment, whether it is real or imagined. Indeed, many are prepared to do so, for as Chopper explains, almost incredulously, 'I've written a best seller and I can't even bloody spell. It's sold over 250,000 copies and it is still selling! I'm writing another one and I'm semi-literate!' The question being posed here is 'Who's fooling whom?' whilst at the same time the film is also asking us to question our own interest in murder and other extreme forms of violence.

CONCLUSION

The future of imprisonment envisaged by *Ghosts* ... did not materialise either in reality or in film. Whilst we could easily point to themes or issues picked out by *Ghosts* ... such as the influence of privatisation and the development of 'super-max' prisons, the calculated, unremitting inhumanity and degradation that is foretold has not so far occurred. In *Buried* we see a different version of the future that *Ghosts* ... was imagining. Emerging from a different media tradition and set within a different criminal justice system, the characters in *Buried* are more human than Lilly, Wenzil or Waychek. In Lee, Barry Shiel and even in Troy we see something of ourselves and of how we might react if we too found ourselves in HMP Mandrake and perhaps this is at the root of why Channel 4 did not re-commission the series. By being able to identify with the characters in *Buried* the audience could no longer feel the thrill of the exotic and the unknown—of 'them' and 'us'—and so the prisoners became ordinary and banal, rather than frightening and monstrous. Ironically, Chopper puts this best when sitting on a stool in a bar talking to two detectives, to whom he might or might not give intelligence, when he observes, 'I'm a bit of a disappointment to you, aren't I?'

From then on his 'yarns' become ever more fantastic—exactly what everyone, especially the viewers, wants.

All of the items reviewed here have argued or concluded that there is a kind of madness and insanity to prison. *Ghosts ...* possesses an almost surreal quality as the prison drifts into the madness that leads to the riot. In *Chopper* prison is depicted as an insane and irrational institution—full stop. Chopper's own violence is completely senseless. He 'bashes people for no reason' and when asked to explain why his crew are at war with the rest of H wing has no answer. In *Buried*, Lee takes his own personal journey into madness, echoing a journey that his brother Troy has already made. Violence is both 'rational', necessary to run the internal prison economy, and at times just senseless, as when Carter, the man convicted of killing his two children in a car crash, becomes a focus for mob violence.

In *Ghosts ...*, *Chopper* and *Buried* violence is one of the main means of identifying the irrationality of the institutions. But this use of violence is, in a sense, double edged. On the one hand it can serve to undermine the legitimacy of prison. The fiction of prison is that as an institution it should be 'unimpeachably humane, but unremittingly severe', although the reality is that it is such an unnatural institution that it will always be difficult for it to live up to this ambition. Revealing the madness of prison serves a useful function to counter the fiction of severe, but humane punishment. In *Buried*, Lee begins his journey as a kind of 'everyman'; a prison innocent, determined to avoid being sucked into the power plays and internal politics of prison culture. But the speed with which prison culture overtakes him is frightening and by episode four Lee has bludgeoned a man to death over 'a rumour'. But why do we wish to watch this descent into madness? What accounts for our fascination with seeing prisoner culture depicted as a Darwinian struggle for survival? One issue that requires further investigation is the gendered nature of the audience for prison drama. To what extent do dramatisations of the male experience of prison play to male audiences, drawn to products which celebrate 'a fascination with the hard man'? Do prison dramas have a tendency towards 'cool masculinity'?

Buried certainly expanded the range of relationships that could be represented within prison drama. It was able to show same-sex activity as both supportive and predatory. It was also able to show relationships across the staff/inmate divide and its representation of the relationship between Lee and his brother Troy was novel for UK TV. Whether it could have done more to indicate the potential for reform is unclear. Perhaps if the show had been recommissioned the opportunities to develop this aspect might have emerged. But if *Buried* becomes available on DVD it will become part of our culture and as writer Jimmy Gardner has suggested, prison is an underdramatised topic and any innovative approach to depicting it is to be welcomed. If the point of both *Ghosts ...* and *Buried* is that prisons and prisoners can too easily become hidden from view, then the significance of the productions is to make them visible again. Why this visibility matters will be addressed in the following chapter which considers the significance of HBO's amoral prison drama *Oz*.

Appendix to *Chapter 6*: Interview with Jimmy Gardner

Jimmy Gardner is from Edinburgh and is 45 years old. He is a graduate of the Leeds Northern School of Film and TV. He started writing scripts for the TV series *The Bill* and *This Life*, before co-authoring *Cops* and *Buried* with Robert Jones.

David Wilson (DW): Jimmy, who did you see as the audience for *Buried*?

Jimmy Gardner (JG): In one sense we were hoping for a similar audience to *Cops* and by that I mean an adult audience. We wanted people to have to work at the drama—for it to be something that they would have to think about. I would also say that we wanted the audience to think that what they were seeing was authentic and to that extent we were also hoping that prisoners would watch it too and feel that what they were seeing was a fair reflection of their experiences.

DW: Were you also hoping that it would be a polemic against the penal system, or was this at the end of the day just entertainment?

JG: We weren't producing a polemic as such, and I don't think that there is an ideology in the series about what prison should or should not be like, although clearly we did draw attention to some of the ludicrous things that can happen. For me polemical drama doesn't work, but you used the word 'entertainment'. I think that is too light a word for what we were trying to create and in one sense we approached the subject because prison has been relatively underdramatised.

DW: So were you surprised that the series seemed to create a great deal of interest in prisons—real prisons as opposed to HMP Mandrake?

JG: I didn't see too much of that reaction other than people saying how grim prison seemed to be. However, I did detect people picking up on a strong theme in the series—should prison be about punishment or about rehabilitation. For me that was very pleasing.

DW: You say that prison is relatively underdramatised, but I suppose when you approached this subject you had to avoid the type of view that is created in *Porridge*?

JG: Well, I think that *Porridge* is a brilliant piece of writing and captures one reality of prison: the humour, the relationships, and the scams but yes, we did want to look at the darker realities of prison. We certainly did want to avoid the *Daily Mail* view that prison is quite a laugh and that prisoners all have colour TVs. Personally I was quite angry that the prison population was rising every year even though the country was getting richer and richer. I wished we had dealt with those broader political issues more and when we did the research for the series we found out all sorts of information that we would have liked to have included dramatically—the urine tests for example, which encourage prisoners to switch from cannabis to heroin use. We did introduce the character Henry in episode three with this in mind, but we had to cut back on this in final drafts. I think that you could say that we were trying to do two things—firstly, make an episodic drama, like *Cops* where issues beneath the surface can be looked at briefly and secondly, follow a single prisoner's journey in prison with all the issues that that throws up. In that sense the series was a hybrid and so there are always going to be compromises. We didn't get to investigate other minor characters' experiences of prison and ultimately we say that prison is terrible but we didn't really say how to make it better—except by implication.

DW: You mentioned reseaching the series in that answer, what sort of research did you do—apart from speaking to me!

JG: We spoke with several serving and just-been released lifers and to a prisoners' writing group about the psychological experience of prison. That was very helpful as most of them described a journey too—from 'angry young man' to 'elder statesman'. That was very insightful and helped us think about the journey that Lee would make in the series. In fact all the lifers told a similar story. We also went to [HMP] Grendon and that was very good too, although we would have liked to have talked to prisoners more. I got the impression that the Prison Service wasn't that keen and so it was almost a cosmetic exercise on their part when they took us around places.

DW: Why do you think that Channel 4 didn't re-commission the series?

JG: Various reasons. Firstly, our ratings. My understanding is that the series started at 1.3 million, but the audience didn't grow. My understanding is that Channel 4 didn't think that that was enough. So, in that sense it was Channel 4's decision, but it was also down to us. Channel 4 could also have made things easier. After all, they scheduled it late in the evening—after Graham Norton, and you have to remember that people have to get up in the morning. *Buried* was not necessarily something that you would want to fall asleep to. I got the impression that people found it interesting, but crucially they also said that it was a bit grim. Perhaps we overdid the bleakness and it was a bit short on laughs. I would say that our other failure was that we didn't develop enough of an ensemble cast of characters and therefore when Lee died Channel 4 could say that the series had come to a natural end.

DW: But, do you think that people are simply not interested enough in prison and prisoners?

JG: Yes, that's true too. People like cop dramas. *Cops* worked well firstly because we got fantastic access and so we really got to know the police's lives and we dramatised many of the anecdotes that they told us. But crucially, and I think that this is where I agree with your question, in doing the research we also found out about the excitement of being a cop. It was exciting and great fun. When you watch a cop drama there's also some action—crashing through doors, driving fast cars, but in prison you obviously don't get that at all. More than that, you get shown a world that you wouldn't want to go to. Being a cop or a doctor is a fantasy—you fantasise about going into that world. You don't fantasise about going to prison. Obviously *Porridge* created a funny community and so the viewer did want to go there, but that created only a very partial impression about what prison is really like.

DW: You've mentioned *Porridge* once or twice, and the fact that prison is relatively underdramatised. Did you watch any prison films that caught your attention when you were researching *Buried*?

JG: *Oz* springs to mind but with one big reservation. When I watched *Oz* I remember thinking that I was really glad that these people were on the inside—locked up, and that I was on the outside. I didn't want people to think about *Buried* like that, but rather to see more of the people behind the label 'prisoner'; more of the compassion and humanity. Not 'them and us'. I did like the production values in *Oz*, which did show the dark side of America, but in *Buried* we came more from a social realist tradition and that allowed us to be more compassionate.

CHAPTER 7

Inside the 'Predatory Prison': *Oz*

> This too I know—and wise it were
> If each could know the same—
> That every prison that men build
> Is built with bricks of shame,
> And bound with bars lest Christ should see
> How men their brothers maim.
>
> Wilde, *The Ballad of Reading Goal* (Part V)

We have previously argued (in *Chapter 2*) that prison film can perform the same function as Oscar Wilde's classic poem *The Ballad of Reading Gaol*. Thus, prison films such as *Brubaker* aim to be both revelatory about prison conditions and to *connote* those conditions as being something that we should be ashamed of, although one problem with the prison film genre is that not all prison films do this. The prisons revealed in, say, *Midnight Express* or *Papillon*, are not really being held up for shame but rather invite their viewers to revel momentarily in the horrors, whilst comfortably assuming that they themselves will never have to serve time on Devil's Island or in a Turkish gaol.

So is prison drama an exercise in revelation, benchmarking the unacceptable prison, or merely an opportunity for us to 'holiday in someone else's misery'? This chapter considers these issues through an examination of the US made TV prison drama *Oz*. First aired in 1997, the HBO TV series provided a controversial, hyper-violent depiction of life inside a maximum security prison, complete with a weekly carnage of inmate fatalities, male rape and other prison violence. But, whereas prior to *Oz*, prison drama had, rhetorically at least, invariably taken the side of the prisoners against the tyranny of the authorities, *Oz* provided a studiously amoral look at the workings of the prison. The claim by Tom Fontana, creator of the show and its writer, that it 'was never about prisoners' rights' (DVD commentary season one, episode two) is to a large extent borne out by what we see on screen. *Oz* featured no heroes and no villains. Everyone was equally bad and, formally at least, the programme never connoted a prison we should be ashamed of. The expression, 'Shit happens' could well have been *Oz*'s motto.

In the US, *Oz* attracted a reasonably large and diverse following. In Britain, shown on C4 late at night, it has only ever had a cult following, presumably attracted by the promise of 'the truth' about prison that people would not see elsewhere. But, in daring to show male nudity, male rape and predatory same-sex relationships, was *Oz* revealing some kind of 'truth' about prison, or has it just been a more sophisticated version of the 'don't bend over to pick up the soap', prison-rape 'jokes' that have come to characterise contemporary popular culture? The discussion below draws on the first two seasons (now available on DVD). Although at the time of writing *Oz* was in its sixth and final season this examination of the first two seasons is more than adequate for gauging its style and tenor. Later in the chapter we consider whether we should see *Oz* as reproducing or challenging current 'myths' about prisons and prisoners.

WELCOME TO *OZ*: MAIN PARTIES AND PLAYERS

The action in *Oz* takes place entirely within its fictitious setting, the Oswald Maximum Security Penitentiary. The show never goes outside of the prison, except for when the crime scenes of its inmates are shown in flashback. Outside shots of the prison are rarely seen and there is no outside set for, say, a prison yard. Yet, despite the fact that *Oz* never strays from its internal set, one of its aims is to show that prison is a product of a wider set of social forces. Whilst the characters are often believable and plausible, they are at the same time stylised and symbolic. Each of the main characters carries a defined 'discourse' or perspective on prison which rarely changes. *Oz* takes the notion of 'the predatory penitentiary' and examines it through introducing the contesting groups that wrestle for its control and direction. It takes the racially divided prison and puts it under the microscope but taking a neutral stance, introducing the diverse parties as all having formal equality.

Perhaps one of the most interesting of the characters is that of Governor James Devlin. Governor Devlin is an actor external to the prison, but one whose decisions affect its fortunes, and who, from time to time, descends on *Oz* to impress upon its Warden and staff his own particular view as to how a prison should be run. Devlin is a law and order conservative, who believes in being tough on crime and tough on prisoners. In the first season he bans smoking and conjugal visits, and reinstates the death penalty. At other times he cuts the prison's budget, or argues for it to be shifted from educational activities to the hire of corrections officers. At the end of the first season Devlin makes the decision to send in the SORT team to put down the riot; a decision which leads to the loss of eight lives. It would be tempting to assume that *Oz* is a liberal show and that Devlin is being set up as the villain but in formal terms this is not the case. Devlin simply articulates that he enacts his 'tough on prisoners' policies because they are popular with the electorate. Much as some might not like his policies, as long as the electorate keep voting him in, they have just as much legitimacy as those preferred by liberal elements within the prison.

Devlin's main foil is Tim McManus, the reform-minded liberal who runs Emerald City, the experimental unit within Oz. McManus is in favour of education and rehabilitative activity and is always trying to make a difference to the lives of his charges. But the character of McManus rarely gets the better of Devlin. When Devlin lets it be known that he intends cutting the prison education programme to fund more officers, McManus attempts to embarrass him by 'leaking' this information in a televised graduation ceremony speech. McManus thinks that he has scored a point off Devlin but in a washroom conversation after the ceremony Devlin acquaints McManus with political realities.

> Crime is down, taxes are down, employment however, is up, mean incomes up, up, up, the Knights made it into the playoffs, even the Ballet is thriving, and as for education—we now have the second highest literacy rate in the USA, so do you

seriously think that the John and Jane Q public give a shit about some drugged out homeboy who's gonna get a diploma knowing that their own little daughters are going to Yale ... enjoy that coffee and cake.

After this exchange McManus is left scratching his head. His preference for reform and rehabilitation is just that, *his preference*. McManus' well meaning interventions are rarely successful and there is never any implication that if only Oz was run on the lines that he would prefer then all would be well. McManus is said by some to have 'a tendency to play God', at times withholding rewards and privileges from his charges in an attempt to influence their behaviour, whilst not always appreciating that neither he, nor even they, can manipulate their behaviour in this way. Coming between McManus and Devlin is Warden Glynn, the man with the responsibility for managing Oz. Glynn is a pragmatic manager, less reform-minded than McManus, whose interest is in maintaining control and order, and staying within budget.

Up against the prison authorities are a highly diverse range of inmates. These are arranged in groupings of Black Muslims, the Italians, the Homeboys, the Aryan Brotherhood, the Latinos and a diverse assortment of others. Some of these others coalesce into identifiable groups as the show progresses (the Irish, the gays). At any one time each of these groups has an identifiable leader, although this is subject to change. Across the first two seasons there was a core ensemble of characters who were the main players within Em City. Firstly, Kareem Said is the leader of the Black Muslims. Said believes that prison is a product of an unjust society. So, whereas McManus wishes to reform the prison and build a better one, Said thinks the need is to reform society. Although Said believes in education, consciousness raising and purposeful activity, he rarely willingly cooperates with McManus. The task of the Black Muslims is to challenge the power structure. Although peaceful and religious, Said also believes in political direct action. Towards the end of season one, Said and the Black Muslims are believed to be planning a riot, although in the end it is started spontaneously by two crackheads who had an argument and then started a fight about a game of checkers.

The main group in opposition to the Black Muslims is the Homeboys. Whereas the Muslims are anti-drugs and in favour of political action, the Homeboys use drugs and struggle to control the prison's drug trade. The Homeboys see Oz/Em City as a Darwinian struggle for survival and the battle for supremacy is one of the main motors that drives the action. Despite their apparently stereotypical representation, individually the Homeboys are all different, with various personalities and life-courses. The leader is Simon Adebisi, a predatory warrior who has little interest in reform or self-betterment. Other members of the group might be swayed by McManus' reform efforts, but reform for them is always harder than McManus might think. Loyalty to the group, the Darwinian struggle for survival and prison culture more generally, militate against them simply making a voluntary decision to 'clean up their act'.

Next in Em City are the Italians who are the remains of the mafia wise guys, with their older members still believing in family codes of honour and means of doing things. The younger generation is more concerned that their power within the prison is waning in relation to other groups. The Latinos are in a similar position. Ethnically identified as a group for survival purposes, some of their members believe that they should have more influence. But, here again, despite their ethnic identification, individuals within the group have their own distinct characters and life-courses, particularly Miguel Alvarez, the one-time leader, who becomes overpowered by prison culture as the show develops. Finally, Oz has its own white supremacist group, the Aryan Brotherhood led by Vern Schillinger. A group of racists who disapprove of drugs, the Brotherhood need to maintain profile and presence to survive the prison culture. Although their leader, Schillinger, believes in 'building a better America' outside prison, inside he behaves in a highly amoral, predatory way.

The character of Tobias Beecher constitutes one of the main focal points of the show. Beecher is a lawyer who has been struck off after having killed a little girl in a drink-drive accident. The main story arc in Oz concerns the manner in which Schillinger manoeuvres the 'prison innocent' Beecher into a predatory relationship. In season one Schillinger turns Beecher into his 'cell bitch', and the subsequent series is an exploration of Beecher's attempts to break free of this relationship and the implications of it. It should be said, that although some viewers might see the white supremacist, predatory rapist Schillinger as a potential figure to identify against, in terms of the show he is coded as having equal worth to everyone else. If Schillinger had not made Beecher his 'cell bitch', then Adebisi or someone else would have done. And, in the world of Oz, if Beecher does not want to experience this kind of relationship then he has to do what is necessary to avoid it or get out from under it.

The second main character is Ryan O'Reily. Not really attached to any group (although at times identified with the Irish), O'Reily is the arch schemer. Playing everyone else off against each other, he is responsible for many of the inmate deaths that occur in Oz. Again, paradoxically, O'Reily is one of the most appealing characters in the show, and someone whom it is possible to follow because of his continuing story arc, even though 'objectively' he is one of the most despicable. But, in Oz's kill-or-be-killed environment, survival of the fittest rules and getting rid of one's rivals is therefore only to be expected. O'Reily's Machiavellian scheming is one of the main entertainment features of the show. Oz is more honest than some other prison dramas in recognising that our fascination with the Darwinian struggle to survive is one of the main viewing pleasures of prison dramas. Both Beecher and O'Reily are depicted as white, although the prison is multi-racial.

The other main character of significance is Augustus Hill. Hill is an African-American wheelchair user, who acts as the show's narrator. He interjects philosophical observations on the proceedings, whilst also being a character in his own right in the ensemble of players.

The corrections officers (COs) vary from the overtly corrupt to the simply world weary. COs collude with inmate fatalities and participate in the illicit economy of the prison. Brutality by COs is not unknown. Some become corrupt because they face an economic struggle to survive. Corrupt COs who dish out brutality are not formally disapproved of. Everyone just does what they need to do to survive.

But, are there any good characters in Oz? Some potential candidates would be Sister Peter Marie, the prison psychologist, a nun who does not wear a habit;

Father Ray Mukada, an Asian-American Catholic priest; and Gloria Nathan, the prison doctor. These three figures are generally coded as being well-intentioned and attempting to do good within the limits of their ability. But, they are not really coded as morally superior to the kill-or-be-killed inmates. Whilst any one of them might on occasion counsel a particular inmate to be less manipulative and less predatory, any inmate who unilaterally took their advice would most likely be found dead the next day. These well meaning professionals generally have no answers considering how to improve the prison culture. Their efforts are often ineffectual and they are all at times seen colluding in decisions or actions that they might have been expected to oppose.

UNDERSTANDING OZ

Oz presents itself as being an amoral, hyper-violent examination of prisons and prisoners. As we have seen, Tom Fontana, the show's creator seemingly distances *Oz* from any penal reform intent. In refusing to privilege any one view of how prisons should be run, the stylistics of the show would seem to support this view. But should we take *Oz* at face value? Does its apparent agnosticism have some purpose or significance? Is its portrayal of 'the predatory penitentiary' defensible, or is *Oz* guilty of constructing a 'skewed and selective representation of prisons and prisoners' (O'Sullivan, 2001)? Does *Oz* contribute to reproducing the notions of criminality which have underpinned the growth of the prison population, or does it challenge them?

The *Corrections Yearbook* (2001) suggests that only some six per cent of US correctional facilities are maximum security institutions. The inmates of *Oz* have invariably been convicted of serious violent crimes. Yet we know that the majority of offenders within US prisons, and the main area of prison growth, is relatively minor offenders, convicted of non-violent crimes (Donziger, 1996). *Oz* would seem to be continuing the media fascination with the maximum security prison. It is possible that it could contribute to the public's misperception of prison and prisoners, confirming their belief that prison is confined to necessary protection against dangerous, violent offenders. But the notion of a predatory penitentiary exists independently of *Oz's* portrayal of it (see, for example, Wacquant, 2001), so rather than merely reproducing this notion maybe *Oz* sets out to explore it. The series could be seen as an examination of 'the worst case scenario'. What if prisons were filled with dangerous, cynical criminals who had committed unspeakable acts outside prison and continued to harm each other with their predatory behaviour in prison? If this were reality, would we then be justified in concluding that prisoners get the prison they deserve?

Arguably there is purpose and intent to *Oz's* strategy of constructing its 'skewed and selective' representation of prison and prisoners. *Oz* experiences a high turnover of new inmates, who are usually introduced some time after their arrival via a flashback to the crime scene of their offence. The crime scene is invariably accompanied by the narrator, August Hill, gleefully telling us what the inmate did, the sentence he received and the time he must serve before he is 'up for parole'. So for example Ryan O'Reily is introduced as follows (with gleeful emphasis):

Prisoner number 973904 .. Ry-an O'Reily ... ha, ha. ha. Convicted July 12th '97 ... Two counts of vehicular manslaughter, five counts of reckless endangerment ... possession of a controlled substance ... criminal possession of a weapon ... uh, ha, parole violation..ha..ha.ha.. Sentence—life imprisonment (ha, ha). Up for parole in 12 years (ah ha ha ...)

The gleefulness with which these recitations are delivered parodies the element of *schaudenfraude* (delight at the misfortune of others) present in any desire to see or know that criminals get their just deserts. This ritual naming of offenders, many of whom are 'minorities', produces a constant stream of violent criminals who have been incarcerated for a spree of shootings and slayings. *Oz*'s tactic of replaying the crime scenes mimics the way that TV presents a continuous stream of images and representations of dangerous (ethnically marked) criminality. Thus *Oz* arguably does two things. Firstly, it undermines stereotypes of (ethnically marked) criminality by overloading them to excess. The constant stream of such offenders suggests that this criminality, if it exists, must be social and structural, rather than simply the product of the acts of free-willed individuals. Secondly, *Oz* goes beyond what we see on the TV news to show the life and personality of the offender after they have been led away. *Oz* humanises the prisoner. It achieves this mainly through having a large ensemble cast in which the vast majority of prisoners who appear on screen have some dialogue and some storyline. *Oz* deliberately tries to employ as little *mise en scène* as possible. There are relatively few crowd shots depicting a mass of inmates connoted as dangerous hardened convicts. Where possible, members of the main cast are used as the incidental players in the action (for example, McManus is talking to Said, Ryan O'Reily is the person mopping the floor in the background). Allowing the participants to have their own storyline allows different personalities to emerge. Adebisi and Wangler are both part of the group identified as 'the Homeboys', but have quite different personalities and characters. Indeed everyone in *Oz* emerges as a strong individual character. Like many other cult TV shows, *Oz* exhibits the paradox that highly stylised characters, who are clearly intended as symbolic carriers of discourses, can at the same time become highly compelling and 'believable'.

But, having said this, although the inmates in *Oz* emerge as strong characters in their own right and indeed all posses their own personal moral code, they all at some point display some kind of 'predatory' behaviour, whether out of offensive intention or defensive reaction. So, for example, the two oldest prisoners, Rebadow and Busmalis, are possibly the least offensive of the inmates in Em City. But on one occasion, when members of the Aryan brotherhood try to muscle in on an escape tunnel that they have dug, the pair weaken the tunnel's supports and deliberately allow the Aryans to go to their deaths. In *Oz* virtually every inmate has caused another inmate's death either directly or indirectly. But again, if everyone participates in 'predatory' behaviour of some form, including COs, this begs the question as to whether such behaviour can be seen as a product of the characteristics and disposition of the individual. And, although *Oz* never formally disapproves of the constant stream of beatings, inmate fatalities brought about by CO contrivance, and so on, the show perhaps does implicitly raise the question of whether we should just accept the fact that bad things occur in prison under some generalised notion that 'shit happens'.

Although *Oz* represents itself as being studiously neutral on prison issues, this neutrality is a bit of a charade. In effect, the show identifies prison as a failing institution. The authorities are shown as being unable to protect their charges from rape, abuse or even murder, unable even to protect their inmates from their own addictions and personal failings. Prison is shown as being no solution to the crime problem. It neither deters crime, nor rehabilitates its prisoners. There are no success stories in *Oz*. Prisoners rarely make it out of the institution alive. Those who do invariably come back. But, although few if any ever actually achieve the desired for change in their life-course, because we come to know them as individuals we see that the possibility of change exists, even if circumstances usually conspire to deprive them of a happy ending. So, despite the fact that the efforts of McManus, Sister Peter Marie and Father Ray Mukada rarely amount to much, would we really say that they should not be there trying? *Oz* maintains the possibility that there is no solution to the problem of prison. It may be, as Said suggests, that the task is not to build a better prison but to build a better society. But, as long as we do have prisons, *Oz* suggests that a good prison should have: a reform-minded liberal running an experimental unit; a nun/psychologist who tries, for example, to develop appropriate provision for prison elders; a doctor who will try, within the constraints of economy, to provide appropriate healthcare; and a chaplain who expresses genuine concern for the spiritual and personal wellbeing of his flock.

We would suggest then that although *Oz* represents itself as being formally agnostic on the origins of the 'prisons crisis' and the solutions to it. The show makes no sense if there is not some kind of problem to be addressed. If prison were a smoothly functioning, valuable social institution then we would have no need to see it. The simple act of showing prison is an agenda setting intervention suggesting a problem in need of consideration.

Whilst in the early days Tom Fontana may have attempted to distance *Oz* from penal reform ambitions, as its sixth season came to a close a clearer statement of intent emerged. In an epilogue to the show Fontana revealed that the 1971 Attica uprising had been one of the significant events of his formative youth. According to him, Attica had prompted a public debate about the reasons for the uprising and the appropriateness of the response to it. But Fontana confesses that he personally had not revisited the issue of prison until filming for his TV series *Homicide: Life on the Street* took him into a Baltimore prison. Stunned by the extent to which the prison was 'rife with fear and racism', Fontana resolved to make a TV series about 'life behind bars'. The result was *Oz*, an attempt 'to put a human face on our faceless prison population' (Fontana, 'Epilogue' in Hill, 2003: 192). The final book produced to accompany the end of the series contained extensive sidebars referencing sources of information on real world prison problems relating to safety, sexuality, mental health, education and so forth.

The Russian philosopher Fyodor Dostoevsky suggested that 'the degree of civilisation in a society can be judged by entering its prisons'. In making prison visible *Oz* sought to allow us to see, without having to go there—although this perhaps leaves the problem of the relationship between the at times hyperbolic representation in *Oz* and its real world referent. If we cannot have an eyewitness account will a (hyperbolic) dramatic representation do in its stead? Whether *Oz* succeeded in raising the profile of prison and what effect its appearance had on public perceptions, goes beyond the scope of the present discussion. But *Oz* certainly found a formula that created a relatively successful and long running men's prison drama, something there have to date been precious few of. If TV can make shows about cops, lawyers, doctors and lifeguards, then why not about prison and prisoners (Fontana, 'Epilogue', in Hill, 2003: 189)?

CONCLUSION

Oscar Wilde wrote *The Ballad of Reading Goal* to reveal the inhumanity of prison and to connote prison as something that we should be ashamed of. *Oz* constructed prison as a hyper-violent, kill-or-be-killed environment, where no one knows exactly why it is like this, or whether anything can be done to change it. It almost dares us to draw the conclusion that no one is to blame for the state of prison and that there is therefore nothing to be ashamed about. Wilde invited us to agree with his assessment of prison, whilst *Oz* dares us to disagree with its own. Wilde stated his critique of prison in the unconditional—this is what prison is like, we should be ashamed of it. *Oz* states its critique in the conditional—if this is what prison is like, should a society that claims to be civilised be tolerating it? *Oz* dares its viewing public to agree with the proposition that whatever happens to prisoners in prison does not much matter. If they 'cannot do the time' then they 'should not commit the crime'. Whilst there may be some who will agree with this proposition, the majority of the audience might come to feel that prisons need to have some standards of decency. If we really support a prison where 'anything goes', then society's standards have been reduced to being the same as the standards of those it dubs 'the worst of the worst'. In which case, as well as prisoners getting the prison that they deserve, society will get the criminals it deserves. The dramatisation of prison in *Oz* suggested that, even in the worst possible case scenario prisoners are still human beings to whom some standard of care is owed if society is to maintain its idea of itself as civilised. It would seem then, that *Oz* was a show about 'prisoner's rights' after all.

CHAPTER 8

On Being 'the Man': The Prison Governor

Walter, Death Row inmate (Morgan Freeman): I want 'the Man';
Warden Brubaker (Robert Redford): I am 'the Man'.

(*Brubaker*, 1980)

Governor (Michael Redgrave) addressing new receptions: If you play ball with us, we'll play ball with you. We want you to work hard and play hard. We believe in all that.

(*The Loneliness of the Long Distance Runner*, 1962)

Prisons operate as hierarchies, not just of prisoners but most obviously of staff. At the top of this latter hierarchy in the UK is the prison Governor and in the US, the Warden (see Bryans and Wilson, 1998 for a general introduction). Unsurprisingly, Governors and Wardens have great powers, or as Gresham Sykes (1958: 42) has described it, 'a grant of power without equal', allowing them to make the lives of their charges tolerable and productive, or dehumanising and miserable. So, when Walter asked to see 'the Man' in *Brubaker*, he was revealing that he understood the nature of the hierarchy in the gaol and thus who would be able to make life better for him, or at least to whom he could complain. Similarly, Michael Redgrave, as the Governor of the borstal Ruxton Towers in *The Loneliness of the Long Distance Runner* (from now on referred to as *Loneliness*), was attempting to set out for new receptions at the prison the nature of its regime, how they could fit in and an implied threat if they did not.

Recognition of the Governor's power in a British context can be gleaned from a variety of governmental reports, especially those of HM Chief Inspector of Prisons and other writings related to the inner working of prisons. For example, Sir Raymond Lygo (1991: ii) thought that governing prisons was the 'most complex and difficult management task that I have encountered' and Derek Lewis (1997: 23), the first Director General of HM Prison Service to be recruited from the private sector, wrote in his autobiography that he had no doubts as to his most pressing task after taking office—'the key group I had to get to know were the prison Governors'. In the US, DiIulio (1987: 255) has argued that the Warden's managerial style was the most salient determinant of whether prisons were safe, orderly, clean and capable of providing inmate amenities and Kevin Wright's *Effective Prison Leadership* (1994) suggested that good Wardens create good prisons.

Yet, given this power, their ability to control the culture of the prison and the impact that a good Governor or Warden can have, it is surprising how rarely they appear in current prison movies. For example, the Warden is missing from *The Green Mile* (1999) and *American History X* (1998) and makes only the briefest of appearances in *Monster's Ball* (2001), to take but three recent, popular, mainstream films. Nellis (1982) has argued that in the 1930s and 1940s reform-minded Wardens (as to which see generally *Chapter* 5) were a major source of screenplays and ideas for prison films. Rafter (2000) has noted the disappearance of the reform-minded Warden, with Wardens over time becoming progressively more ludicrously evil, for example as portrayed by Donald Sutherland in *Lock Up* (1989) or Gary Oldman in *Murder in the First* (1995). Cheatwood (1998) has noted that in the 'sci-fi' prison the Warden has disappeared almost entirely, becoming either an external controller (*No Escape*) or a technological controller (*Fortress*).

This chapter looks further at the way Governors and Wardens are presented in film by considering two British films, *The Loneliness of the Long Distance Runner* (1962) and *Scum* (1979), and two American films, *Brubaker* (1980) and *The Shawshank Redemption* (1994). Do cinematic prisons give us any clues as to what constitutes 'good governing'? Do fictional Governors or Wardens help us to push further the argument at the heart of this book that fictional accounts of prisons, prisoners and prison staff matter and can perform penal reform functions? We have suggested that these penal reform functions are particularly acute when the film popularises critical accounts of the penal system, or presents 'benchmarks' as to what constitutes a socially acceptable standard of decency and that these functions are at their most effective when a Hollywood star acts as an informal endorser of the position implicit in the film. It is no surprise, for example, that Warden Brubaker, 'suggested by' the campaigning book by Thomas Murton, who had been a Warden in the Arkansas penal system (see below), was played by Robert Redford and that the viewer is expected to support the positions that he adopts. In these ways, we suggest that the fictional Governor or Warden comes to symbolise something much broader than the power that he exercises in the gaol and thus also acts as a signifier about the use, or abuse, of power in the community in which the film is set and the time when it is located.

ON BEING 'THE MAN'

Bryans and Wilson (1998: 27-8), in what remains the only book dedicated to explaining in detail the role and function of the Governor in British prisons, use two job adverts from 1967 and 1997 to show how the type of person and the qualities needed to be a Governor have changed over time. The recruitment literature for 1967, only four years after *Loneliness* was released, reads: 'Duties demand a lively interest in social problems and a good understanding of the modern methods of handling them', which reflects the social work ethos of the 1960s. Thirty years later, recruitment literature for the Prison Service's Accelerated Promotion Scheme (APS) suggests a more complicated and managerial picture:

> Being a prison Governor is probably the most complicated people management task you will ever come across. The daily challenges of the Prison Service are immense. Maintaining a balance between our duty to protect the public by keeping offenders securely in custody and our duty to help people in prison address their problems is never easy. Add to this a commitment to our staff and to the effective use of resources and you'll begin to appreciate what the job involves.
>
> That's why the people we recruit onto the APS have got to be exceptional. We welcome graduates from any discipline, and from any race, ethnic origin, religion or gender, because we are only interested in your personal qualities and abilities.

Stamina, enthusiasm, leadership, organizational flair, numerical and analytical ability should accompany strong interpersonal skills, but without plenty of self-confidence you'll never make it.

Bryans and Wilson (1998: 32-3) suggest that there are four elements to the role of Governor in British prisons: leading; interpreting; resourcing and representing. Thus, for example, a Governor's ability to influence events is linked to the way that he exercises leadership and authority, maintaining a balance between the legitimate expectations of staff and prisoners. As he has a total overview of the prison and its place within the wider criminal justice system, the Governor is able to interpret and then reconcile competing demands between various penal objectives, political expediency and humanity and ensures that his establishment is appropriately resourced. Finally, the Governor is a public figure who represents the establishment in the community and in the media.

These personal qualities—which are just as valid in an American context—also lead to and dovetail with what Barak-Glantz (1981) has described as the four models of 'prison management': authoritarian; bureaucratic lawful; shared-powers; and inmate-control. In essence, the chief characteristic of an authoritarian model is the domination of the Governor or Warden over the staff as well as the prisoners. Within extremely broad limits, the Governor or Warden can do as he or she pleases. A bureaucratic-lawful model of prison management is often implemented as a response to the authoritarian model and general principles, rules and regulations are applied by the central administration to the Governor or Warden and they in turn apply them to their staff. The third model, shared-powers, refers to a situation in which rehabilitative goals lead to the democratisation of the prison, with some powers being given to prisoners, who begin to form a recognisable pressure group. 'Treatment-orientated' Governors and Wardens often adopt this model, with only minimum levels of controls and democracy characterises the decision-making process. The inmate-control model involves prisoner groups taking control of the prison by creating 'no go areas', organizing activities and settling disputes amongst themselves. Prisoners can divide in this model on the basis of, for example, ethnic groups or religious denomination and can create relatively well-organized structures with clear leadership and a chain of command. Their actions and behaviour often support deviant behaviour as a means to gain further power or regime privileges.

It is, of course, difficult to identify actual prisons which equate exactly with each type of model, although, for example, DiIulio (1987) described the Texas penal system as operating a 'control' model, similar to the authoritarian model, with emphasis placed on prisoner obedience, work and education, all set within a paramilitary style of organization. On the other hand, the Michigan penal system was seen as a 'responsibility' system, equated with the shared-power model, in which the focus was more on grievance procedures, with prisoners given some responsibility for running their own lives. However, it is relatively easy to read those prison movies which feature a Warden or Governor within these models of prison management and, for example, it would be perfectly possible to analyse *Brubaker* as an attempt by Warden Brubaker to introduce a shared-powers model of prison management at Wakefield State Penitentiary after years in which the prison was run on an authoritarian model. Indeed, one of Warden Brubaker's first decisions is to set up an Inmate Council.

Celluloid Governors and Wardens

The Loneliness of the Long Distance Runner
Loneliness (directed by Tony Richardson, 1962), based on the short story by Alan Sillitoe, who also wrote the screenplay, is set in Ruxton Towers borstal—a type of young offender institution that survived until 1983, based on the public school system, and to which young offenders were sent to serve an indeterminate sentence. Thus, a young person was sentenced to 'borstal training' but not given a specific date when he would be released. Release was a matter for the borstal staff to decide, rather than the courts, on the basis of the young person's attitude, work habits and educational attainment whilst incarcerated. This gave the staff—especially the Governor or 'House Masters' a great deal of personal discretion and power. In *Loneliness* we follow the fortunes of the rebellious Colin Smith (Tom Courtenay), who has been sent there for breaking into a bakery and stealing just over £71 with his friend Mike (James Bolam: who was to reprise aspects of this role in the long running BBC TV series *The Likely Lads*). Colin has just watched his father die of cancer. His mother, now flush with the compensation that she received from the factory, where her husband had been a union leader prior to his illness, establishes a new relationship with Gordon, her 'fancy man', who effectively moves into the house, thus establishing a tug-of-war with Colin as to who is the 'head' of the household. Indeed, this subtext of Colin finding a suitable replacement for his dead father, or metaphorically becoming the father himself is echoed throughout the film. Thus, when Colin makes it to the top of the inmate hierarchy within Ruxton Towers, the other prisoners, using borstal slang, describe him as 'the daddy', which has added poignancy.

The film opens with scenes of Colin running freely in the countryside, with *Jerusalem* playing in the background, and in effect establishing a sense it is dealing with larger themes about the nature of England—this 'green and pleasant land' and of Englishness. Very quickly these images of freedom are replaced by those of handcuffs and of six boys, including Colin, being taken into Ruxton Towers in a minibus, an opening scene later used in *Scum*. We then see the Governor, played by Michael Redgrave, who wears his Harrow tie throughout and who explains that, 'It is a great day for us—something I have been working for a long time.' It transpires that what is 'great' about the day is that Ranley School—a local public school, has agreed to share its sports day with the borstal and the Governor has set his heart on the borstal winning the Challenge Cup for the cross-country. In this way the English class structure forms a none too subtle backdrop and the struggle to win the cross-country race becomes a metaphor for the social and economic changes that England is experiencing. In a key scene, told in flashback, Colin and Mike sit at home watching a fictional party political broadcast on behalf of the Conservative Party (on the TV bought with his dead father's compensation money) in which a politician asks for a 'spirit of rededication, such as we have at a coronation or at a royal wedding' and who reminds his audience of their prosperity, which he accounts for on the basis of a 'new mood of self-discipline' and the fact that 'our young people have never been affected by the Continental disease of existentialism'. Colin and Mike sit laughing uncontrollably and turn the volume down completely. Gordon, the 'fancy man', the new head of the household and a representative of 'old England', enters the room and attempts to turn the sound back up but Colin resists, before being thrown out by his mother.

Initially the Governor—yet another representative of 'old England', pins his hope on Stacy—the 'daddy' of the iconically named Drake House—to win the race, but he soon shifts his allegiances to Colin, which sets up a competition between the two prisoners and thus provides an echo of his tug-of-war with Gordon. Stacy, recognising that Colin is faster and that he is no longer the Governor's favourite, eventually absconds and is beaten by the staff after his recapture, whilst Colin is given greater and greater freedoms to help him win the cup. Thus, reflecting his power, he takes Colin out of the factory shop in which he is working and puts him to work in the gardens and even allows him to run unescorted in the countryside, so as to build up his stamina. Later, after Mike has been sent to the borstal too, Colin is described to him as 'the Governor's blue-eyed boy', which prompts Mike to ask, 'who's bloody side are you on?' Even after the prisoners riot in the dining room—partly out of sympathy with Stacy, a scene which would again be used in *Scum*, the Governor refuses to cancel the sports day on the basis that 'We should not make too much of this spot of bother' and the fact that the sports day would be 'a great day in borstal history'. The Governor's philosophy is 'a healthy mind in a healthy body', although this does not go down well with the newly arrived house master, Mr Brown, who asks, 'Isn't life a little more complicated than a football match?' However, the Governor is dismissive of all this 'psychiatric stuff that they shove at us', although it is Brown, using word association with Colin who uncovers the recent death of his father—'gun—horses; knife—smoke; car—crumpet; father–dead'. Nonetheless, Brown is told that 'it pays to play the Governor's game' and the Governor's game is athletics. Indeed, he advises Colin that there can be no 'higher honour than representing your country at the Olympic Games—the greatest invention ever made by civilization', which both echoes the bombastic party political broadcast and leaves Colin and the viewer in no doubts as to the importance of the race for the Governor.

On sports day the public school boys of Ranley nervously enter the changing rooms in their blazers and soon there is some good-natured banter with the borstal boys about food and smoking, which serves to establish that they have things in common. 'We should get together and start a revolution', shouts one of the prisoners but the public school boys are too busy getting changed into their pristine, white track-suits to take this seriously. (The public school would not revolt until six years later, in Lindsay Anderson's *If...*) Gunthorpe, Ranley's star runner, played by a young James Fox, comes over to shake Colin's hand and then all the runners are lined up and introduced to a visiting army major, as if they are about to go into battle. The race starts and it is quickly apparent that Colin can win if he chooses, but as he enters the finishing straight first—the soundtrack from earlier scenes from the film playing in his ear—he hears Mike asking again, 'Whose side are you on?', that seems to remind him that winning this race is not his ambition, but the Governor's and that this England is not one that he particularly likes. He stops and despite being urged on by the crowd, he refuses to run another step until inevitably Gunthorpe—the natural heir of 'old England' passes him and without as much as a backward glance (there is going to be no revolution here) crosses the line. Soon Colin is back in the borstal's factory shop and the film ends with a close-up of the gas masks that the prisoners are making, an echo of war and fighting, which suggests that this is all that the working-class are fit for.

Scum

Scum (1979) (director Alan Clarke), written by Roy Minton, is also set in a borstal, but some 17 years later, just prior to the borstal system's abolition. It too follows the story of one prisoner's progress—4737 Carlin, played by Ray Winstone, and whom we first see with Angel, a black prisoner, and Davis, who has absconded from an open prison, handcuffed in the prison van, echoing the opening scene in *Loneliness*. Carlin is subsequently introduced as 'the daddy, the hard case', who had assaulted an officer at his previous establishment and who has therefore been sent to his new borstal to be 'sorted out'.

Because of this the staff have ensured that Carlin's progress in the gaol is as difficult as possible, by having him deliberately assigned to a dormitory occupied by Pongo Banks—the established 'daddy', and two of his cronies, Eckersley (Ray Burdis) and Richards (Phil Daniels). On the first night, Banks beats up Carlin and tells him, 'Right, Carlin, I run this fucking gaff. You just keep your fucking mouth closed—you ain't no daddy here' and in effect the action in *Scum* centres on Carlin's efforts to replace Banks and climb the inmate hierarchy. Along the way, Davis is raped in the greenhouse by three other prisoners, an event witnessed by a smiling, almost approving officer and he eventually commits suicide, which prompts a dining room riot, all played against a background of violence, corruption and casual racism, something that *Loneliness* did not tackle, but which by 1979 had become an issue within the criminal justice system. Angel (Davidson Knight), for example, is described by the staff as a 'nig-nog—straight out of the banana tree' and a 'black, Brixton bastard'. The suicide of Davis is especially gruesome, given that he rings his cell bell and tells the officer, 'I feel lonely and frightened, Sir. I'm depressed and don't know what to do'. The officer responds by telling Davis to get 'his subnormal head down' and he promptly cuts his wrists. Realising what he has done, he rings the cell bell again, but the officer simply ignores it.

Carlin's progress is aided by Archer (Mick Ford), a vegetarian who wants to read Dostoevsky and is thinking of becoming a Sikh. He informs Carlin that the 'Governor is a religious nut', with strong Church of England beliefs and so it is clear that through his faith, Archer is rebelling. He is called up to see the Governor, Mr Baildon (Richard Butler), who has purchased plastic boots for Archer to wear, given that he had refused to wear leather because of his supposed vegetarianism (he later welcomes a sausage given to him by Carlin). The Governor, whilst professing to 'respect another man's beliefs', asks, 'Have you read the *Life of St Francis of Assisi*?' Archer says that he has not, but that he is now 'strongly drawn to Mecca'. 'Mecca, Archer!' the Governor explodes, 'You'll see the chaplain tomorrow and there will be no more talk about Mecca in this establishment!'

Throughout *Scum* various people—prisoners and staff—claim to be 'in charge' of, or 'running' the borstal. Pongo Banks, the established 'daddy', senior officer (SO) Sands—'I run a wing—right, Carlin?', the house master, Mr Goodyear and indeed the Governor himself all claim to be in charge. However, what is of interest is that it is clear that the staff have to use the prisoners to run the borstal and thus do not object to, or try to control the inmate subculture that produces 'daddies', violence, sexual assault and racism, but rather condone the brutality. Indeed, when it is clear that Carlin has replaced Banks as 'the daddy', Mr Goodyear (John Grillo), Carlin's house master, calls him into his office and reminds him that 'the gift of leadership entails responsibility' and that Carlin should therefore set an example to the other prisoners and 'keep order'. Whilst reminding Carlin that 'I run this wing', it is clear that Mr Goodyear is asking Carlin for help—something that he is only too pleased to give, in return of course for favours—in this case occupancy of a single cell. 'I think that can be arranged,' suggests Mr Goodyear and the deal is done.

That deal is important. It symbolises that Carlin is not trying to oppose the system, but rather to get as much out of it as he can. He knows the system is corrupt and violent, but he is equally adept at being corrupt himself and can clearly use his fists. Archer, on the other hand, refuses to compromise in any respect and in a well-known scene with one of the officers, Mr Duke (Dennis Castle), assigned to guard him whilst the other prisoners are at chapel, Archer explains, 'The only thing that I will take away from borstal is evil—how can anyone build a character in a regime based on deprivation?' He continues, 'Mr Duke, I don't want to underestimate your lifetime's work, but the punitive system does not work. My experience of borstal convinces me that more criminal acts are imposed on prisoners than criminals on society.'

Carlin is uninterested in this type of theorising, as is the Governor, who wanders through the gaol on his daily rounds almost oblivious to the regime that surrounds him. He enters the kitchen and briefly tastes the meal that is to be served to the prisoners—'Fine, Mr White, excellent'—and then signs to say that the food has been tasted. He goes to the punishment block, where prisoners are standing outside their door awaiting his arrival. 'Name and number for the Governor!' shouts an officer; a name and number are duly given, to which the Governor replies, 'Everything all right?'—'Yes, Sir'. 'Good,' says the Governor, as the officer pushes the prisoner back into his cell. And, after the prisoners have rioted, when it becomes clear that Davis has committed suicide, the hollowness of the Governor's Christian beliefs mirrors the hollowness of the borstal's regime when he addresses the assembled prisoners. First, he takes away their earnings and privileges until the broken 'public property is paid for.' Then, 'With regard to our absent friend I would remind you all that sad and unfortunate accidents occur in institutions like this as they do on the outside. I will not tolerate any more outbursts. There will now be a minute's silence for our departed friend'.

Brubaker

Brubaker (1980) (director Stuart Rosenberg, who also directed *Cool Hand Luke* in 1967) was 'suggested by' the book by Thomas Murton, who had been a Warden of two prison farms in Arkansas between 1967 and 1968 and who had been appointed to modernise and reform the state's penal system (Nellis, 1982: 41). As the phrase 'suggested by' in the credits indicates, the film takes numerous liberties with the book (the screenplay is by W. D. Richter and Arthur A. Ross) and, for example, the opening scene which has Henry Brubaker (Robert Redford) enter Wakefield State Penitentiary disguised as an inmate is one such (although as Nellis advises, a former Warden at Sing Sing—Thomas Mott Osborne, had had himself committed to Auburn Penitentiary in 1913 under an assumed name (Nellis, 1982: 12)).

This artistic licence allows Brubaker to experience for himself various corrupt practices: prisoners selling their blood and buying medical treatment; prisoner on prisoner rape; maggot infested food; an overcrowded dormitory with too few bunks; and prison trusties, led by 'Captain' Eddie Caldwell (Everett McGill), who inflict corporal punishment on other prisoners, the 'Rankmen', with leather belts, rifles and electric shocks—known as 'phone calls'. Brubaker only reveals his true identity after his meeting with Walter (Morgan Freeman) and marches up to Warden Renfrew's office to relieve him. The old Warden has some advice for the new one—'The smartest thing that you ever did was come in here incognito; the stupidest was coming forward. You want it? You got it'. Thereafter, the action centres on Brubaker's efforts to deal with the problems that he has inherited and his negotiations with the politicians and the state's Prisons Board, headed by John Deach (Murray Hamilton).

Brubaker makes some immediate changes—he abolishes the beatings and suggests that he wants to turn the prison into 'a twentieth century farm' by growing vegetables and raising cattle. He asks Roy Purcell (Matt Clark)—the Warden's clerk—to buy him a dozen pairs of sunglasses and it soon becomes clear that these are for Walter and his fellow Death Row inmates, who are to be allowed exercise in the sunshine, after years of being left in the darkness. Brubaker enlists the support of two trusties—Larry Lee Bullen (David Keith) and Coombes (Yaphet Kotto). He offers Bullen the job of running the motor pool and Bullen agrees, but suggests that 'You're one weird fucking individual' and 'I haven't got you worked out yet if you are a good or a bad thing'. This suspicion is continued by Coombes, who lets Brubaker know that, in the beginning, 'Everyone's a reform Warden' and points out that the new clothes that they are wearing were procured for them by Warden Renfrew. 'One day', suggests Coombes, 'we could all just stop playing the Man's game, put down our rifles and take off'. However, gradually both Coombes and Bullen come over to Brubaker's side.

The same is not true of the many interested parties on the outside. In one humorous scene, the corrupt lumber merchant, C. P. Woodward (M. Emmet Walsh), who has been using the prisoners as poorly paid labour, comes by with a prune cake to ingratiate himself with Brubaker and in passing bid for repairing the Rankmen's dormitory roof, which he had earlier built only two years previously, but which has now collapsed. Brubaker is incensed, but Woodward suggests, 'You've got to get on top of this shit pile, Henry, and then the job's not so much of a ball breaker'. He also reminds Brubaker that, 'This is a community. We don't ostracise the gaol; we accept it. It's a two-way street. Let things runs like they've been running for a hundred years. Don't fuck with tradition'. But this is exactly what Brubaker intends to do. As Woodward is shown the door, he asks the Warden's clerk (an echo of Mike in *Loneliness*), 'Whose team are you on,

Purcell?' 'What can I say?' replies Purcell, 'He's the coach for now'. 'Short season', snaps back Woodward.

That Brubaker's season was indeed to prove short was not so much a result of the hostility from the local community—of Woodward and his ilk—but rather his failure to overcome or accommodate the political reaction to what he was uncovering at the gaol and how he was attempting to move the prison forward. His biggest supporter, Lillian Gray, the State Governor's aide, tries to explain that it is 'a very complex world out there', but Brubaker is in no mood to compromise. He tells the prison's board to 'give me a year and leave me alone' and argues with John Deach, the head of the board, that he wants to reform the prison and allow the prisoners 'to have responsibility'. Deach in turn points out that he thinks that Brubaker's degree in penology is not a sufficient basis on which to make demands; that the prisoners are 'reckless'; that he does not want 'to make life easy for men like that'; and, that people 'don't want to hear that their taxes are being raised to pay for murderers and rapist'. Clearly, this is not a meeting of minds and Brubaker walks out, quickly followed by Lillian, who warns him that, 'They'll pull the plug on all of this' and 'If you are not in the system, you cannot change it'. Brubaker retorts, 'Prison reformers—pseudo reformers, are the real obstacles to prison reform', and reminds her that 'The prisoners now think of themselves as human beings'. Lillian warns Brubaker that if he does not 'figure out how to play these people' then he will 'self-destruct'.

Brubaker discovers that an elderly prisoner, Abraham (Richard Ward), who had been kept in the gaol after his sentence had ended and who had told him about there being bodies buried in the prison's fields, has been murdered before he could take him to where these graves were located. Undeterred, Brubaker has the prisoners start digging up the fields looking for the dead bodies, which again merely antagonises the politicians, who are clearly aware of what he will find and the scandal that will be caused. The state senator who sits on the prison's board tells Brubaker, 'You've got to stop digging'. He suggests that 'Wakefield is one of the best conceived prisons in this country, Sir.' He is prepared to concede that 'Wakefield State Penitentiary is an imperfect institution, much like the United States itself. She is nonetheless a grand experiment. Government of the man, by the man, for the man. It is the only prison in this country which has shown a profit'. However, it is clear that the senator is prepared to release funds to support Brubaker's reforms—as Lillian points out, 'Stop digging. We've got leverage. Don't concentrate on the dead, but on the living', but Brubaker is not going to be bought off. And, as he resigns/is sacked, he points out that he 'can't play politics with the truth'. The climactic ending has already been described in *Chapter 4*.

The Shawshank Redemption

The Shawshank Redemption (1994) (director Frank Darabont), based on the 1982 short story by Stephen King called *Rita Hayworth and Shawshank Redemption*, is concerned with Andy Dufresne (Tim Robbins), a banker who has been wrongly convicted of the murder of his wife and her golf-pro lover and his subsequent imprisonment in Shawshank. Inside the gaol, which is in Maine but actually filmed at Mansfield Reformatory, Ohio, we follow Dufresne's trials and tribulations from 1946 to his escape in 1975 and much of the narrative is told in voice-over by Dufresne's friend, Red (Morgan Freeman). The early action within the prison centres on Dufresne's attempts to fight off 'the sisters'—a predatory group of prisoners who want to bugger and rape him—and his eventual triumph over them, partly achieved by enlisting the support of Captain Hadley (Clancy Brown), whom Dufresne has advised on how to deal with the inheritance tax that he is about to pay on monies left to him by his rich brother. Dufresne's tax advice is soon in demand from other staff in the prison and we quickly see him getting better jobs and privileges—most notably being allowed to work in the library with an old prisoner (echoes here also of Abraham in *Brubaker*) called Brooks Hatlen (James Whitmore). Dufresne eventually escapes, having carved a hole in his cell's wall, which he had originally covered up with a large poster of Rita Hayworth (and thereafter of Marilyn Monroe and latterly Raquel Welch) and Red subsequently joins him, having gained parole. The final credits of the film roll as Dufresne and Red walk towards each other on a beach by the shore of the Pacific Ocean.

Into this brief narrative outline we have to add the central and crucial character of Warden Norton (Bob Gunton). According to Kermode (2003: 44), the Warden is 'the greatest invention' of Darabont's screenplay and someone whom he describes as 'sublimely demonic'. Kermode (2003: 45) also asserts that the Warden is meant to represent the reincarnation of Richard Nixon and the period of Dufresne's imprisonment does match the political career of the former, disgraced President (who was eventually impeached for, amongst other things, 'obstruction of justice' and 'abuse of power' but pardoned). Throughout the film the Warden does indeed obstruct justice and abuse his power, most notably in having Tommy Williams (Gil Bellows) killed, after it became clear that Williams could prove that Dufresne was innocent of the crime for which he had been convicted. After all, the Warden did not want to lose Dufresne, who had been acting as an accountant for his corrupt business ventures and who, if he had been released, could have reported him to the authorities. Instead Dufresne has to escape and he takes the money that he has been lodging for the Warden for himself and for Red and lets the press know what has been happening. In these circumstances, with the police cars coming to arrest him, the Warden commits suicide.

It is difficult to be too precise about Warden Norton's motivation, but in a telling scene, which seems to be located in the narrative in 1963—the year of the assassination of President Kennedy—he announces to the assembled public and press the launch of his 'Inside Out Programme' (echoes here too of the importance of sports day in *Loneliness*, which was to be 'a great day in borstal history'). The press carefully note down the Warden's words—'No free ride', he tells them, 'but rather a genuine progressive advance in corrections and rehabilitation' which is to provide prisoner labour, 'properly supervised ... at a bare minimum of expense to Mr and Mrs John Q Taxpayer' and which will be a 'valuable service to the community'. Of course, it soon transpires where the money is really going and Dufresne's job is to launder it. Nonetheless Warden Norton's lies are accepted at face value and his duplicity and greed only revealed much later after Dufresne has escaped.

THE DIFFERENCE BETWEEN WINNING AND LOSING

What, if anything, can we learn from our celluloid Governors about the way in which prisons should be run, or the processes through which they might be made better? And, what moral might we discern in the differing degrees of success or failure achieved by the screen protagonists introduced above?

The fictional prisons outlined in *Loneliness*, *Scum*, *Brubaker* and *Shawshank* pose a series of questions about who exactly were the winners and losers in the encounters they describe. It is relatively easy to see that *Loneliness* asks whether the figure of Colin Smith should be seen as a 'losing winner' or a 'winning loser'. It would appear that he had the race in his grasp and needed only to cross the winning-line to secure 'easy time' throughout his borstal training. Is it then that in making his token show of defiance Smith 'blew it,' and became a 'losing winner'? His gesture maintains the integrity of his own principles and allows him to retain the respect of Mike. But the final scene of the film would seem to undercut this interpretation. The Smith that we see returned to the workbench is far from triumphant and cocksure, and he will pay the price for a token show of defiance that no one really saw, or cares about. The real 'winning loser' in *Loneliness* is our governor of Ruxton Towers, for although Smith's show of defiance has robbed him of his 'great day for borstal', in the wider scheme of things this is relatively small beer. Smith will pay the price for his actions, the Governor's authority is reasserted and nothing really changes. *Loneliness* may have shown borstal to be an institution that was only interested in a symbolic show of rehabilitation, but even in the screen version the institution has not yet lost its control over its inmates, nor its legitimacy with the viewing public. In real life the borstal training system would endure for another 21 years relatively unchanged.

This brings us to *Scum* and here it is the Governor, Mr Baildon, who is 'a winner who lost'. The riot is put down and its leaders thrown bloody nosed into the cells of the punishment block. The Governor's speech to his assembled charges is met with no show of resistance, as he assures them that Davis's death is 'just one of those tragic things'. Authority is reasserted, but at a cost. We the viewers have seen that borstal isn't working, and in real life the system of borstal training was abolished in 1983, four years after the appearance of *Scum*. While it is not being suggested here that the one event was in some way caused by the other, the fact that by 1979 even the film makers had tumbled the bankruptcy of borstal as an institution, and were able to represent this on screen, may have signalled to politicians and policy makers that the secret was out.

Brubaker, it has been said, poses the liberal's dilemma: whether to work within the system for small change, or to hold out for radical change and be rejected by the system. The character of Lillian clearly believes that Brubaker is a 'losing winner'—he had leverage and the possibility of resources but threw his winning hand away. Nellis (1982) believes that Brubaker was always a loser; the authorities never ever wanted more than a semblance of penal reform, and the autonomy of the Warden has been overstated. Penal reform takes place, if at all, within the wider system. Our analysis is somewhat different. For us Brubaker is a 'winning loser'. In his refusal to 'play politics with the truth' he has benchmarked change. By the end of the film the regime of the Arkansas prison farm has lost its legitimacy, both with its inmates and us the viewing public. The 'real world' significance of this is less clear. Did the Arkansas Prison farm go the way of 'super-max' (King, 1999b) or become the twentieth century farm Brubaker wanted it to be? Maybe we need a sequel, *Brubaker 2: The Return to Arkansas*, to tell us what happened.

Tellingly, this last point brings us to *The Shawshank Redemption*. This film is not *Brubaker 2*, not a return to Arkansas, and indeed not any kind of investigation into, or comment on, real world penal conditions in the US past or present. It is an adaptation of a Stephen King novella. But, as a fictional representation, what might we learn? Of our four films, *Shawshank* is undeniably the most pessimistic about the role of the Warden and the potential for penal reform. When Warden Norton announces his Inside Out programme we have a view of penal reform as being nothing more than the same old package wrapped up in new rhetoric ('meet the new Boss, same as the old Boss'). Prison is a waste of space however it is run, rehabilitation is 'just a politician's word' and 'salvation lies within'. There is little point in Andy and Red waiting for a process of penal reform which never really occurs. They must find their own salvation, for Andy through escape, and for Red through breaking his parole. But this is just a fantasy resolution to the problem of prison for prisoners. Back in the real world, for most if not all prisoners, the possibility of escape to a beach in Mexico is, as Red would put it 'a shitty little pipe dream', or as Stephen King put it 'a pipe dream in a shitty little prison yard' (Kermode, 2003: 69). *Shawshank's* pessimism about penal reform and its 'outlaw ending' make for a great film about hope triumphant over adversity, but do little to provide us with any model for thinking about how prisons can and should be run.

CONCLUSION

It is quite clear that Shawshank fails as a prison, as does Ruxton Towers as a borstal. However, this benchmark of failure is just as much a failure of wider social and cultural phenomena as it is of each institution. Ruxton Towers fails because England in the 1960s is changing and Colin represents 'new England' rather than the culture and values of the old. Similarly, Shawshank fails because the Warden represents a failure of American politics, which dies with the assassination of President Kennedy—the year that Warden Norton launches his 'Inside Out' programme to a credulous media. Thus, the benchmarking that takes place in each film is not particularly helpful to penal reform but rather provides a yardstick with which to judge society as a whole. The prison, the prisoners and the staff—especially the Governor and Warden—come to represent something much larger than their lives inside and instead they reach out to us from behind the prison walls to tell us something about ourselves.

On the other hand, *Scum* and *Brubaker* are very much concerned with benchmarking the acceptable and unacceptable faces of incarceration. *Scum* lets the viewer know that the borstal, no matter what it might be trying to achieve, was failing to deliver anything that could reasonably be defended and it is no coincidence that the film—which was originally made for the BBC—was banned and only saw the light of day when the BBC's rights lapsed back to author Ray Minton. *Scum* caused a great deal of public furore when eventually released and whilst we do not argue that there was a cause and effect here, it is no surprise that the borstal system, which had existed since 1908, came to be seen as corrupt and in need of reform—and indeed was soon replaced temporarily by youth custody in 1983 and later by detention in a young offender institution.

Brubaker did not cause a great deal of furore on its release, but it did get nominated for an Academy Award for its screenplay—a not inconsiderable achievement given that it was the penal system that was being portrayed as the 'bad guy', rather than the Warden or a specific prisoner. And, in having Robert Redford play Henry Brubaker the viewer is left in no doubt as to which side to be on and with whom to identify. When Redford argued that you cannot 'play politics with the truth' and that prisoners are 'human beings' who should be given 'responsibility', he articulated a message about penal reform for an audience that had probably never before considered the matter—and crucially would believe him, rather than a politician or penologist. Here the audience was being asked to identify with a model of prison management that was characterised by the sharing of power with prisoners, rather than the authoritarian models that had hitherto dominated the prison film genre. Not only was this radical for a film, it was also radical for the American penal system, which all too soon was prepared to forget Henry Brubaker and accept the logic of the 'super-max' prison. Ironically, Redford did receive an Academy Award in 1980, but not for his acting skills in *Brubaker*. In the year that *Brubaker* was released, Redford won the Oscar for Best Director of *Ordinary People*—a film about a dysfunctional American middle-class family.

CHAPTER 9

In and Around the Penal State: Escaped and Released Prisoners

Your number is going to be given to you as a sequential number, Son,
It's not a random set of numbers, Son,
That number means something ... it's your number, it's your number now,
You know what that number represents ... Son?
Two hundred and seventy six thousand, and listen carefully to me and you'll understand a little bit about what makes me so angry.
We have less than 500,000 people in the District of Columbia, Son,
And now only 70 per cent of them are Black.
Now what's 70 per cent of 500,000 ... Do the math!
We've got 350,000 Black people in DC.
Of the 350,000 half of them are female, aren't they!
Well what's that? Use the math, Son—the math.
Less than 175,000 people are males like yourself,
Not all of them are over 21 years of age, half of them are kids, now then,
Tell me, if we've only got 75–80,000 adult males in the District of Columbia and here's the number 276,000 today ...
Figure it out for yourself, we've exhausted the 21-year-olds, the 20-year-olds, 19-year olds, we're working on 18.
We're moving down the line, Son, by the time we cross 300,000 we'll be down to 16- and 17-year olds.
We're wiping out our race in Washington DC.
And here you are there playing these silly ass little games.
Well we've got something for you, Son,
Welcome to the DC jail.
You might make it out of here, you might not.

(Admitting Corrections Officer to Ray Joshua, *Slam*, 1998)

You can make the Governor very happy. He's got a great reputation for never forgetting anyone who's done right by him.

(Warden of the Attica State Correctional Facility to Jake Shuttlesworth, Spike Lee's *He Got Game*, 1998)

Boat drinks are drinks that are drunk on a boat. Or near a boat. Or while wishing you were on a boat. Or near someone who is wishing they were on a boat. They tend to be colourful, sometimes too colourful. They tend to have fruit in them. They tend to taste almost, but not quite, booze-less and they tend to pack a hidden wallop. As a general (but not infallible) rule boat drinks have two main ingredients: rum and a paper umbrella.

(Stephen Gwyne's Boat Drinks Page (personal web page))

In the film *Things to Do in Denver When You're Dead* (1998), a group of petty criminals who have messed up on a job that they were engaged to carry out on behalf of their mobster boss, are informed that a contract has been taken out on their lives and that they will be executed as the price of their failure. On receiving this news, one of the characters remarks that, there will be no 'boat drinks' for him then. 'Boat Drinks!', the film suggests, is a toast used by criminals to flag their hoped for 'happy ending'. For what (cinematic) criminal does not dream of pulling off that 'one last big job', leaving him free to retire to the sun, enjoying his evening cocktail 'boat drinks' on the proceeds of his ill-gotten gains? In *The Shawshank Redemption*, Andy dreams of his own version of 'boat drinks' in fantasising about retiring to Zihuatanejo, Mexico, where he can maybe do up an old boat and take his guests out charter fishing. But, despite the fact that *Shawshank* grants Andy his wish, Red probably got it right when he dismissed Andy's fantasies as nothing more than 'shitty pipedreams', or as Stephen King put it, 'pipedreams in a shitty little prison exercise yard' (Kermode, 2003: 69).

The happy ending provided in *The Shawshank Redemption*, is no more than a fantasy resolution to the problem of prison for prisoners. Very few real world prisoners are ever likely to effect a revenge sequence as fulsome as that perpetrated by Andy. Combining escape with cleaning out the Warden's bank accounts packed full with ill-gotten gains is not a likely real world scenario. In fact very few prisoners ever do successfully escape from prison and fewer still successfully elude capture. For most, serving out one's time is the main means of 'escape'. And, other than for short-term prisoners, the main uncertainty associated with this is unpredictability regarding eligibility for parole. In the light of this the fascination with escape demonstrated by the prison film would seem a little overblown. Nevertheless, the prison-break movie is a standard of the genre. Witness a host of titles such as: *Prison Break* (1938), *Crashout* (1955), *Big House USA* (1955), *The Defiant Ones* (1958) through to *Breakout* (1975), *Midnight Express* (1978) and *Escape from Alcatraz* (1979). Released and paroled prisoners also show up from time to time: Dustin Hoffman as paroled con Max Dembo in *Straight Time* (1978), Denzil Washington as the temporarily released con on a 'special mission' in *He Got Game* (1998), and Mark Wahlberg as Leo Handler in *The Yards* (2000).

More recently the 'going-to-prison' movie has made an appearance in *Slam* (1998) and *25th Hour* (2003). The cinematic shift from the 'escape-from-prison' movie to the 'going-to-prison' movie probably has some basis in penal realities. For whereas there are said to be some two million people currently incarcerated in the US, the headline figure should read that there are, at the present time, some 6.7 million people under some form of supervision from the Criminal Justice System, when taking into account the estimated 4.7 million Americans supervised whilst on probation or parole (Bureau of Justice Statistics, 2002). A further estimated eleven million Americans are admitted to locked facilities each year, and an estimated 30 million Americans have a criminal record (Donziger, 1996). Such large numbers indicate a general expansion of the reach of the penal state. As long ago as 1990, urban theorist Mike Davis suggested that parts of US cities were in danger of becoming 'vast outdoor prisons' (Davis, 1990).

The UK faces a similar set of issues, on a smaller scale. At present whilst the prison population of England and Wales stands at an all time high of over 74,000, this has been accompanied by the increased use of a variety of community sentences and parole options, giving England and Wales the highest proportion of offenders in Europe subject to some form of electronic monitoring (or 'tagging') (Nellis, 2003: 1). Scotland is also witnessing a record prison population, at a time when the official position of the Scottish Executive is to work for a reduction of prison numbers and when there has been a significant increase in the number of offenders receiving community sentences (Scottish Executive, 2003). For both the UK and the USA options intended as alternatives to incarceration would appear to have become 'add-ons'.

The tendency for alternatives to custody to become add-ons leaves opponents of prison growth with a lot of work to do. The prison populations in both the UK and the USA are predicted to increase. Although Mathiesen (2000) has argued that this could be halted through a strategy of *decriminalisation*, the scope for this at present would seem to be limited. Realistically, opponents of prison growth need to champion alternatives to custodial sentences. And they need to do this in a context where supporters of prison growth can be expected to counter such efforts, actively arguing and organizing against any reduction in the prison population through extensions to parole. For those who support prison as an incapacitating measure, opposing parole is a logical extension of their position and emphasising the re-offending of those on probation or parole is their major weapon. As Mathiesen (2000) and Donziger (1996) argue, the media have a tendency to overplay the significance of crimes committed whilst prisoners are out on parole, although Nellis (2003) suggests that, in England and Wales, there has been a significant increase in the number of offenders serving non-custodial sentences subject to some form of tagging without significant media or public disquiet. But still, opponents of prison growth would appear to be running in order to stand still. If they are to effect a reduction in the prison population they need to promote effectively the value of community sentences and at the same time construct persuasive arguments as to why early release is desirable.

ESCAPED AND RELEASED PRISONERS IN FILM

Should we be optimistic or pessimistic about prisoners who have escaped, or who are released from custody? Will they resume their offending behaviour, or desist from their life of crime? And what influences their choices? In this section we will consider some examples of films which consider these issues.

The Defiant Ones
Released in 1958, *The Defiant Ones* is an 'escaped prisoner movie' set entirely outside of prison. When the prison van goes off the road and crashes, chained together cons Sidney Poitier (Noah Cullen) and Tony Curtis (John 'Joker' Jackson) make a break for freedom. The remainder of the film is about the manhunt to track them down. From the outset we seem to be on the side of the escaped cons, although it is not clear why, other than that they are the film's star names. From the start the two display animosity and racial tension. Chained together they need to exhibit a more than minimal amount of cooperation if they are to evade recapture but Jackson wants to head south, whilst Cullen regards this as unthinkable and insists that they head north. Cullen suggests that he knows of a place where the freight train crosses by a swamp where they can

jump a train ride to freedom. They head north, bickering all the way. When Jackson saves Cullen from drowning in a swollen river he insists, 'I didn't pull you out. I just stopped you from pulling me in'. Pursuing the pair is a patient sheriff who has continually to reign in his makeshift posse who want to call in the National Guard/let lose the dogs. The sheriff believes that if they simply keep tracking their quarry, they will get their men.

During a scene in which they take a rest from travelling, Curtis and Poitier reveal to each other something of the nature of their crimes and their attitude to them. Poitier has been imprisoned for fighting back against a man who was racially abusing him. Curtis is a petty criminal who believes that crime is a rational response to limited opportunities. Both believe that prison is a disproportionate response to their offending behaviour and both exhibit a fierce determination to avoid recapture. Subsequently they arrive at a secluded farm, which is run by a lonely young widow and her young boy. Here they are able to break their shackles, but plan to stay the night before attempting to jump the freight train. During the night the young widow takes a shine to Curtis, seeing him as a route out of her miserable life. She tries to persuade him to ditch Poitier and to leave with her. Curtis and Poitier agree to separate, but when his new found love-interest reveals that she has misdirected Poitier through the swamp, Curtis goes after him to save his friend. Reunited they make it to the railway track just as the train is passing through. Poitier makes it aboard, but Curtis is being left behind. Reaching back to pull him aboard, Potier loses his grip and they/both fall back to earth. The manhunt arrives and the sheriff faces down his posse who want to release the dogs, then simply walks up to the men and arrests them.

The Defiant Ones succeeds in generating sympathy for the prisoners. With our hearts we want them to win, even if with our heads we know that they will not. The overall theme of the film is clearly the inevitability of the law. The calm patient sheriff knows that his quarry will run out of luck somewhere along the line. But, even had Jackson and Cullen caught the train that they missed by a fingertip, nothing much would have changed. They would still have had to steal to live, or attempt to pass incognito fearing discovery at any minute. The film is optimistic about the ability of human beings to change; certainly Curtis/Jackson becomes less racist and more principled as the film progresses. But it is pessimistic about the impact of release. If nothing has changed in the wider society then the conditions which produced offending behaviour in the first place will re-emerge, the more so for those on the run. Escape is no route out of offending, nor back into respectable society, which is, by the end of the film, the ideal that both Poitier and Curtis might want.

Straight Time

Poitier and Curtis suffer from the fact that their escape attempt was an illicit bid for freedom. But what if their release had been secured by more conventional means? How would they have fared then? The released-prisoner movie *Straight Time* (1978) provides some clues. Small-time crook Max Dembo (Dustin Hoffman) is paroled from prison, obtains a job, finds a girlfriend and tries to go straight. The film starts by being pretty much on Hoffman's side. His apparently genuine attempt to go straight is made more difficult by his bully-boy parole officer, who is on his back looking for any minor breach to send him back to prison. Max's circle of friends consists of other petty criminals, one of whom shoots-up in Max's room, leaving the evidence. On discovering a tell-tale piece of silver foil, Max's parole officer tells him that he is either 'using' (drugs) or allowing his premises to be used for that purpose. Either way he is in breach of his conditions of parole.

Hoffman subsequently falls out with his parole officer and returns to crime. But his inept crime spree does not last long—and by the end of the film he has accepted the inevitable, ditched his girlfriend and, as the closing titles tell us, was soon caught and returned to prison. But the film sells Hoffman short. His character, Dembo, is blown off course far too easily. It is hard not to conclude that his return to offending was fairly inevitable. Whether the message of this film is that criminals are incorrigible offenders, or that prison makes criminals incorrigible offenders is not entirely clear. Whichever, Crowther (1989: 147) suggests that this is the kind of film which gets the idea of rehabilitating the ex-prisoner a bad name

McVicar
As previously discussed in *Chapter 2*, *McVicar* (1980) is a significant film treatment of prisoner escape and the decision to desist from crime. The extent to which the film is an accurate portrayal of McVicar's life and his decision to reject crime is, in a sense, not particularly relevant. The question is, what 'imaginative resources' does the film provide the viewer with for thinking about the issue of rehabilitation versus punishment? One possible reading is that it invokes a standard cliché of a man being redeemed by a (heterosexual) 'love interest' and that romantic success is being used as reward for male decency. But arguably this is not really being fair to the film which, although it clearly does validate family life and family relations, does so in the context of a critique of prison as an institution which denies prisoners access to the things that might help re-integrate them into society. The film ends with a closing title expressing McVicar's view that: 'Being a thief is a terrific life. The trouble is they put you in prison for it'. McVicar would appear to be suggesting that if we did not have prison as the penalty for crime he would still be offending today, although the substance of the film suggests that the awfulness of prison alone is not sufficient to motivate people to desist from offending. We need to look further than this at what does have that effect as the film leaves us with the strong impression that society is better off for McVicar having renounced his glamorised criminal identity and opted for reintegration. Neither the police nor prison were, of themselves, sufficient to protect the public from his activities.

The Yards
The Yards (2000) is the most metaphorical of the four films we discuss here. It tells the story of Leo Handler, a young man just out of prison and apparently hoping to go straight. But rather than be found a job by his parole officer, Leo seeks work within his network of family and friends. Unfortunately for him, his uncle's rail engineering company is involved in corruptly obtaining contracts for work on the New York subway rail system and in sabotaging their competitor's business. Leo drifts into hanging around with Willie, the person who organizes the kick-

backs and sabotage and who is dating the daughter of his Uncle Stolz, head of the family and the company. Leo comes to be present when, during the course of a sabotage mission, Willie kills a subway night-watch man and he himself assaults a police officer putting him in a coma. The rest of the film concerns the efforts of his family, other corrupt businesses and politicians, to ensure that he stays out of sight or takes the fall for the murder.

It is not really explained why Leo turns down the offer from his parole officer to find him a job, nor why he declines his uncle's offer of an apprenticeship. Opting to join the business straight away as Willie's assistant is clearly going to lead to an involvement in questionable activities and should have been avoided if Leo really had intended going straight. But the point of *The Yards* is more metaphorical. Having been deserted by those he trusted, Leo comes to realise that he will have to identify Willie as the real perpetrator of the murder if he is to survive. A deal is worked out amongst the subway contractors, politicians and police that will leave Willie to carry the can for the murder and keep the subway contracting corruption under wraps. All looks to be heading towards a successful conclusion until Willie, who realises that he has been cast out, visits the family house for one last time and fights with Erica, the daughter of Uncle Stolz. Erica, for whom Leo has secretly been carrying a torch, falls from a balcony and dies. Now the point of the film becomes apparent. *The Yards*, a slow paced film which only just manages to maintain its viewers' interest, leaves it to the last one minute 30 seconds to kick in. Leo rejects the deal that would have kept the corruption under wraps and chooses instead to testify to the District Attorney. The film ends with him testifying that, despite his criminal record, he wishes to rejoin society and, recognising that he is breaking a code of silence, he proceeds to name everyone involved in the corruption conspiracy and cover-up.

Whilst *The Yards* is not a realistic examination of the problems facing the usual paroled con, it is in the end quite an effective de-glamorisation of crime. And, at a general level, it does portray a young man exercising choice and rejecting crime. But although apparently set in present day New York, the film is shot in a style similar to a 1970s 'mob film' and indeed the story could easily refer to an earlier piece of New York history. As a result, it does little to address the specifics of the choices made by those under the supervision of the criminal justice system in the present period.

IN AND AROUND THE PENAL STATE

Slam (1998) concerns the decisions of a young African-American man facing a gaol sentence for possession of 'weed'. Spike Lee's *He Got Game* (1998) tells the story of a man out from prison on a special mission to recruit his basketball playing son for the state Governor's alma mater university. The first represents, in our view, a 'black realist' perspective on crime and offending which argues that African-American men should take responsibility for their offending behaviour. The second carries on from the first with the proposition that, to the extent that black criminality is converted into legitimate entrepreneurial capitalism, then this can and should be accompanied by a reduction in the prison population.

Slam

Slam (1998) tells the story of Ray Joshua, a young African-American man who spends his life in inner-city Washington DC writing free-style verse, buying ice cream for the neighbourhood kids, and dealing 'weed' to make a living. In an arranged meeting, his friend Big Mike (a fellow neighbourhood operator), is shot and seriously injured. Fleeing the scene of the shooting, Ray is arrested and found to be in possession of a small amount of marijuana. For this he is remanded in custody to the Washington DC gaol. Here life goes from bad to worse, as it turns out that the word is that Ray set Mike up for the shooting. Ray is told that he needs to join a gang for protection, which he refuses to do. Just as it appears that serious violence is about to occur in the prison yard, Ray slams into one of his free-styling verses, acts a little crazy and 'dances' his way out of trouble. His performance is watched by Lauren, the prison education teacher who is also a poet. Lauren invites Ray to her creative writing class and then later takes up with him whilst he is out on bail, introducing him to her circle of friends and encouraging him to perform his verse in public.

Whilst out on bail Ray is faced with a major dilemma. His public defender lawyer has told him that if he contests his drugs possession charge he is looking at an eight-to-ten-year sentence if found guilty, whereas if he 'cops a plea' he is looking at two-to-three years, with the possibility of being out in 18 months with good behaviour. Ray is incredulous that he is in the position where *possession* of a small amount of 'weed' is going to send him to prison. Over the course of a weekend, during which he successfully performs his verse in public for the first time, he has to decide what to do—should he 'Cop' (enter a plea of guilty) or 'Rock' (take the case to trial), or abscond? He complains to Lauren that he cannot even comprehend his choices. There must be another way out—some kind of 'magical trapdoor'. Here it should be remembered that Lauren is a prison educator whom we have already seen speak passionately about the injustice of the experience of the incarcerated black male, yet a totally unsympathetic Lauren remains unmoved by Ray's complaints of injustice and tells him that he has no choice but to cop a plea, do his time, and use it wisely to develop his writing.

Perhaps the main surprise in *Slam* is that it is only Ray who thinks he has a dilemma. *Slam* has an entirely black main cast and an almost entirely black incidental cast. None of them has much sympathy for Ray. He is arrested by black cops, who sing doo-wop in their patrol car whilst waiting for action. He is remanded to prison by a black judge, who is mightily unimpressed that Ray has been caught in possession whilst fleeing the scene of a shooting. He is defended by a black public defender lawyer who lays out his 'Cop or Rock' options in the most matter of fact manner. Ray is welcomed to the DC gaol by a black corrections officer, who tells him in no uncertain terms how heartily sick to death he is of the continuous stream of young black males coming through his gaol. He is befriended by a black prison teacher, later girlfriend, who, as already stated, is surprisingly unsympathetic to Ray's seemingly justifiable indignation. What is going on here?

Slam is a film shot in the style of black independent cinema. It was directed by a white director (Marc Levin), but co-written by Levin, Richard Stratton and the two main cast members Saul Williams (Ray) and Sonja Sohn (Lauren). Whilst some might question whether a white writer/director can articulate an authentic black perspective on mass incarceration, the perspective advanced by the film, which might be dubbed black realism, is not that incomprehensible. The argument is pretty much similar to that advanced by black intellectuals such as Cornell West (1992) in his *Nihilism in Black America*. West argued that there was very little point in blaming social deprivation or racial inequality for black violence and black criminality. Tackling the problem of nihilism in black America required that those who committed crimes should be held responsible. *Slam* is firmly of the view that whatever the structural factors of social deprivation or racism, young African-Americans can still exercise choices. Ray rejects the option of joining a gang and uses his poetry to reaffirm non-violence. On being bailed from prison he takes a message to Mike, from the leader of the Black Muslims, that non-violence must be the way forward. Ray persuades Mike that there should be no retaliation for his shooting and Mike agrees with the hope that 'the bullet that took [his] sight will be the last fired'. *Slam* is a 'stop-the-violence' movie which suggests that black America will need to be its own salvation. *Slam* is also a 'getting out of the 'hood through talent' movie, although this perhaps is not that obvious, given that Ray's talent is poetry not basketball. But how realistic is this message of beating mass incarceration through black achievement? Can black America 'pull itself up by it's bootstraps' without help from white America?

He Got Game
Released in the same year as *Slam*, Spike Lee's *He Got Game* (1998) picks up and develops the theme introduced by the former. It tells the story of Jake Shuttlesworth (Denzil Washington), who is serving a one-to-15 year sentence in the Attica Correctional Facility for the manslaughter of his wife. His son, Jesus Shuttlesworth (Ray Allen), is at the time the number one rated high school basketball prospect in the country. The action takes place over the week when Jesus has to make 'the most important decision of his life'—whether to go pro and sign for an NBA team, or continue his education and take a sports scholarship. The pressure on Jesus seems intense as nearly everyone—family, friends, girlfriend and coach—whilst claiming to have his best interests at heart, are trying to influence his decision for personal motives. Into this mix is thrown Jake, who is released on parole for a week to attempt to persuade Jesus to sign a letter of intent to take a scholarship at Big State—the state Governor's alma mater university. If Jake succeeds the Governor will use his influence to secure early parole. As the Warden of Attica pitches it: 'You can make the Governor very happy. He's got a great reputation for never forgetting anyone who's done right by him'; although he continues with the implied threat that, 'He's also never forgiven anyone who's done him wrong'.

In review and comment the film is most often discussed as 'Spike Lee takes an unsubtle and obvious sideswipe at the exploitation of the African-American male in and through basketball'. Or alternatively, it is seen as a story of reconciliation between father and son. Whilst the issue of prisons and prisoners gains an occasional mention, they are rarely seen as central to the film. In our view *He Got Game* is not, in any way, shape or form a complaint about, or critique of, the exploitation of the black male in and through basketball. It is an argument about the need to reduce the prison population through the extension of parole and early release for those who might benefit from it. Whereas it has been suggested that Spike Lee is against the tagging (electronic monitoring) of offenders, seeing it as an extension of racist oppression (Nellis, 2003), the exact opposite is true and *He Got Game* is an argument *for* the use of electronic monitoring for those securing early release.

The headline story is about Jesus Shuttlesworth, the number one basketball prospect. While he is arriving at his career decision everyone wants a piece of the action. His Uncle Bubba is anxious not to be 'cut out of any deal that's about to go down': there must be jobs for the family from the stream of riches about to flow. Girlfriend Lala (Lay-la not La-La) is being paid-off to steer Jesus in the direction of a high-powered sports agent claimed to be 'a friend of the family'. His high school coach advises Jesus to make his own decision, but then offers him money in return for information on what that decision is likely to be. And a cast of other minor characters proceed to either warn Jesus of the temptations and pitfalls that await him, or to serve them up to him. And then there is just out of prison Jake, who arrives to tell Jesus that he needs him to choose Big State, if he is to have any chance of securing early parole.

There is little doubt that Lee represents the politics of basketball as a somewhat corrupt. As Jesus tours the colleges that are more than interested in offering him a sports scholarship he is greeted by a stream of (white) college girls, of implied availability, supposedly willing to offer themselves to influence his choice of destination. Indeed Jesus succumbs to the temptation of two female 'students' laid on for him in a college dorm. But, despite this main story, *He Got Game* is not about basketball and Lee said all that he wanted to say on the subject of exploitation within that sport in his cameo appearance in the basketball documentary *Hoop Dreams* (1994). That film more than adequately documented the pitfalls that could befall the aspiring sports star.

So if the film is not about basketball, what it about? And, why did Lee create the whole basketball storyline if all he wanted to do was tell a story about a reconciliation between an estranged father and his son? The answer is that *He Got Game* is about prisons and prisoners. Its point is the deal, brokered by the Warden of Attica on behalf of the state Governor, which offers Jake reduced time if he can deliver Jesus to Big State. We need to run this on a little to see what happened and how this storyline turned out. Jake accepts the deal and is released on an unofficial parole, minded by two 'Rottweiler' parole officers and fitted with an electronic tag. He returns to Coney Island, Brooklyn knowing that his task is not going to be particularly easy. Jake was imprisoned for having ('accidentally') killed his wife during a domestic dispute. The killing arose out of an argument about how hard Jake was pushing his son Jesus at basketball. Jesus, who witnessed the killing, has since disowned his father and now wants nothing more to do with him. Over the course of a week, Jake attempts a reconciliation with Jesus telling him that he loved his mother, but that nothing that he can do will bring her back. Jake, six years into a 15-year sentence, tells Jesus honestly that he needs him to go to Big State. Jesus remains unmoved by this, just another piece of surplus information cluttering up what he already knows is 'the biggest decision he will ever make'. On the night that the decision is to be made father and son play one-on-one on a Coney Island basketball court. The deal is that if Jake wins, Jesus will sign a letter of intent committing him to Big State. If Jesus wins, Jake will turn around, walk out of his life and never bother him again. Jesus wins and the parole officers arrive to return Jake to Attica. By morning Jesus has weighed his options and gives his decision via a statement read out in his absence by his coach at the press conference. Jesus will go to Big State and his statement thanks everyone who supported him in his decision—including his father.

Back in Attica a surprised Jake Shuttlesworth is again called in to see the Warden. Jesus has signed for Big State, although no one knows why. What are the implications of this? The Warden is a little uncertain. On the one hand, the Governor has got what he wanted and hopefully will come good on his promise. But on the other hand, Jake never actually succeeded in getting Jesus to sign the letter of intent—part of the bargain. So, although the Warden is hopeful, we are left waiting to see if, given a little bit of time, the Governor will be able to work something out. This ending is deliberately ambiguous. The imprisoned black male awaits to see if the (white) state Governor will deliver on his reputation for 'remembering those who have done right by him'. The next we see of Jake, he is shooting ball in the yard at Attica. In what is, in effect, the final scene of the film he walks, basketball in hand, towards the wall stepping into the 'Out of Bounds' zone. With one finger squeezing the trigger of his high-powered rifle an armed guard calls to Jake to stop his advance, turn around and step back, or else be shot. Jake stops and hesitates for a moment before throwing the ball over the wall. It sails through the air and, in what must be the almightiest throw in history, travels all the way to Big State, before coming down and bouncing onto the court where Jesus is having his first solo warm-up practice. Black success and black 'failure' are connected by the throw of a basketball.

We now turn to substantiating the view that *He Got Game* is about prisons and prisoners by considering two questions. Firstly, what did Jake achieve during his week on parole and what is the attitude of the film towards electronic monitoring (EM)? When Jake is released into the care of the 'Rottweiler' parole officers, he is bunked in a sleazy hotel. The first thing they do is fit an EM device to his ankle, whilst plugging an electronic base unit into his phone. This device is to discourage him from absconding, to monitor Jake's presence in his hotel room (effectively a home curfew), although it is dramatic licence to imply that it would be able to track his movements wherever he went. Nellis (2003: 21) suggests that *He Got Game* is a disparagement of EM, representing it as a facet of racial oppression. In one scene Jake buys a pair of trainers and is mildly embarrassed when the young black assistant spots the tag on his ankle. Jake passes it off as being 'for his arthritis', to which the shop assistant knowingly replies that his brother also wears one for his 'arthritis', and the two agree that there seems to be a lot of 'arthritis' going around Coney Island. Whereas Nellis (2003: 11) reads this scene, in the context of the rest of the film, as indicating EM as an aspect of racial oppression, it can just as easily be seen as its opposite. Jake is only mildly embarrassed by the discovery and his interaction with the assistant suggests that in this particular community the tag could be seen as a non-stigmatised form of community penalty—especially if we consider the balance-sheet of what Jake achieved during his weeklong furlough from prison.

The Coney Island into which Jake is released is a long way from being a 'vast outdoor prison', its current epidemic of 'arthritis' notwithstanding. It provides opportunities for valued social interaction. It is the place where the people who were most affected by Jake's crime still live. Whilst on parole, Jake reconnects with his family (daughter and son) and effects a reconciliation with the latter. At the same time, he befriends Dakota, a prostitute who works out of the room next to him at the hotel where he must reside. She allows herself to be beaten by her pimp, because 'he loves her' and 'they're going to get married', and because she 'has low self-esteem and was abused as a kid'. Although this subplot is widely decried as stereotypical and clichéd, and not particularly well executed, it allows Jake to have a small victory. Having suggested to Dakota that she should leave her pimp, towards the end of the film we see her apparently doing this, riding the bus out of town to visit Jake in Attica. On the minus side, during his week out Jake has had a minor loss of temper, when he is involved in a street scuffle with the assistant to the agent who is trying to manipulate Jesus through his girlfriend Lala.

What prevents Jake from re-offending or absconding whilst on parole? It could be suggested that it is neither the watchful parole officers (whose bark is worse than their bite), nor the monitoring device (which may or may not be able to track his every move). Nor is it really that Jake avoids re-offending because a successfully accomplished mission might help secure his eventual release. Rather, what stops him is that his purpose on being released is to effect a reconciliation with his son, the person most affected by the crime he committed. *He Got Game* is an argument in favour of Restorative Justice—'I loved her, but there's nothing that I can do to bring her back now'. It favours early parole for those who can benefit from it and argues that EM is acceptable (although probably tokenistic and ineffective) if used to reduce the prison population (rather than to expand the net of social control). Jake's furlough will have been worthwhile even if it does not secure him permanent release. But, the bigger point of *He Got Game* is that it should secure that release. The deal with the Governor should still stand. Jesus made the right choice, so Jake should be 'remembered'. The moral of the story is that if black youth can be persuaded away from crime and channelled into legitimate activities, then this should be rewarded with a reduction in the prison population. The question posed by the Governor's yet to be fulfilled promise is: If black America shows that it can play ball with white America, will white America play ball with black America? Like *Slam, He Got Game* sees black achievement as the route out of mass incarceration.

But is this unrealistic thinking? Is this to collude with the fallacy that although *anyone* in America can become a leading basketball prospect, slam poet, or President, not *everyone* can? In a recent documentary, made by PBS/BBC and broadcast as *Amercia Beyond the Colour Line*, the Harvard, African-American scholar Henry Louise Gates Jnr investigated black success on America's East Coast. As well as visiting obvious examples such as Colin Powell, Gates investigated a wider range of black success stories. Interviewing Russel Simmons, the founder of Def Jam records, now valued at $250 million, Simmons revealed how his entrepreneurial activity had started with selling 'weed', before graduating to being a DJ and then music impresario. He now has his own fashion label and controls a range of diverse businesses. The point of the Simmons interview was to flag up the extent to which ghetto entrepreneurial behaviour had already moved out of 'illegitimate' into legitimate activities.

More generally, talking to black corporate businessmen and even to America's first black chess Grandmaster, Gates was upbeat about the extent to which black success was fanning out beyond its traditional bastions (sport and entertainment). Of course Henry Louis Gates Jr is not likely to be everyone's favourite black intellectual. And not everyone will favour such a pro-capitalist solution to racial disadvantage—although as one inmate in *Slam* argued— 'America is a capitalist society, we are capitalists'. It may be that social mobility for a few will not necessarily improve the lot of African-Americans more generally, nonetheless at least *Slam* and *He Got Game* attempted to suggest a route out of mass incarceration. And, as has been suggested above, in *He Got Game* this route includes a shift towards Restorative Justice, as much as it involves black success through basketball.

STARS AS ENDORSERS/DISPARAGERS

One of the problems with criminal justice processes is their tendency to render offenders faceless. If crime can be presented as a freely-willed, rational act of a callous individual, then this simplifies the problem of how to respond. Criminals can be sent to prison, for punishment—end of story. Whilst this might be comfortingly simplistic, it does not make for a very effective system as it can be shown that criminals offend for any number of reasons and there are any number of ways in which people may be helped not to offend (such as drug treatment, education, offence confrontation and so forth). But such provision will not be developed if simplistic notions of punishment inform common sense and in turn influence politics, policy and practice. In this context, any of the films discussed above might be viewed as welcome to the extent that they try to put faces to offenders, and suggest that they have a life before and after the crimes that they have committed. All of these films, including *Straight Time*, which is the least sympathetic, have the potential to create some empathy with the offender. Some might be seen as going further. It has been suggested, for example, that *He Got Game* can be seen as attempting to cultivate a sentiment in favour of Restorative Justice and of reducing the prison population. But can such films garner support for their implicit premises? Does the production of a film mean that it will succeed in diffusing its intended sentiment to its audience?

Endorsers
One relatively underdeveloped area of film studies is a consideration of the ways in which stars, either as players or directors, might act as 'informal endorsers' of the 'political' positions implicit in the films associated with them. We earlier discussed the Robert Redford movie *Brubaker*, a film revealing corruption and wrongdoing on an Arkansas Prison Farm. Here we suggested that the fact that the part of Brubaker was played by Robert Redford is by no means insignificant. Redford brings to the film a well-known screen persona and so when he, as Brubaker, tells us that he cannot support the regime, we are receiving this message from a friendly face, someone we may be inclined to trust.

There is a similar process to be detected in the death-penalty films of 1990s Hollywood cinema. A number of household name stars and directors made a series of films questioning, at least on the surface, the death penalty. Is there something significant in the fact that Tim Robbins, Sharon Stone, Clint Eastwood, Frank Darabont, etc. directly or indirectly associated themselves with an anti-death-penalty cause? Did their collective efforts in any way signal that if these stars think that we might need to take another look at the death penalty, then we the public might come to agree also that we should perhaps revisit it?

Disparagement
It should be emphasised that if there is any such effect in play then we are considering a contested process. If films can garner support for their implicit 'political' position, then those who oppose that position are likely to wish to discredit the film in question. It is quite easy to see that such processes of disparagement do in fact occur. Any film which tackles any 'social issue' runs the risk of being dubbed 'controversial', a tag often sufficient in itself to discourage some people from seeing it. The impact of a film can be undermined in other ways, for example, by what is said about it in review and comment. When a star name appears in, or directs, a social issue film, their efforts may well be greeted with a, 'Gee … I usually like his or her work … but this film just plain sucks', etc. In all of the films discussed above the stars have a potential to operate as informal endorsers and therefore to attract discourses of disparagement.

In thinking about how the reception a film receives might influence its ability to diffuse its intended message the most interesting case to consider out of the films discussed above is probably *He Got Game*. The lead role is played by Denzil Washington, an 'A' list Hollywood star, who is known for having appeared in a wide range of Hollywood productions. Washington should have been a good bet as a star able to act as an effective endorser for the perspective advanced by the film. Indeed, his portrayal of Jake Shuttlesworth is sometimes praised in reviews generally unsympathetic to the film. But we need to understand that here Washington is starring in a film directed by Spike Lee, where the film is branded more by its director than its star. And it is here that the processes of disparagement take over. Lee's films are invariably greeted with a degree of hysteria in review and comment. In one review of *He Got Game* it's director is branded as: given to anger, paranoia, propaganda and egotism, and is said to have 'a chip on his shoulder the size of a planet and aspirations often [as] laughably outsized'. The film itself is referred to as being 'uneven' and 'ludicrous'. Other reviews referred to it as being 'preoccupied with sex and trashy dialogue', 'misogynist', and so forth. Lee's later film, the going-to-prison movie *25th Hour*, starring Edward Norton, fared even worse, being referred to in one review as a 'turgid, bombastic and outrageously self-satisfied movie'.

Such processes of disparagement can operate to limit the impact of a film although they cannot entirely counter a successful film. It is worth doing a quick check on the popularity of some of the movies being discussed here, evidenced by reactions to them on the Internet Movie Database, contrasting a number of films on the basis of 'votes cast' and 'score-out-of-ten' achieved, as illustrated in Table 9.1.

This relatively unscientific comparison shows what we perhaps might already suspect. Namely, that Spike Lee's films generally do not achieve mass popularity. The relatively watchable *He Got Game* (heralded by some as a return to form by Lee) gains only the same rating and fewer votes than the completely formulaic 'knock-off' Robert Redford prison-romp *The Last Castle*. The Spike Lee directed *25th Hour* just pips the Oscar nominated, but not particularly outstanding, revenge movie *In the Bedroom*, but on fewer votes. None of these films achieves the vote or rating of a successful (IMDb Top 250) movie like *American History X*. Finally *Slam*, discussed above, scored a respectable 7.1 but based on only 440 votes. Although this is only a rough and ready way of gauging the impact of a film, comparisons are nonetheless instructive.

It is not being suggested here that films such as *Slam*, *25th Hour* or *He Got Game* have no impact or are not worth making. They clearly are part of the cultural resources available to us for understanding the penal state. But equally these films are on the margins of popularity and limited in their cultural reach.

Table 9.1: *Viewer ratings of films on the Internet Movie Database*

Film	Score (out of 10)	Votes Cast
He Got Game	6.5	2,800
25th Hour	7.7	6,200
In the Bedroom	7.5	7,400
The Last Castle	6.5	4,500
American History X	8.3	36,000
Slam	7.1	440

CONCLUSION

If films can operate to humanise the prisoner, to tell the story of their crime, and to remind us that offenders have a life before and after the crimes that they have committed, then we should want more, not fewer, mainstream Hollywood films which attempt to tackle the expansion of the penal state. In both the UK and US most prisoners have been convicted of relatively minor offences and could be helped to address their offending behaviour through appropriate programmes. They are never likely to make sufficient money from pulling off 'one last big job' to retire to the sun for 'Boat Drinks!' We perhaps need more movies that reflect this fact.

CHAPTER 10

Film, Television and Popular Culture: A Note

There has in recent years been an upsurge in interest within criminal justice circles concerning the effects of popular culture on penal reform issues. Cultural products including films, TV programmes and even music videos can be seen as carriers of ideas about the law, crime, criminals and punishment. Any number of journals on crime and culture are now produced and recent contributions in books and articles would include Rafter (2000), Sarat (2001), Herman (2003), Nellis (2003) and Mason (2003a).

We see our work as a contribution to this debate and in this final chapter make some suggestions as to why those with an interest in penal reform should take an active interest in dramatic representation.

PRISON DRAMA AND PENAL REFORM

In the UK an established network of penal reform organizations exists and continuously seeks to exert an influence on penal policy and practice, through influencing policy-makers, politicians and practitioners directly, or by seeking to raise the profile of penal affairs issues within the media so as to influence the *general public*. These organizations use the mass media to comment where possible on the growth of prison numbers, the financial and social costs of prison and the standards of prison regimes. But despite these efforts the available research still shows that the general public are poorly informed on prison issues. So, for example, the Rethinking Crime and Punishment initiative reported that there existed a widespread view that the courts were not tough enough on offenders. This view is maintained despite the fact that when asked to recommend a sentence for a given crime the public are either in line with, or more lenient than, what current sentencing practice would suggest.[1]

The tendency for the prison population to continue to rise, despite the best efforts of reformers to argue that prison is an expensive and counter-productive mistake, has led some commentators to suggest that attempting to influence public opinion by conventional means is a futile approach. Mathiesen (2000) in particular has argued that the (news) media have a tendency to reduce everything to 'sound bite politics' and 'entertainment'. He favours the creation of an *alternative public space*. This would be a grass roots network of campaigning organizations who would organize public meetings and flows of information and influence outside the sphere of the mainstream mass media (2000: 194). His advocacy of this idea seems to derive mainly from a view that the mass media will never give more than superficial coverage to social issues, particularly crime and punishment. Whilst there is nothing wrong with attempting to create the campaigning grass roots network Mathiesen envisages (and which may already exist in substance if not in formal terms), it could be suggested that his views are

---

[1] See further at www.rethinking.org.uk

overly influenced by his assessment of TV news media. Popular film and TV products *can* carry valuable penal reform arguments and information and may have distinct advantages as a means of propagating awareness of the issues that underlie dramatic representations—something that reform groups would do well to consider and engage with.

One area being investigated by criminologists is the ideological limitations of particular films or TV programmes (Rafter 2000; Sarat, 2001; Herman, 2003). Products which represent themselves as in some way progressive often turn out on closer examination to be ways of reproducing already dominant ideas and ideologies. Our approach to the reading of films (or TV programmes) does not assert that all readings are equally valid, but we do believe it legitimate to propose that one reading is better than another. We have also tried to recognise that there are certain cultural products for which we do not, as analysts, understand either their manner of operation or their full social significance—the films *The Shawshank Redemption* and *The Green Mile* might be intances of this, but also the Brit-pic prison movies of the turn of the century. These films may operate in very subtle ways to reshape the ways in which people see the world. Even if we can get our readings 'right', we may have done no more than catch up with what the producers (intuitively) understood.

A SUMMARY OF THE CASE FOR FURTHER STUDY

In both the UK and the USA the prison populations have expanded to new highs and attempts to promote alternatives to prison have merely served to increase the total numbers of citizens under the supervision of agencies of the criminal justice systems. Concern about this has been reflected in the TV series *Oz*, *Bad Girls* and *Buried*. In film, some of the more thoughtful reflections on the expansion of the penal system came from the margins of film popularity (*Slam*; *He Got Game*). Mainstream Hollywood has done little to address prison critically and indeed prison could be seen as coming to represent an iconography of cool masculinity that can be attached to a range of films. Having said this, the abolitionist case against the death penalty was well represented in 1990s Hollywood cinema. One conclusion to be drawn from this would be that we need more mainstream prison drama not less. We also need to make more use of the prison drama we do have both as an educational resource for thinking about prison and prisoners and as a potential means of delivering sound information. The general public are unlikely to be won over, for example, to the cause of reducing prison numbers simply by criminologists conducting rational debate about the relative effectiveness of different sanctions. We need to supply an emotional argument and this is something that film and TV drama is ideally suited to doing—a fact that the producers of such drama may have long been intuitively aware of.

Drama consists not just of a moving image but also a narrative story. From *Porridge* to *Bad Girls* any attempt to tell a story about prisons and prisoners is preferable to the mug shot, the often still and stark black and white image which demonises offenders and reduces criminals to little more than symbols of the crimes they have committed. We need more prison drama not less—and more discussion about the prison drama that we do have if we are to move beyond simplistic and counter-productive responses to crime and criminals.

Finally, to draw together some further key points, our argument is that:

- prison regimes are generally worse at any given time than the public think: worse than they would accept for themselves if incarcerated
- prisons have to conceal or deny their inhumanity and irrationality to maintain legitimacy
- prison film performs a penal reform function when it popularises critical accounts of the penal system, when it translates the insights of first hand experience into a wider domain. It can perform the penal reform functions including: revelation; benchmarking; news/memory and empathy.
- films and TV prison dramas can act as benchmarkers, either by connoting the prisons that they describe as falling below socially acceptable standards of decency, or by flagging up what are considered to be the characteristics of a good prison
- the prison of the past can be used to put pressure on the standards of the prisons of the present and the future
- some prison films reveal little about real world penal practices, or the pains of incarceration and some, rather than connoting disapproval of prison, endorse it as a form of 'cool masculinity'
- most prison films carry some degree of humanisation and empathy
- Hollywood films featuring household name stars may be particularly suited to carrying out penal reform functions of endorsement or disparagement with well-known stars acting as 'informal endorsers' or 'disparagers' of the position implicit in a film
- producers of TV prison dramas have become more sophisticated in their representation of prison. Contemporary 'cult TV' prison dramas such as *Bad Girls*, *Oz* and *Buried* should be seen and understood as the results of producers attempting to find new ways to give 'voice' to prisons and prisoners
- with large numbers of people under the broad supervision of the criminal justice system in a variety of forms—including on probation and on parole—film needs to move beyond the 'pure prison movie' and address the experiences of people 'going to prison' and 'getting out from prison'
- reducing the prison population requires not just arguments countering the effectiveness of custody but a broader set of arguments encouraging us to rethink the nature and purpose of punishment: ultimately a shift in thinking from punitive to Restorative Justice
- there is a need to provide the general public with a non-technical, non-expert understanding of the issues and in particular of Restorative Justice
- representations of prison in film and TV can be ideally suited to 'penal reform education', by providing resources through which to explore the many issues that surround crime and punishment.

We hope that this book will act as a stimulus to interested parties to explore further the recesses of these often complex issues. We hope that many readers, when watching prison film and TV prison drama, will do so in a fresh light.

Bibliography

Abbott J. (1982), *In the Belly of the Beast*, New York: Random House
Barak-Glantz I. (1981), 'Towards a Conceptual Scheme of Prison Management', *Prison Service Journal*, Vol. 61, Part 2, 42-60
Barker M. (2000), *From Antz to Titanic: Reinventing Film Analysis*, London: Pluto
Beckett K. and Western B. (2001), 'Governing Social Marginality: Welfare, Incarceration and the Transformation of State Policy', in Garland D. (ed.) (2001), *Mass Imprisonment: Social Causes and Consequences*, London: Sage
Bordwell D. (1985), *Narration in Film Fiction*, Madison: University of Wisconsin Press
Boyle J. (1977), *A Sense of Freedom*, London: Pan Books
Braithwaite J. (1989), *Crime, Shame and Reintegration*, Cambridge: Cambridge University Press
Bryans S. and Wilson D. (1998), *The Prison Governor: Theory and Practice*, Leyhill: PSJ
Bureau of Justice Statistics (2002), *Probation and Parole in the United States, 2002*, Online at: http://www.ojp.usdoj.gov/bjs/abstract/ppus02.htm
Campbell D. (2000), 'Anger Grows as US Jails its Two Millionth Inmate', *Guardian*, 15 February
Cavadino M. and Dignan, J. (1996), *The Penal System: An Introduction*, London: Sage
Chadder V. (1999), 'The Higher Heel: Women and the Post-war British Crime Film', in S. Chibnall and R. Murphy (1999), *British Crime Cinema*, London: Routledge
Cheatwood D. (1998), 'Prison Movies: Films about Adult Male Civilian Prisons: 1929–1995', in F. Bailey and D. Hale (eds.) (1998), *Popular Culture, Crime and Justice*, Belmont: Wadsworth
Clowers M. (2001), 'Dykes, Gangs and Danger: Debunking Popular Myths about Maximum-Security Life', *Journal of Criminal Justice and Popular Culture*, Vol. 9. Issue 1 (also available online at: http://www.albany.edu/scj/jcjpc/vol9is1/clowers.html)
Crowther B. (1989), *Captured on Film*, London: Batsford
Curthoys A. and Docker J. (1989), 'In Praise of Prisoner', in J. Tulloch and G. Turner (eds) (1989), *Australian Television: Programmes, Pleasures And Politics*, Sydney: Allen and Unwin also available online at: http://www.wwwentworth.co.uk/library/dockcurt.htm
Davis M. (1990), *City of Quartz: Excavating the Future in Los Angeles*, London: Verso
Denzin N.K. (2001), *Reading Race*, London: Sage
DiIulio J. (1987), *Governing Prisons: A Comparative Study of Correctional Management*, New York: Freedom Press
Donziger S. (ed) (1996), *The Real War on Crime*, New York: Harper Perennial
Edgar K. and O'Donnell I. (1998), 'Mandatory Drug Testing in Prisons—an Evaluation', *Home Office Research Findings*, No. 75, London: Home Office
Fitzgerald M. (1977), *Prisoners in Revolt*, London: Penguin Books
Fitzgerald M. and Sim J. (1979), *British Prisons*, Oxford: Basil Blackwell
Flynn N. (1998), *Introduction to Prisons and Imprisonment*, Winchester: Waterside Press
Foucault M. (1979), *Discipline and Punish: the Birth of the Prison*, Harmondsworth: Penguin
Garland D. (ed.) (2001), *Mass Imprisonment: Social Causes and Consequences*, London: Sage
Goffman E. (1975), *Asylums*, London: Pelican. First published 1961
Gregory S. (2002), *Forget You had a Daughter: Doing Time in the 'Bangkok Hilton'*, London: Vision
Henry J. (1952), *Who Lie in Goal*, London: Gollancz
Henry J. (1954), *Yield to the Night*, London: Gollancz
Herman D. (2003), ' "Bad Girls Changed My Life": Homonormativity in a Women's Prison Drama', *Critical Studies in Media Communications*, 20.2
Hill A. (2003), *Oz: Behind These Walls–The Journal of Augustus Hill*, New York: Harper Collins
Hogg R. (2002), 'Prisoners and the Penal Estate in Australia', in D. Brown and M. Wilkie (eds.), *Prisoners as Citizens: Human Rights in Australian Prisons*, Sydney: The Federation Press
Human Rights Watch (2000), *Out of Sight: Super-Maximum Security Confinement in the United States*, available online at: http://www.hrw.org/reports/2000/supermax/
Kermode M. (2003), *The Shawshank Redemption*, London: bfi publishing
King N. (1999a), *Heroes in Hard Times: Cop Action Movies in the US*, Philadelphia: Temple University Press
King R. (1999b) 'The Rise and Rise of Supermax: an American Solution in Search of a Problem', *Punishment and Society*, 1.2, 163–184
Leech M. and Cheney D. (2002), *The Prisons Handbook*, Winchester: Waterside Press
Lewis D. (1997), *Hidden Agendas: Politics, Law and Disorder*, London: Hamish Hamilton
London Evening Standard (2003), 'Sitcoms Miss the Boiling Issues', 16 July

Lygo R. (1991), *Report on the Management of the Prison Service*, London: HM Prison Service
Mason P. (1995), 'Prime Time Punishment: the British Prison and Television', in D. Kidd-Hewitt and R. Osborne (eds) (1996), *Crime and the Media: The Post-modern Spectacle*, London: Pluto Press
Mason P. (1998a) 'Systems and Process: The Prison in Cinema' *Images* Online at www.imagesjournal.com/issue06/features/prison.htm.
Mason P. (1998b) 'Men, Machines and the Mincer: The Prison Movie', *PicturingJustice*, Online at www.usfca.edu/pj/articles/Prison.htm.
Mason P. (ed) (2003a), *Criminal Visions: Media Representations of Crime and Justice*, Cullompton: Willan
Mason P. (2003b), 'The Screen Machine: Cinematic Representations of Prison', in P. Mason (2003), *Criminal Visions: Media Representations of Crime and Justice*, Cullumpton: Willan
Mathiesen T. (1990), *Prison on Trial*, London: Sage
Mathiesen T. (1995), *The Driving Forces Behind Prison Growth: the Mass Media*, Washington D.C.: The Sentencing Project
Mathiesen T. (2000), *Prison on Trial*, Winchester: Waterside Press, 2nd edition
McVicar J. (1974), *McVicar: By Himself*, London: Arrow
Morey A. (1995), ' 'The Judge Called Me an Accessory': Women's Prison Films 1950–62', *Journal of Popular Film and Television*, 23 (2): 80–8
Morgan S. (1999), 'Prison Lives: Critical Issues in Reading Prisoner Autobiography', *Howard Journal*, Vol. 38, No. 3
Mulvey L. (1975), 'Visual Pleasures and Narrative Cinema', *Screen*, 16.3
Murton T. and Hyams J. (1969), *Accomplices to Crime: The Arkansas Prison Scandal*, New York: Grove Press
Nellis M. (1987), 'A Reasonable Aesthetic of Punishment: British Prison Films 1930–86', (unpublished) paper presented at the British Criminology Conference, 15 July 1987
Nellis M. (1988), 'British Prison Movies: The Case Of "Now Barabbas"', *Howard Journal of Criminal Justice*, Vol. 27, No. 1
Nellis M. (1993), 'Remembering Joan Henry', *Prison Writing*, No. 3
Nellis M. (2002), 'Prose and Cons: Offender Autobiographies, Penal Reform and Probation Training', *Howard Journal of Criminal Justice*, Vol. 41, No. 5
Nellis M. (2003), 'News Media, Popular Culture and the Electronic Monitoring of Offenders in England and Wales', *Howard Journal of Criminal Justice*, Vol. 42, No. 1
Nellis M. and Hale C. (1982), *The Prison Film*, London: Radical Alternatives to Prison
Oshinsky D. (1996), *Worse than Slavery: Parchman Farm and the Ordeal of Jim Crow Justice*, New York: Free Press
O'Sullivan S. (2001), 'Representations of Prison in Nineties Hollywood Cinema: from *Con Air* to *The Shawshank Redemption*', *Howard Journal of Criminal Justice*, Vol. 40, No. 4, 317-334
O'Sullivan S. (2003), 'Representing "The Killing State": The Death Penalty in Nineties Hollywood Cinema', *Howard Journal of Criminal Justice*, Vol. 42, No. 5
Parish J.R. (2000), *Prison Pictures from Hollywood*, Jefferson, NC: McFarland & Co.
Pfeil F. (1998), 'From Pillar to Postmodern: Race, Class and Gender in the Male Rampage Film', in J. Lewis (ed) (1998), *The New American Cinema*, Durham NC: Duke University Press
Pratt J. (1999), 'Norbet Elias and the Civilised Prison', *British Journal of Sociology*, Vol. 50, No. 2
Pratt J. (2002), *Punishment and Civilisation*, London: Sage
Querry R. (1973), 'Prison Movies: an Annotated Filmography 1921-Present', *Journal of Popular Film*, Vol. 2, Spring, 181-197
Querry R. (1975), *The American Prison as Portrayed in the Popular Motion Pictures of the 1930s*, (unpublished) PhD, University of New Mexico
Rafter N. (2000), *Shots in the Mirror: Crime, Film and Society*, Oxford: Oxford University Press
Rethinking Crime and Punishment (2003), Bid Guidance Document, available online at: www.rethinking.org.uk
Roffman P. and Purdy J. (1981), *The Hollywood Social Problem Film*, Bloomington: Indiana University Press
Ryan M. and Kellner P. (1990), *Camera Politica: The Politics and Ideology of Contemporary Hollywood Cinema*, Bloomington: Indiana University Press
Salgado G. (ed) (1972), *Coney Catchers and Bawdy Baskets*, London: Penguin
Sarat A. (ed) (1999), *The Killing State: Capital Punishment in Law, Politics and Culture*, New York: Oxford University Press
Sarat A. (2001), *When the State Kills: Capital Punishment and the American Condition*, Princeton NJ: Princeton University Press
Sayer A. (1984), *Method in Social Science: A Realist Approach*, London: Hutchinson

Schlosser E. (1998), 'The Prison-Industrial Complex', *Atlantic Monthly*, December 1998
Scottish Executive (2003), 'Prison Population at Record Level', available online at: http://www.scotland.gov.uk/pages/news/2003/09/SEjd310.aspx
Shelly J.F. and Wright J.D. (1995), *In the Line of Fire: Youths, Guns, and Violence in Urban America*, New York: Aldine de Gruyter
Simon J. (2001) 'Fear and Loathing in Late Modernity: Reflections on the Cultural Sources of Mass Imprisonment in the United States', *Punishment and Society*, 3.1, 21–34
Smith D. (1989), *North and South: Britain's Economic, Political and Social Divide*, London: Penguin
Sparks R. (1992), *Television and the Drama of Crime*, Buckingham: Open University Press
Sykes G. (1958), *The Society of Captives*, Princeton: Princeton University Press
Travis A. (2002a), 'Crowding Fuels Prison Violence', *Guardian*, 29 August
Travis A. (2002b), 'Three Prison Riots in a Week as Overcrowding Hits Record Levels', *Guardian*, 9 May
Travis A. (2003), 'UK now Europe's Jail Capital', *Guardian*, 27 February
Tudor A. (1995), 'Genre' in B. Keith Grant (ed) *The Film Genre Reader*, Austin: University of Texas Press
Turner R. (2000), *Coal Was Our Life*, Sheffield: Hallam University Press
Wacquant L. (2001), 'Deadly Symbiosis: When Ghetto and Prison Meet and Mesh', in D. Garland (ed), *Mass Imprisonment: Social Causes and Consequences*, London: Sage
Walmsley R. (1999), 'World Prison Population List', *Home Office Research, Development and Statistics Directorate: Research Findings No. 88*, London: Home Office
Walmsley R. (2000), 'The World Prison Population Situation: Growth, Trends, Issues and Challenges', (unpublished) paper presented at the Association of Paroling Officers International Conference, Ottawa 2000 available online at http://www.apaintl.org/Pub-Conf2000-PlenaryWalmsley-En.html
Walmsley R. (2003), *World Prison Population List*, 4th Edition London: Home Office
West C. (1992), 'Nihilism in Black America' in G. Dent (ed) (1992), *Black Popular Culture*, Seattle: Bay Press
Wilde O. [1898] (1992), *The Ballad of Reading Goal*, New York: Dover Publications
Wilson D. (1993), 'Inside Observations', *Screen*, 34(1) 76–9
Wilson D. (2002), 'Millbank, the Panoptican and their Victorian Audiences', *Howard Journal of Criminal Justice*, Vol. 41, No. 4
Wilson D. (2003), 'Lights, Camera, Action' *Prison Report*
Wilson D. and Ashton J. (1998), *What Everyone in Britain should Know about Crime and Punishment*, London: Blackstone Press
Wolfensberger W. (1980) 'The Definition of Normalization: Update, Problems, Disagreements and Misunderstandings', in R. J. Flynn and K. E. Nitsch (eds.), *Normalization, Social Integration and Community Services*, Baltimore: University Park Press
Wood R. (1986), 'From Buddies to Lovers', in R. Wood (1986), *Hollywood from Vietnam to Regan*, New York: Columbia University Press
Woolf Lord Justice (1991), *Prison Disturbances, April 1990: Report of an Inquiry*, Cm. 1456
Wright K. (1994), *Effective Prison Leadership*, New York: William Neil Publishing

Index

Please note that select *Filmographies* appear at the end of *Chapters* 2 and 4. The index includes films appearing in text headings only: otherwise it is by subject matter.

abuse 42 69 77 96 99 100 104 120 133 134 154 165
academic viewpoints 25
action-adventure 78 79 94 95 109
administrative era in the USA 76
Alcatraz 27 67 72
Allen, Rob iv
'alternative public space' 183
alternatives to custody 10 21 25 78 88 99 171
alternative traditions 68 74 80 85
America, see *USA, Hollywood*
'answer films' 106
anti-authority 46 56
anti-hero 44 85 129
approved school 38 39 41
architecture 11 28 138
Arkansas 101 157 162 167
arson 140
assault 9 19 43 161
Attica Penitentiary, New York/uprising 31 61 73 75 87 154 176 178
Auburn Prison, New York 71 163
Australia 236, 137 *et seq*
  and see *Ghosts ... , Prisoner Cellblock H*
authority
  abuse of 42 69 and see, generally, *abuse*
  inevitability of 42 44 47
  outwitting 129
  reasserted 65 67 69 91 166
  resistance to 46 56 127
  struggle against 64
autobiography 11 18 26 19
awfulness of prison 26 46 86 121 173
'babes-behind-bars' 71 74 89 120
'bad faith' 106
Bad Girls 8 116 *et seq*
Ballad of Reading Gaol, The 29 148 154
Barlinnie Special Unit 20
baron, see *'top dog'*
Big House, The 81
Big, Mr, see *'top dog'*
black actors/prisoners etc. 47 52 74 79 111 137 141 150 161 169 174 175
black humour 142
'black realism' 174 176
'blaxploitation' 74 176
'boat drinks' 170 182
borstal 38 41 43 129 156 157 161
Boyle, Jimmy 19 31 42 46
breaking the spirit 71
'bricks of shame' 148
bribing the audience 123
British 48 70
  British Board of Film Censors 36
  Britishness/Englishness 51 54 159
  British Social Realism 41 44 128
'Brit-pic' 51 184
Brokedown Palace 110
Brubaker 101 156 157 162
brutality/brutishness 31 38 43 52 63 111 151 162
buddies 64 89 108
bullying 44 124 129 142
Buried 117 136 *et seq*

camp/camping it up 127
Cannon City Prison, Colorado 99
capital punishment 38 49 79 91 112 149 180 184
caring relationships 133 134
CCTV 138 *et seq*
celebrity 46
censorship 47 97
chain gang 100
chaplain 154 161
Chino Prison, California 72
Chopper 136 137 142 144
cliché 51 52 59 64 71 81 91 107 120 122 127 135 173
Clowers, Marsha 120
comedy/comedic tradition 36 128
common sense 17 18 27
community corrections 9 170 178 185
concern 42 47
confinement, fascination with 93
Conlon, Gerry 48
containment in the USA 73 *et seq* 80
convention 82 90 127
Convict 99 36
convicts
  'in skirts' 39 122
  depiction of 15
correctional supervision 105
corporal punishment 98 99 102 163
corruption 41 67 74 102 120 142 151 161 163 173
county gaols (USA) 78 96 112
Criminal, The 41
crisis 42
critique 42 *et seq* 129 173
cruelty 41 82
cult 24 44 56 95 116 117 123 185
  'made as cult TV programmes' 118 128 148
daddy ('prison daddy') see *'top dog'*
danger/dangerousness 17 78 96 130
Dannemora Prison, New York 71
Darwinian struggle 150 151
Death Row 16 105 112 *et seq* 156 163
  and see *capital punishment*
decency 50 81 98 114 142 155 173 185
defiance 46
Defiant Ones, The 171
demonisation 184
denial/counter denial 103
Depression, heyday of USA prison film 70 94
deterrence 12 154
Devil's Island 27 148
Dickens, Charles 29
discounting 16
disparagement , see *endorsement /disparagement*
disturbances 9
documentary /pseudo documentary 61 105 138
Dostoevsky, Fyodor 88 154 161
drama
  imaginative apparatus, providing 16 21 55 78 88 98 100 111 173
  limits of plausibility, setting 19 27
  non-technical significance 21 185
  perceptions, shaping 19 58 *et seq* 74
  role of prison drama 14
  'softening ' of prison in 27 37 40
dramatic approximation 124 125
dramatic licence 16 17 126 178
drugs 31 85 110 111 123 125 130 139 141 150 173 174 175
  drug testing 141
Durham Prison 45

190 *Images of Incarceration*

educational aspects 39 40 104 123 135 175 184 185
electronic monitoring (EM) 171 177 178
empathy through drama 101 113 128 131 180 185
endorsement/disparagement 180 181 185
Englishness, see under *British*
escape 16 45 50 62 64 67 72 99 108 165 169 *et seq*
escapism 63
Esmée Fairbairn Foundation iv
eras, prison film eras 69 70
    and see *periodisation*
exhaustion of genre, impact etc. 82 83 135
experiental accounts 26 31 39 45 56 57 95 97 104 107 121 185
    actively discouraged 36
experimental unit 154
fantasy symbols/endings 74 89 97 118
    rebellion 74 90
    sexual fantasy 89
fear 154
'feel good', see *heartwarming tales*
feminism 133 134
fiction
    generally 17
    source of ideas etc. as 14 25 123 135 184
film, meaning of 42
    and see *prison film*
fight scenes 122
flashback 72 149 152 159
Foucault 142
Gardner, Jimmy 137 141 143 145 146
gender aspects 23 25 74 87 125 145
Georgia, USA 100
Ghosts . . . 136 *et seq*
Goffman, Irving 11
going straight 46 172
Goodtime Girl 38
Governor 16 41 117 137 143 149 156 *et seq*
    academic, artistic, dramatic etc. 50
    celluloid 159
    ineffectual 50
    middle-class 122
    pompous etc. 52 128
    power 156 159
    progressive 122
grass 52 64 110
Greenfingers 53
Gregory, Sandra 18 26 motif 90
Grendon Prison 141 147
gun crime 13
Hans, Jimmy 50
happy/unhappy ending 51 58 67 68 85 86 95 103 126 170
harassment 122
hard case/man, see *'tough guy/nut'*
'hard core' prisoners 52 109
    mellowing 52 54
healthcare 154
heartwarming tales/'feelgood' factors 51 58 65 95 109
heavy, see *'tough guy/nut'*
He Got Game 176
henchmen, see *'tough guy/nut'*
Henry, Joan 39 121
Herman, Didi 132
hero/heroine 89 101 103 120 132 148
    and see *anti-hero*
heterosexuality, negative 132
Hill, The 41
Holloway Prison 39 122
Hollywood 36 58 *et seq* 88 *et seq* 114 180 184 185

'left Hollywood' 74
Home Office 36
homo-eroticism 89
homosexuality 38 73 87 143
hostile environment 122 129
house of correction 28
hulks 29
humanisation of prisoners through drama 37 98 101 113 131 153 154 155 180 182 185
hunger strike 140
I am a Fugitive from a Chain Gang 100
icon/iconography 79 82 160 184
Incentives and Earned Privileges Scheme 32
induction/initiation/reception rituals 40 43 81 82 83 139 156 159 169
injustice 45 58 110 113 127 128 129
'innocents' (prison innocents) 40 41 44 53 64 67 69 71 75 81 89 112 140 145 151
Internet Movie Database vi 182
interpreter 131
intimidation 38 43 52 129 142
James, Erwin 141
Jones, Robert 141
justice restored 64 67 89 108 112
juxtaposition 126 128
labelling/labels 40 130 143 147
legitimacy 44 77 90 93 97 99 129 145 149 166 167 185
lesbian aspects 122 123 132
Lewis, Derek 156
Loneliness of the Long Distance Runner, The 41 156 157 159
lovable rogues 51
'love interest' 51 53 108 139 173
Lucky Break 50
Lygo, Sir Raymond 156
Lynds, Elam 71
Made in Britain 46
Map of the World, A 111
mass incarceration 59 65 76 79 87 91 96 109 176 179
Mathiesen, Thomas 13 28 57 171 183
Mattock, Kath 141
maximum security 14 75 96 109 114 148 152
    and see *'super-max'*
McVicar 45 173
McVicar, by Himself 31 45
McVicar, John 45
Mean Machine 51
media 9 13 17 79 96 136 183
medical model 71
medication 31
metaphor 53 54 159 173 174
Michigan 158
middle-class people and/in prison, 'posh' aspects 29 38 40 50 90 112 121 130 131
Millbank Penitentiary 28
misperceptions, see *perceptions*
moral centre/tales/amorality 55 132 133 152 166
movies/drama
    artificiality 18
    benchmarks, providing 22 44 98 104 113 135 148 157 185
    cult 24 44 56 95 116 117
murder 102 139 140 144 154
Murton, Thomas 101 103 157 162
mutiny at Dartmoor 30 37
Nellis, Mike iv 34 36 37 38 41 61 81 91 106 156
new fish 108
newsreel footage etc. 72
'normalisation' 12
nostalgia 31 34 49 *et seq* 54

novelty 82
official cooperation 37
old-timers 51 53
'on-the-run' 75
open prison 53 72 122
optimism 37 *et seq* 71 72 172
Osborne, Thomas Mott 163
'outlaw ending' 108 167
overcrowding 9 32
Oz 117 143 147 148 *et seq*
'paddling' 99
pain 98 105 110 185
'pantomime baddy/goody' 124 127
parody 120 128
parole 173 174 176
penal change 97
penal reform(ers) 9 10 20 26 40 41 56 71 84 87 88 92 95 *et seq* 114 121 130 135 157 183 185
    fictional 37 84 164
Pentonville Prison 29
'perfect friendships' 90 108
perks, favours, see *privileges*
periodisation 34 69 70 80 *et seq*
pessimism 167
plausibility
    setting limits of 19 27
    residual 78
plays, prison plays, operas etc. as a device 50 54
pleasures, viewing 116 123 129 135 151
plot/characters/theme/stock plot etc. 64 69 82
politics/politicking 72 91 *et seq* 100 149 158 159 163 164 174 180 181
popular culture 14 24 109 148 183 *et seq*
pornography 139
Porridge 7 15 24 27 37 42 116 128 129 146 147
predatory prison/prisoners 73 75 76 78 86 96 120 122 139 148 *et seq* 165
prison
    'crisis' 8 9 154
    characteristics 11
    culture 10 145 150 152 156
    doctor, psychiatrist etc. 71 72 132 141 151 154 160
    futility/irrationality etc. 57 97 121
    Governor, see that entry
    'gritty' etc. 27 46 111
    growth 60
    'infernal prison' 110
    institution, as 141
        failing 154
    management models 158
    'new generation prison' 136 *et seq*
    officer, see *staff*
    population 9 10 76 78 88 137 171 179 184 185
    'prisons fiasco' 57 97
    prison film, see below
    purpose of, conflicting ideas 13
    reform 9 10 84 150
    regime 10 53 68 70 77 88 183 185
    historical 27 et seq
    lifer 45 48 77 96 105 117 125 130 147
    USA 70
    representations in drama 106 130
    sci-fi 75 78 79 94 157
    'secret world'/hidden 14 18 36 55 89 90 135 136 145
    traumatising effect of 48 55
    and see *predatory*

prisoner
    code 73 96
    collaborator 124
    economy 139
    'heart of gold' 51
    hierarchies 141 156 159 161
    hostility to authority 44
    incorrigible 41 68 104 173
    mutual support 131
    people, prisoners as 143
    reluctant leader 58 59
    subcultures 85 90 162
    used to keep order 43
    young 138
    and see *trusties*
Prisoner Cellblock H 121 *et seq*
prison film
    American tradition 37 58 *et seq*
    box office 94
    British 24 *et seq* 159
    contribution to USA prison growth 58
    defining 33
    disappearance of the British prison film 48
    functions listed 98
    genre/formula 53 58 *et seq* 70 80 *et seq* 89 91 107
        changing genre 66 69 83
    Hollywood, in 44 88 *et seq* 108 157 182
    ideology 91 184
    issues 60 et seq
    Prison Film Project iv
    'prison-in-film' 60
    'prison-related film' 60
    protest cinema 81 91
    traditions, genres etc. 22 23 24 33 37 40 58 70 159
    unpopularity 93
privileges, perks, favours 43 139 150 158 162 165
    and see *Incentives and Earned Privileges Scheme*
protection 175
protest 9 16 19 42
    fictional 42 43 131
punishment 12 21 25 41 82 102 173
    beatings 85 99 102 108 139 142 160 163
    block 127 130
'purposeful activity' 9 33 150
psycho 52 139
racial aspects 17 23 46 47 51 62 74 75 76 86 87 96 109 111 112 119 137 148 154 161 172 177
Rafter, Nichole 58 *et seq* 63 *et seq* 69 *et seq* 81 89 107 157
rape 43 75 86 148 154 161 163 165
'rat', see *grass*
'reading' film etc. vi 106 184
reality 7 8 *et seq* 27 *et seq* 54 55 60 69 76 122 123 167 170 185
    penal reality in the USA 70 104 167 176
reception into prison, see *induction*
recovery 52 53 55 108
redemption, prisoners of 52 104 108
    and see *Shawshank Redemption, The*
regular John 69 76 81
rehabilitation 9 10 26 40 72 150 154 173
    era of in the USA 71
released prisoners 62 68 106 169
religious aspects 43 154 161
resistance to authority, see *authority etc,*
respect by film makers 40
Restorative Justice 21 78 88 179 180 185
reform
    offenders, of 52 104

and see *penal reform*
'repressive tolerance' 73
restriction, era in Britain 36
Rethinking Crime and Punishment iv 10 183
rethinking prison 9 21
revelation 98 100 122 129 138 148 185
revenge 105 108 111 113 170
review 181
riot 9 16 29 31 32 64 67 71 72 73 74 114 125 138 149 160 161
   copycat 32
   fictional 44 131
   Parkhurst 31 42
   Zoot Suit 85
   and see *Attica*
romance 116 132 173
   and see *'love interest'*
roof-top protest 16 31
sadism 41 64 72 142 144
sanitised view of prison 7 15 110
Santa Fe Prison, New Mexico 75
Sarat, Austin 112
sarcasm 52
scam 16 37 125
'screw'
   nasty etc. 50
   predatory 124
   relationships with prisoners 16 123 (sexual) 125 (sexual) 132
   and see *staff*
Scum 43 129 157 161
selective view of prison 15
self-harm 9 112 140
segregation 127
Sense of Freedom, A 19 31 46
sentimentality 51
sexual exploitation 71 74 83 111 120 143
   glamour, use of 51
   prisoners, of 39 45 122 143
sexuality 132
Shawshank Redemption, The 107 157 164
'shit happens' 148 153
sit-down protest 31
Slam 175
'slopping out' ended 33
snitch, see *grass* 52
social aspects
   baromoter, film as 55
   building a better society 154
   messages 39 40 124 125 129 135
   realism 44 147
   shaping society, films 58
   and see *British Social Realism*
solitary confinement 15 19 28 43 46 67 71 72
'spiv movie' 38
spoof films 65
staff
   good/well-intentioned 152
   hierarchy 156
   hostility/grudge etc. 42 52
   invisible 142 143
   normal people 54
   perpetual war against 139
   prisoner relationships 85 122 132 145
   support 131
   tensions 42
   unflattering depictions 42 43 58 129 142
   unpleasant 123
   unsympathtic 131

stereotypes 150 153
Stir 136 137 138 142 144
Straight Time 172
Stranger Inside 111
Strangeways Prison (Manchester) 32 49
'stock' plots, see *plot*
suicide 9 15 29 32 43 142 (staff) 161 165 (Warden)
suspending disbelief 144
'super-max' 11 52 76 104 114 140 167 168
Sykes, Gresham 156
symbols 149 184
tattoo 139
television drama/movies (main entries) 47 49 99 105 106 111 148 185
'tent city' 78
Texas, USA 78 158
Tomorrow La Scala 54
'top dog' 43 74 82 111 125 129 159 161 162
total institution 11
tough guys/'tough nuts', heavies, henchmen etc. 41 43 45 46 69 76 145 161
'tough on crime' 25 31 77 149
transformation 53
translating information into reality 33
transportation 28
transvestite 139
treadmill 28 29
trusties 102 163
truth
   in sentencing 96
   about prison 97 116 117 123 148
tunnelling 16 153
unacceptability 148 185
unconscious acceptance/understanding 16 22
unrest 42
USA 58 *et seq*
victims of abuse/crime/system 21 105 120 134
Victorian prisons 36
villains 124 148
violence 17 19 41 42 44 52 76 129 137 138 144 145 148 161 175
voice 114 121 130 185
voyerism 121 122
Warden 58 59 102 108 149 156 176
   autonomy 70 102
   celluloid 159 *et seq*
   evil 58 59 120 157
   fair/wise/reform-minded vi 64 68 69 70 72 76 81 87 97 101 156
   good 59
   meglomaniac 69
warder 41
Weak and the Wicked, The 39 121 *et seq*
West, Cornell 176
whipping 71 99
white supremacy 151
Who Lie in Gaol 39 121
Wilde, Oscar 29 155
Winters, Larry 48
women-in-prison/experiences/sub-genre 18 23 38 47 66 71 74 83 89 96 111 112 116 120 127
Woodhill Prison 136
Woolf Report 32
working-class depictions 41 44 54
Yards, The 173
zoo 144